Contents

5 MEDIA CHOICE 2 – BELOW-THE-LINE

6 ADVERTISING RESEARCH – PRE-CAMPAIGN, DURING CAMPAIGN, POST-CAMPAIGN

7 LEGAL CONSTRAINTS AND ETHICS

8 CREATING THE MESSAGE

12.99

659

Advertising

Sandra Cottier Bunting

Hodder & Stoughton

GROUP

For Neil, my husband, thank you for your support, help and understanding, and in loving memory of my dear parents, Dora and Jim Cottier.

Cataloguing in Publication Data is available from the British Library

ISBN 0 340 63157 0

First published 1996
Impression number   10 9 8 7 6 5 4 3 2 1
Year   1999 1998 1997 1996

Typeset by Fakenham Photosetting Ltd, Fakenham, Norfolk. Printed in Great Britain for Hodder & Stoughton Educational, a division of Hodder Headline Plc, 338 Euston Road, London NW1 3BH by the Bath Press

Acknowledgements

The author and publisher would like to thank the following organisations for the use of illustrations and information in this publication:

The Advertising Standards Authority Ltd; Amstel Beer; Asda Stores Ltd; The Automobile Association; BCA; Baxters of Speyside Limited; Ben & Jerry's; Boots the Chemist; Business & Market Research plc; Cadbury Limited; the Campaign Report; Citroën; Clinique Laboratories Ltd; Comet Group plc; Creative Magazines (*Ads International* magazine); Daewoo UK Ltd; Dollond & Aitchison The Opticians; Ford Motor Company Limited; Freemans; GrandMet Foods (UK); GUS Catalogue Order Limited; H J Heinz Company Limited; Häagen-Dazs UK Ltd; Halifax Building Society; Haymarket Marketing Publications Ltd (*Marketing* magazine); Headline Book Publishing Ltd; The Independent Television Commission; Infoplan (Vittel); Jameson; Kellogg Company of Great Britain Limited; Landmark Express Ltd; Littlewoods Pools; Lloyd's of London (Insurance); Lowe Howard-Spink Marschalk Ltd (*Today* newspaper); Loyd Grossman Sauces; Victoria Mather and Sue McCartney-Snape (*Absolutely Typical. The Best of Social Stereotypes from the Telegraph Magazine*, Methuen, 1996); MFI; Mr Lucky Bags Ltd; The National Magazine Company (*She* magazine); National Westminster Bank plc; Nestlé UK Ltd; Next Directory Ltd; NTC Publications Ltd (*The Advertising Association's Advertising Statistics Yearbook 1993, Marketing Pocket Book 1996, Admap* magazine); Premier Waters Ltd (Evian); Proctor & Gamble Ltd; Profilex Ltd; RAC Ltd; Renault UK Ltd; Research International UK Ltd; Rowenta; The Ryvita Company Ltd; Saatchi & Saatchi; Safeway Stores plc; Scott Limited (Andrex); SWEB Retail Ltd; Terry's Suchard; Unilever plc; United Biscuits (UK) Ltd (McVitie's Group); Volvo Car UK Ltd; Walkers Snack Foods Ltd; Walsall Metropolitan Borough Council; William Reed Publishing Ltd (*The Grocer*); The Writers Bureau.

1

Advertising

AIMS

- to define the term 'advertising'
- to identify the elements of the promotional mix
- to take a brief look at the origins and development of advertising over time

Unit 20 Advertising
Working towards:

- **Element 20.1**

    – Performance Criteria:
      2 Recommend focus of appeal to be used for target audience

- **Element 20.2**

    – Performance Criteria:
      3 Select a suitable media mix to reach target audience

- **Element 20.3**

    – Performance Criteria:
      2 Prepare a suitable style of advertisment for a chosen medium

1.1 WHAT IS ADVERTISING

The American Marketing Association's definition of **advertising** is: 'Advertising is a paid form of non-personal presentation and promotion of ideas, goods or services by an identified sponsor.'

THE PROMOTIONAL MIX

There are four main elements which together make up the promotional mix. These are:

- advertising
- personal selling
- public relations
- sales promotions and merchandising

Advertising is the method used by a wide variety of organisations to:

- communicate a message to a selected audience
- persuade people to buy a product or service
- highlight specific features/qualities inherent within the product/service

To achieve these objectives, advertisers use the most cost-effective and appropriate media which will best reach their target market.

STUDENT ACTIVITY

Work in pairs and visit your nearest library. Obtain copies of a variety of newspapers and magazines. Choose a selection of six

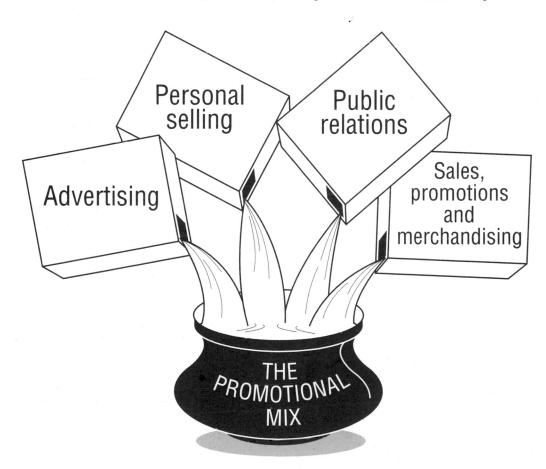

Fig 1.1 Elements of the promotional mix.

advertisements and identify:

1 *the target audience for each*
2 *how each advertisement tries to persuade people to buy the product/service*
3 *which of the six highlight specific features/qualities of a product/service.*

Discuss your findings and your ideas regarding each advertisement with the rest of your group.

1.2 HISTORICAL DEVELOPMENT – A BRIEF RÉSUMÉ

CRIERS AND TRADE/STREET SIGNS

Several thousand years ago, the Greeks used criers to 'advertise' their wares.

Trade signs were also used by the Greeks, but more especially by the Romans who used them as inn signs. Trade signs were an early form of advertising which is still in use today: the three golden globes of the pawnbroker for instance.

Advertisements also appeared on walls, especially near what were termed 'gathering places', i.e. street corners, the baths or any other public place where the local population met to chat.

PRINTING

In the latter half of the 15th century, advertising began to grow with the development of printing. At this time, newspapers were priced at one penny, and only the rich could afford them.

Most advertisers used handbills and posters.

THE 17TH CENTURY

Advertising in the press continued to grow, and by the mid-17th century, a publication entitled *The Publick Advertiser* appeared. It was the first paper to consist totally of advertisements, and it too cost one penny.

In 1662 the Printing Act came into force which restricted printing and, for the most part, placed responsibility for it in the hands of the Master Printers. By 1695 the Act had lapsed and the number of Master Printers had decreased from 59 to 20 during this period of 33 years.

By the end of the 17th century many goods were advertised on handbills and posters, and in newspapers and periodicals.

THE INDUSTRIAL REVOLUTION

During this period, the population was growing rapidly. In addition, there was a large increase in the quantity of manufactured goods being produced. With the improvements made in transportation, this made it easier for the advertiser's message to reach the new urban population. This period thus saw advertising grow to become more commonly used in product promotion.

In London, a wide variety of newspapers developed in the 18th century which ultimately led to an increased growth in advertising during this period. For the first time, advertisers were able to decide which newspaper best reached their specific customers.

THE 19TH CENTURY

During the first half of the 19th century, a tax was levied on both individual advertisements and newspapers. However, in 1853 – in the case of the former – and 1855 – in the case of the latter – the tax was abolished. The result was a large expansion in the variety of newspapers, as well as in the number of advertisements which appeared in them. In newspapers, advertisements were used to build up a mass market for the product being advertised.

Posters were the second most popular kind of advertising media during this century, because these included visuals and colour as well as text – newspapers were unable to include illustrations in their advertisements. Handbills were also widely used and were given to passers-by in the street.

ADVERTISING AGENCIES

Advertising agencies began to appear in the 1880s. An agency's role at this time was to offer advice to advertisers regarding the most suitable media to use to advertise products/services, but by the beginning of the 20th century, agencies were also *creating* the advertisements on behalf of their clients. Interestingly, the use of **branding** also began to increase during this period.

At the same time, technology was being used more and more in the production of newspapers – for example, rotary presses, which improved the speed of printing.

ENAMEL SIGNS

In the late 19th century, an increased number of companies began to use **enamel signs** to advertise their products. More particularly, products such as chocolate and soap were advertised in this way. The advertisements were displayed in railway stations, on the sides of buildings and on buses.

The second half of the 19th century and the first decade of the 20th century proved to be one of the greatest growth periods in advertising history. The advertising industry at that time was not dissimilar to the industry as we know it today.

Fig 1.2 The design for a 17-foot enamel sign to be erected on the Brighton loop line.

THE 20TH CENTURY

Advertising almost ceased during the First World War because companies found that they had full order books. In addition, a shortage of paper resulted in the Government producing a Paper Restriction Order in 1917 to limit the use of paper.

The nature of advertisements changed during this period. The Government used advertisements for their army recruitment campaigns, and also as a way of giving information to the population nationwide.

During the interwar period, the use of market research to assess market potential grew. This made advertising more effective.

A variety of new media ideas developed during this period, some of which were: neon signs; aerial messages; moving models in shop windows; pavement advertisements; and a whole host of other ingenious ideas.

During the Second World War, it was important for advertisers to keep a high profile. Again, the Government proved to be the major advertiser during this period. Paper shortages once more brought restrictions.

During the first few years of the postwar period, many restrictions remained in force.

However, advertising began to show an upsurge during the early 1950s, and new brands were developed as the restrictions were lifted. At the same time, however, the cover charges on all newspapers were increased, and the downturn in demand which ensued took several years to reverse.

Our social life and tastes in entertainment were significantly changed by the introduction of commercial television in 1955.

In the early 1960s, newspapers and magazines met with a number of difficulties, e.g. labour disputes, a higher cost of production and the impact of television advertising. Several newspapers disappeared as a result.

Cinema was also losing its appeal.

RADIO

Radio Luxembourg was the first commercial radio station to broadcast in Britain – in 1933.

The popularity of commercial radio increased during the 1960s with the growth in the number of 'pirate' radio stations operating from ships lying off the British coast. These closed down under force in the mid-1960s and were replaced by onshore commercial radio stations in the early 1970s.

Fig 1.3 Four advertisements for Heinz's 'Joy of living' campaign which began in 1947. The advertisements highlight the pleasures of eating, nourishment and natural flavours, and the use of fine ingredients.

11

THE 1990s

- Posters are no longer as popular as they were in the Victorian era
- Enamel signs, so popular in the first few years of the century, have almost disappeared (except as collectors' items)
- The number of cinemas has reduced by almost 25 per cent since the Second World War ended
- Advertising agencies are now more widely used by companies to advise on content as well as on what media to use to advertise products/services

The arrival of radio, film and television earlier in the century meant that advertising had arrived in a big way, and was here to stay.

STUDENT ACTIVITY

You are to work in groups of three.

1 Choose a product which is currently being advertised either in newspapers/magazines or on radio/television.

2 Trace the advertising history of the product over the past 50–100 years.

3 Produce three visual examples of earlier advertisements for the product, and

(a) identify the target market
(b) interpret the message.

4 Think of a unique way in which you might advertise the product of your choice today, and:

(a) identify your proposed target market
(b) explain the advertising message.

5 Produce at least two visuals of your ideas. Explain which media you would use to advertise the product and why.

Present your evidence in an oral presentation lasting 10 minutes. Explain the visuals and ideas behind your advertisements.

1.3 CASE STUDY: ROWNTREE'S CHOCOLATE CRISP – BETTER KNOWN AS KIT KAT!

Chocolate Crisp was launched in 1937, and the change of name to Kit Kat occurred in 1939. The following extracts supplied by Nestlé plot the development of the Kit Kat chocolate bar up to its 50th anniversary in 1987.

Fig 1.4 Rowntree's Chocolate Crisp, launched in 1937.

Chocolate Crisp was created in 1937. The Kit Kat name was not adopted until two years later, although the Company had registered the name 'Kit Kat' in 1911. It had been used as a nickname for the product initially.

Fig 1.5 Kit Kat during the Second World War.

THE 1940s

Kit Kat advertising charted the progress of events. The illustrated ladies started the war on their bikes, on their ponies, strictly on their own. By the middle of 1940 they had become a different breed, some wearing the uniforms of Wrens or nurses, others driving tractors, wielding spanners, hefting boxes of ammo.

The value of Kit Kat as a wartime food was evident. But food rationing now hit the confectionery industry. It was announced that because of the shortage of milk 'there will be no more Kit Kat until after the war.' Soon after re-launch in 1945 the pack had to be changed from red to blue to signify that continuing shortages prevented it from being made with milk.

Happily, the blue livery was withdrawn in 1947. The advertising joyfully proclaimed that 'Kit Kat is thickly spread with rich chocolate praline and wrapped in scrumptious full cream chocolate.'

THE FRONTIERS OF THE FIFTIES

A new consumer group emerged – Teenagers, with new-found spending power and plenty of expensive interests: fashion, haircuts (crewcuts for the boys, beehives for the girls), pocket-sized tranny radios, coffee bars – and pop music.

Kitty the Kat first appeared in Kit Kat advertising in the late 1940s. In the 1950s she was depicted looking out from behind a pint bottle of milk: a clear and compelling illustration of the 'rich full cream milk' strategy.

In the mid-1950s production improvements meant that, instead of the wafer becoming soft and absorbent from atmospheric moisture, it could now be guaranteed crisp. The kitten became a more active participant, responding to the 'snap' of the bis-

13

cuit rather than just relating to the pinta.

Kit Kat first went on television in 1957 with a series of spots. The theme was 'Have a break – have a Kit Kat' which, with resulting sales increases of 22 per cent, proved television to be a powerful new advertising medium.

THE SWINGING SIXTIES

Kit Kat advertising reflected the changes that were taking place in society. Changes not just in spending power, but also in the pattern of shopping.

In 1965 we opened our first ever purpose-built plant for the two-finger Kit Kat at York.

The abolition of retail price maintenance for confectionery in the early 1960s enabled the grocery trade to cut-price sweets to the consumer. Supermarket shopping spread rapidly. The bargain six-pack of two-finger Kit Kats was introduced in 1963 and by 1968 accounted for over 20 per cent of total Kit Kat sales. The advertising of 'Have a break – have a Kit Kat' remained, although tactical use was made of the line at different times, such as 'Have a holiday break – have a Kit Kat' and 'Have a lunch break – have a Kit Kat.'

It was all good for business. By the end of the decade Kit Kat had established itself as the Company's leading brand and as a lead in the grocery trade.

THE EVENTFUL SEVENTIES

Kit Kat entered the 1970s as Rowntree's biggest brand, but with sales that had been declining since 1966. This decline had been brought about by price increases in the late 1960s.

In the early 1970s decimalisation gave Kit Kat a chance to improve the value offered to the consumer. The weight of Kit Kat was increased. The traditional Kit Kat colours of red and cream were changed to the much brighter combination of red and white. The cream lines on the pack were removed and the Kit Kat oval enlarged to give the product lively modern packaging. In response to these moves, sales increased by 66 per cent between 1970 and 1975.

THE 1980s – THE GOLDEN DECADE

From the very start, Kit Kat was targeted at satisfying a genuine consumer need for a delicious, value-for-money 'meal between meals'.

It has been able to meet this need because firstly it has always been a good product, and secondly sound production techniques have always ensured it was a good buy.

The result has been that Kit Kat is renowned for its reliable and consistent quality.

The 1980s no less than previous decades have already seen many changes in society which have had enormous influence on the consumer market as a whole and Kit Kat in particular.

There has been a huge growth of 'snacking' as a result of changes in household structure, increasing leisure, mobility, disposable income, the number of women working and the decline of the traditional school dinner.

During the first half of this decade the Countline Market has grown by 41 per cent. Four-finger Kit Kat has more than matched this growth, with a sales increase of 54 per cent. The Chocolate Biscuit Countline Market during this period has increased by 23 per cent – a growth rate that has been completely outstripped by Kit Kat six-pack's phenomenal 71 per cent increase.

Today our advertising is concentrated in the two main media: posters, where the powerful colours of pack and product are used to dramatise the 'Have a break' theme; and TV.

(Adapted from information supplied by Nestlé Rowntree)

Fig 1.6 A poster advertisement, showing Kitty the Kat, which appeared in 1951.

This is the 'story' to 1987. Rowntree's were subject to a take over by Nestlé a few years ago.

STUDENT ACTIVITY

Working in small teams of three or four, you are to:

1 bring the 'story' up to date
2 explain the message contained within current advertising of the Kit Kat bar
3 determine which media are currently used
4 ascertain what themes/ideas are to take Kit Kat forward through the 1990s
5 find out what Kit Kat's current share of the Countline market is
6 produce bar charts and pie charts to illustrate the numeric information you ascertained in 5 above.

Produce a short formal report detailing your findings.

15

REVIEW YOUR PROGRESS

1 What are the four elements of the promotional mix?

2 Why do companies use advertising?

3 How did people advertise their products/services before printing was developed?

4 When was the Printing Act introduced, and what were the consequences of its introduction?

5 What were the major events which took place during the Industrial Revolution which had a major impact on the development of advertising?

6 What media have been developed during this century which have had a major impact on the way that companies advertise their products/services?

2

Buyer behaviour

AIMS

- to identify and explain the behaviour of the following types of buyer:

  - consumer
  - industrial/trade
  - service

- to identify, explain and gain an understanding of models of buyer behaviour

Unit 20 Advertising

- Element 20.1

  - Performance Criteria:
  2 Recommend focus of appeal to be used for target audience
  4 Select appropriate media for teaching target audience

Marketeers must understand why people buy one product as opposed to another. We will first take a look at consumer buyer behaviour, and then later in the chapter take a look at what factors impact on the buying behaviour of industrial service-sector markets.

2.1 INFLUENCES ON THE BUYING DECISION

Buying decisions will be made based on a number of facts. Some of these facts derive from basic economics, i.e.:

– how much money the individual has available to spend
– the price of the products, and consequently the individual's idea about what is 'value for money' when a substitute product may be a realistic alternative – e.g. an 'own brand' as opposed to a well-known brand.

STUDENT ACTIVITY

Look at the figures in Table 2.1 which show trends in average earnings on a weekly basis for the years 1983 to 1993.

1 What trends can you identify from the figures illustrated?
2 From these trends, do you think there is more or less disposable income in families? What reasons can you offer to support your ideas?

Now look at the figures in Table 2.2.

3 What do these figures tell you in terms of:

(a) sources of income
(b) disposable income per head?

4 What effect on spending can you predict from your analysis of both sets of figures?

Discuss your findings with your group.

Table 2.1 Trends in average earnings per person [a] per week in the UK.

	At current prices		At constant 1993 prices [b]	
	Average earnings [c] per week (£)	Annual percentage change (%)	Average earnings [c] per week (£)	Annual percentage change (%)
1983	148.77	8.5	246.33	3.7
1984	157.67	6.0	248.72	1.0
1985	171.00	8.5	254.29	2.2
1986	184.70	8.0	265.57	4.4
1987	198.90	7.7	274.62	3.4
1988	218.40	9.8	287.44	4.7
1989	239.70	9.8	292.64	1.8
1990	263.10	9.8	293.42	0.3
1991	284.70	8.2	299.95	2.2
1992	304.60	7.0	309.37	3.1
1993	316.90	4.0	316.90	2.4

[a] *Wages and salaries of those in full-time employment, excluding those whose bill is affected by absence.*
[b] *Deflated by the Retail Prices Index (1993 = 100).*
[c] *Prior to 1971, data is derived from average salaries per unit of output. Subsequent data is derived from the earnings index of all adults in employment.*
Source: *Employment Gazette, NTC.*

Table 2.2 Distribution of personal income in the UK.

	Percentage					
	1986	1988	1989	1990	1991	1992
Income						
Income from employment	63.7	63.8	64.1	64.1	63.5	61.9
Income from self-employment	10.5	11.8	12.3	12.5	11.3	10.5
Rent, dividends, interest	10.2	10.7	10.8	10.7	11.2	12.5
Social security benefits	14.8	13.0	12.2	12.1	13.4	14.5
Other current transfers	0.6	0.5	0.5	0.4	0.4	0.4
Total income per head (constant 1992 £)	8,316	9,092	9,292	9,322	9,271	9,493
Direct taxes (% total personal income)						
Income tax	12.2	12.1	12.1	12.6	12.3	11.8
Social security contributions	7.8	8.0	7.4	7.1	7.0	6.8
Community charge	–	–	0.1	1.8	1.6	1.4
Other current transfers	0.6	0.6	0.6	0.5	0.5	0.5
Disposable income per head (constant 1992 £)	6,598	7,213	7,412	7,270	7,288	7,543

Source: *Central Statistical Office, NTC.*

WHAT MOTIVATES US TO BUY?

The motivation to take action is triggered by a specific need. For example, the need to eat motivates us to take action to buy or make some food to eat.

Motives are the spur which make us take action. If we are not accepted by a particular group, we try to change our behaviour to become more acceptable. Similarly, if we are hungry, we take action to rectify the need and thus reduce tension.

Because motives are derived from needs, motives can lead us to take action to purchase a product/service. However, motives do not tell us *which* product/service to buy from the variety on offer: there are other influences that persuade us to purchase one particular product/service as opposed to another.

STUDENT ACTIVITY

*T*able 2.3 *compares the changes which have occurred in weekly household expenditure during the period 1983–1992.*

In small groups, discuss the content of the table and try to identify reasons why you feel these changes have occurred. What might be the economic/social issues which have had an impact on these trends?

Table 2.3 Changes in weekly household expenditure, 1983–92 (at constant 1992 prices).

	Ranked by change in amount spent	% chg	Ranked by change in share of weekly household expenditure	% chg
Top twenty categories				
1	Milk products	188.7	Life assurance & pensions	1.4
2	Purchase/run other vehicles	185.2	Purchase of vehicles	1.3
3	Insurance etc.	171.9	Furniture	0.7
4	Medicinal, dental etc. costs	154.1	Rent, rates etc.	0.4
5	Domestic help etc.	126.8	Floor coverings	0.4
6	Floor coverings	116.3	Educational expenses	0.4
7	Educational expenses	86.3	Milk products	0.4
8	Pocket money	85.1	House maintenance	0.4
9	Furniture	85.0	Other foods	0.4
10	Cocoa, drinking chocolate etc.	71.8	Purchase/run other vehicles	0.4
11	Theatre, sports & other events	70.6	Theatre, sports & other events	0.3
12	Contents insurance	69.6	Domestic help etc.	0.3
13	Horticultural goods	57.4	Medicinal, dental etc. costs	0.3
14	Life assurance & pensions	54.4	TV, video & audio equipment	0.3
15	Other foods	48.0	Insurance etc.	0.3
16	Purchase of vehicles	47.5	Pocket money	0.2
17	Medical & surgical goods	45.2	Contents insurance	0.1
18	TV, video & audio equipment	39.3	Horticultural goods	0.1
19	Soft drinks	37.0	Medical & surgical goods	0.1
20	House maintenance	36.5	Postage & telecommunications	0.1
Bottom twenty categories				
74	Bus & coach fares	−21.0	Pork	−0.2
75	Rail fairs	−22.0	Bacon & ham (uncooked)	−0.2
76	Fuel oil and other fuel	−24.7	TV licence & rental fees	−0.2
77	Betting & gaming	−25.6	Bread, rolls etc.	−0.2
78	Hot fish & chips	−31.4	Mutton	−0.2
79	Beef & veal	−32.0	China, glass, hardware etc.	−0.2
80	Hats, gloves etc.	−32.5	Footwear	−0.2
81	Flour	−32.5	Poultry	−0.3
82	House purchase	−32.6	Leather, jewellery etc.	−0.3
83	Bacon & ham (uncooked)	−33.8	Maintenance of vehicles	−0.4
84	Eggs	−37.4	Beer, cider etc.	−0.4
85	Donations etc.	−38.4	Gas & electrical appliances	−0.4
86	Pork	−39.6	Gas	−0.4
87	Mutton	−42.9	Coal & coke	−0.4
88	Cigars & snuff	−45.1	Beef & veal	−0.4
89	Pipe tobacco	−46.8	Electricity	−0.5
90	Sugar	−49.2	Cigarettes	−0.7
91	Butter	−54.4	Milk, fresh	−0.8
92	Milk, fresh	−55.3	Donations etc.	−2.1
93	Coal & coke	−60.7	House purchase	−3.1

Note: *Figures represent the average weekly expenditure of all households.*
Source: *CSO Family Expenditure Survey, NTC.*

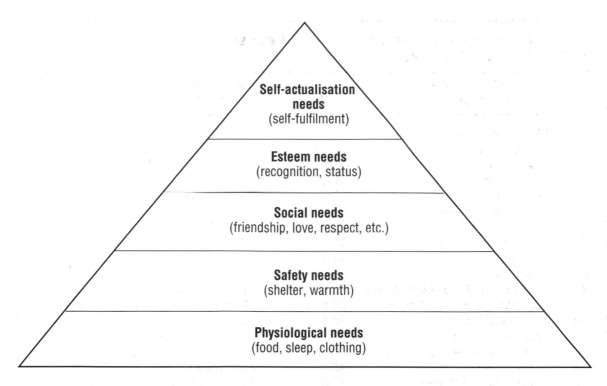

Fig 2.1 Maslow's Hierarchy of Human Needs.

A family may decide they wish to go abroad on holiday, but in order for them to be able to afford such a holiday it may be necessary for them to:

– reduce their spending on other items, i.e. leisure activities, or delay the purchase of 'luxury' items such as designer-label clothes, the latest model of a motor car, etc.
– organise for one or both partners to take on additional paid work to increase the family's income.

The marketeer must therefore understand the needs and wants of all individuals, as well as what motivates them to make a buying decision.

A THEORY OF MOTIVATION

If we look at Maslow's Hierarchy of Needs model in Figure 2.1 shown above, we can see how lower-level needs (the need for food, clothing and warmth), must be satisfied first before higher-level needs (an individual's ability to achieve his or her full potential), can be satisfied.

Maslow identified the need for self-esteem, which is linked to earning the respect of others. The way the consumer views him- or herself gives clues to individual behaviour. Maslow's theory further suggests that behaviour will be affected initially by physiological, safety and security needs, but that sociological needs which relate to self-image are also important influences on buying decisions.

STUDENT ACTIVITY

Design a questionnaire which will help you to assess the reasons why your family and friends purchase the following:

1 *a particular make and model of car*
2 *clothes from a specific store*
3 *a specific make of 'trainer' footwear*
4 *a specific brand of jeans*
5 *a particular type of canned soft drink.*

Try to identify the motives which influence the buying decision in each case.

Produce your findings in an appropriate visual, and explain your findings to your group.

PERSONALITY

We are all unique individuals with a variety of personality traits. Personality traits are partly inherited from our parents (Freud suggested this), whilst others are developed from our personal experiences and what type of 'social conditioning' we were subjected to as children, i.e. girls playing with dolls (mother role), boys playing with guns etc.

Some of us react in a compulsive way whilst others make decisions after carefully analysing all of the facts. It is usual to have several dominant traits which have an impact on our behaviour.

Various attempts have been made to classify these traits into types of personality (stereotyping) like those in the illustrations in Figure 2.2.

The bolshie teenager

She has been to India on her gap year and, having returned to the throbbing sophistication of Gloucestershire and Chelsea, is readjusting to materialism. Her father has manfully suppressed his horror about the stud in her nose — 'It was wicked. This guy called Sanjay did it for me in Varanasi' — and her mother now whips nervously through Royal tabloid stories at breakfast before confining their entrails to the log basket. Not that she need worry — the bolshie teenager doesn't wake for frivolity patrol until noon, by which time she expects her laundry, a mélange of trailing purply cotton, to have been processed by the daily. Her emaciation and spots first induced a maternal rush of fillet steak and M&S pawpaws, but she just said, 'My body can't handle this rich food, Mum,' in the moment she could spare from peak-time telephone conversations with friends about her culture shock. God, isn't anyone in touch with reality? Everyone here just seems to think Harvey Nichols is Mother Teresa. Calcutta is seriously cool — God, the fragility of existence — and the dhurries will look amazing in her study at Newcastle University.

VICTORIA MATHER

ILLUSTRATION BY
SUE MACARTNEY-SNAPE

Fig 2.2 Some social stereotypes (from Absolutely Typical. The Best of Social Stereotypes from the Telegraph Magazine, *Methuen, 1996*).

The Unwanted Guest

The unwanted guest is the pimple on life's dinner party. Always asked at the last moment because someone more amusing has dropped out, his asset is availability; his defects arrogance, a malodorous three-piece tweed suit and yellow teeth. However, he knows everyone, regardless of whether they know him, has an opinion about everything and serves as a platonic walker for women in between lovers. His Roman Catholicism (which consists of the fashionable Latin mass at Brompton Oratory) is harmless; his corruscating dismissal of Tom Stoppard's *Arcadia*, which most Sloanes find an impenetrable bore, rather comforting even if overblown by words like 'vacuous pyrotechnic semantics'. A Wykehamist with a first in Greats from one of the smaller Oxbridge colleges, Crispin thinks he is Stephen Fry. He never stops talking but doesn't listen, his conversation consisting of lumpen anecdotes punctuated by voracious eating, for he knows not when another dinner invitation will supplement his diet of peanuts and Muscadet scavenged at publishing parties. Grandly parsimonious, he sports bicycle clips and boasts that his ideal holiday is walking from Toul to Rome like Hilaire Belloc. This actually means he will be staying indefinitely at your villa in Tuscany.
VICTORIA MATHER

The Masterful Servant 2: the cleaning lady

Sophie Young-Married tidies the house before the cleaning lady arrives. Mrs Green, who calls her Sophie although Sophie calls her Mrs Green, used to work for the previous occupants of The Old Manor, a stentorian dowager with four labradors, and sees no reason why anything should change.

Sophie thinks she's like Mrs Danvers with Pledge, but help is impossible to find in the village since everyone went to work in the hypermarket. So she makes Mrs Green cups of tea ('Typhoo please, dear, not that nasty Earl Grey'), listens to the saga of her bunions and is suitably grateful to have the dust rearranged in her drawing room. Mrs Green implies by heavy wheezing that every photograph frame and bibelot is a personal affront and made such pointed remarks about drip-dry and easy-care that Sophie gave up insulting her with the ironing and now sends the sheets to the laundry.

As a gesture of approval, Mrs Green gave her a very woolly marrow, personally cultivated by Mr Green. Thanking her profusely, Sophie thinks of Spanish Maria and the simple life left in London.

VICTORIA MATHER

ILLUSTRATION BY SUE MACARTNEY-SNAPE

If marketeers can find links between purchasing decisions and personality types, this would result in cost-effective marketing decision-making.

SELF-IMAGE

We all have our own idea about what we look like and how we behave. We may even have an inflated idea of our own ability. Purchasing decision-making is affected by the way we see ourselves, viewed from the following viewpoints:

- you as you really are (real self)
- you as you would like to be (ideal self)
- you as you think other people see you (looking-glass self)
- you as you see yourself (self-image)

STUDENT ACTIVITY

Perception/self-perception exercise

Work in teams of five or six with people you know well. Produce a table like that illustrated below and try to think of each member of your group individually. Choose a model of car, type of food etc. which you feel best describes each person (including yourself). When you have completed the table for your group, give constructive feedback on why you chose the models, food types etc. for each person within your group, including yourself.

	Name	Name	Name	Name	Name
Food					
Car					
Musical instrument					
Fruit					
Adjective					

Were you, or other members of your group, surprised by the results? Are your perceptions of yourself very different from those of your peers?

On your own, carry out a reflective exercise and identify: what you have learned about the way you perceive yourself; how this differs, or not, from the way your fellow peers perceive you. What surprised you, if anything?

PERCEPTION

We each interpret information in different ways, and so our own perception of a particular event will differ from someone else's perception of it. Our perceptions are influenced by our personality, our background and our ability to select information which is of interest to us as individuals. For these reasons we ignore a wide variety of advertising communication each day except for that which particularly interests us. Marketeers therefore often decide to repeat advertisements regularly in order to cement the message and ensure that it is received by their intended audience.

LEARNING

Our buying decisions will be based on actions and decisions we have taken in the past. It is believed that human behaviour is learned by trial and error as well as from personal experience. It is therefore important for marketeers to reinforce the positive experiences and correct any negative ones.

BELIEFS AND ATTITUDES

Our beliefs and attitudes, which are built up through experience and background, have an impact on our buying decisions. Attitude is our approach to the way we think. Our attitude may be always to buy a particular type of vehicle or brand of washing powder. We may decide that we should always 'buy British' wherever possible. These attitudes influence our purchasing decisions.

2.2 SOCIAL INFLUENCES ON THE BUYING DECISION

The culture we have experienced as individuals helps to form our own values and beliefs, and influences all decisions which we make. Cultures within countries vary in a number of ways, including religious beliefs, preferred foods, dress, etc. The main components which influence culture are shown in Figure 2.3.

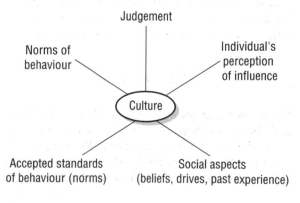

Fig 2.3 Influences on culture.

25

Culture has an impact on the decisions we make as purchasers, i.e. on:

- what we buy – the type of goods/services, the colour we choose etc.
- where we buy – supermarket, corner stores, mail order etc.
- when we buy – what day of the week (a possible religious impact on this decision)
- why we buy – the impact of culture both on what we identify as a need and on the motives which make us buy

STUDENT ACTIVITY

Look at Table 2.4 which details the readership profiles of national newspapers:

1 Which newspaper has the largest circulation in each of the following categories?

(a) male readership all ages
(b) female readership all ages
(c) all people aged 55+

Table 2.4 The national press and its readership.

	Tabloid/ broad- sheet	Circulation (1) '000	Adult Readership (2) '000	%	Men %	Women %	15/34 %	35/54 %	55+ %	ABC1 %	C2DE %	scc £	Mono £	4 colour £
Population profile					48	52	37	32	32	45	56			
National dailies														
The Sun	T	3,517	9,857	22	56	44	45	30	24	27	74	118	28,000	32,500
Daily Mirror	T	2,680	7,864	17	55	45	35	32	32	28	72	100	25,900	32,800
Daily Mail	T	1,775	4,723	10	50	50	30	35	35	61	39	82	26,664	30,000
Daily Express	T	1,497	3,903	9	53	47	29	31	39	56	44	85	23,765	31,500
The Daily Telegraph	B	1,025	2,715	6	55	45	23	36	41	84	18	78	24,500	42,500
The Star	T	773	2,478	5	65	35	49	35	16	22	77	38.50	10,780	15,092
Daily Record (Scotland)	T	755	1,941	4	52	48	39	34	27	31	69	35.50	9,295	11,620
Today	T	538	1,743	4	61	39	41	38	21	43	56	24	5,712	6,188
The Guardian	B	416	1,457	3	56	44	42	37	21	77	23	35	15,500	17,000
The Times	B	366	1,185	3	59	41	36	40	25	84	16	34	15,000	20,000
The Independent	B	347	1,148	3	58	42	43	40	17	81	18	32	14,000	18,000
Financial Times	B	290	745	2	68	32	36	45	18	88	13	63	28,224	35,500
National Sundays														
News of the World	T	4,620	12,516	28	51	49	44	32	25	28	71	125	29,750	34,500
Sunday Mirror	T	2,674	8,825	19	50	50	39	33	28	32	69	110	28,500	36,250
The People	T	2,032	6,025	13	53	47	33	33	35	29	71	77	20,550	27,300
The Mail on Sunday	T	2,030	5,999	13	49	51	37	37	26	62	38	108	27,300	37,000
Sunday Express	T	1,727	4,964	11	50	50	29	31	41	62	38	105	29,864	38,623
The Sunday Times	B	1,224	3,538	8	54	46	40	39	20	79	22	105	47,000	55,000
Sunday Post (Scotland)	T	1,051	2,981	7	48	52	24	31	44	33	67	39	8,846	10,600
Sunday Mail (Scotland)	T	868	2,218	5	51	49	38	35	27	33	67	35	10,995	13,850
Sunday Telegraph	B	578	1,911	4	53	47	28	34	39	79	22	56	25,000	29,500
The Observer	B	509	1,619	4	55	45	34	39	28	77	23	51	23,750	29,700
The Independent on Sunday	B	385	1,238	3	56	44	46	38	15	80	20	32	14,000	18,000
Sunday Sport	T	258	1,212	3	79	21	66	25	8	25	76	25	6,125	6,750
Weekend colour magazines														
Sunday	–	4,620	12,084	27	51	49	44	32	25	29	71	–	–	30,000
Sunday Mirror Magazine	–	2,674	8,569	19	50	50	39	33	28	32	68	–	–	25,000
TV First	–	2,032	5,666	13	51	49	33	33	35	29	71	–	–	19,000
You Magazine (The Mail on Sunday)	–	2,030	5,959	13	48	52	38	37	26	62	38	–	–	17,875
Sunday Express Magazine	–	1,727	4,818	11	49	51	28	31	41	61	38	–	22,400	22,400
The Sunday Times Magazine	–	1,224	3,485	8	53	47	41	39	21	78	22	–	11,000	16,000
Telegraph Magazine	–	1,025	3,410	8	53	47	23	36	40	82	19	–	15,000	15,000
The Observer Magazine	–	509	1,577	3	53	47	33	39	29	78	22	–	7,000	10,400
Independent	–	347	1,614	4	57	43	45	37	17	82	17	–	–	6,250

Sources: (1) ABC data January–June 1993. (2) NRS July 1992–June 1993. (3) BRAD August 1993, single insertion rate.

(d) readers who fall within socio-economic groups A, B and C1.

2 How might the information contained in this table assist you if you were a marketeer about to launch a new type of healthy snack food product?

Discuss your ideas with fellow members of your class/group.

STUDENT ACTIVITY

Work in pairs. Visit your school/college/town library. Using the social classifications in the Table 2.5, produce a list, broken down into socio-economic classification groupings, of class-related purchasing priorities for each grouping. Debate your findings with other members of your group.

SOCIO-ECONOMIC GROUPS AND THEIR IMPACT

The socio-economic classification in Table 2.5 is used by marketeers and in market research to identify the level of disposable income for each social group. This is most commonly used in the UK and is based on occupation.

Some individuals move between classes, but factors which affect an individual's behaviour will usually stay the same or change very slowly over a long period of time.

Individuals within certain 'lower' classes aspire to move up to the next 'social class'. This is more commonly found in Western societies and depends on increases in the income per capita of the population which will show an upward movement in the lower classes.

For people with the financial means, and by putting a ceiling on the spending powers of those higher up the 'social ladder', it is possible to achieve upward mobility. This could result in an increase in the market size at the higher levels, i.e.:

Table 2.5 Classification of consumers by socio-economic groups.

Social grade	Social status	Chief earner's occupation
A	Upper middle class	Higher managerial, administrative or professional
B	Middle class	Middle/intermediate, managerial, administrative or professional
C	Lower middle class	Supervisory, clerical, junior managerial, administrative or professional
D	Skilled working class	Skilled manual workers
E	Working class	Semi-skilled and unskilled manual workers
F	Those at the lowest levels of subsistence	State pensioners, casual or lowest-grade workers

Source: National Readership Survey, London.

– the purchase of private education
– buying a home instead of renting a property, etc.

Other, more reliable socio-economic groupings have been offered, such as:

– MOSAIC
– ACORN

THE MOSAIC SYSTEM

CCN developed MOSAIC, which identifies 12 main groups – split into 52 subgroups – and is based on lifestyle and on residential districts related to postcodes.

THE ACORN SYSTEM OF CLASSIFICATION

ACORN was developed by CACI in 1978 to provide 'A classification of residential neighbourhoods.' This is a geodemographic classification system using information which is stored on a database. It covers 125,000 census districts, each given a number identity which also includes postcodes. The latter are:

– linked to product-usage data, and
– based on national surveys.

ACORN correlates information about the population – i.e. sex, age, occupation and socio-economic status – which is related to the numbered districts.

ACORN further provides detailed Market Segmentation Data which can be used for:

– direct mail shots
– to study catchment-area trends (some large supermarkets have used this data to decide on site location and store development).

ACORN also identifies relevant types of residence, i.e. house, bungalow, flat, etc.

Other classifications are available which identify every address in the UK by postcode, making a flexible and comprehensive record of all types of customer.

Other information termed 'psychographics' or 'behaviour graphics' details the individual's interests, opinions, etc. This helps to identify groups of individuals who enjoy similar interests, opinions, activities etc., and consequently gives pointers to their buying behaviour.

SOCIAL GROUPS

Societies have many different social groupings, which are determined by:

• cultures
• lifestyles
• social class

Social groups are made up of a number of people who share similar beliefs, values, behaviour, interests etc., and behaviour within the group will be affected by both individual and group influences. Individuals within the group will conform to accepted standards of behaviour. Members of the same tennis club, for instance, will have certain accepted standards of dress, as will members of the local golf club. The level of conformity for an individual will depend on how much the individual relates with the group and the benefit derived by the individual from belonging to a specific group.

If individuals can be influenced by a social group, this has implications for marketeers. The individual's decision to buy/consume a product/service will be affected as much by influences within the social group as by other behavioural patterns.

STUDENT ACTIVITY

Work in pairs. Find out from your partner the following information:

1 What type of clothes does he or she wear at home?

2 What type of clothes does he or she wear at school/college/work?

3 What type of clothes does he or she wear when he or she goes out in the evening or at the weekend with friends?

Table 2.6 ACORN geodemographic groups.

Category	Group	Socio-economic group	Population (% of)
A	Suburban areas – wealthy high achievers	A, B, C1	15.1
	Rural communities – affluent greys	A, B, C2, D	2.3
	Retirement areas – pensioners who are prosperous	A, B, C1	2.3
B	Family areas – executives who are affluent	A, B, C1	3.7
	Family areas – workers who are prosperous	A, B, C1, C2	7.8
C	Town and city areas – wealthy urban dwellers	A, B, C1	2.2
	Metropolitan areas – professionals who are prosperous	A, B, C1	2.1
	Inner-city areas – executives who are well-off	A, B, C1	3.2
D	Areas with mature home-owners who are middle aged and comfortable	A, B, C1	13.4
	Home-owners who are skilled workers	C1, C2, D, E	10.7
E	Mature communities – who are new home-owners	C2, D, E	9.8
	Multi-ethnic areas – people who are white-collar workers and who are better off	C1	4.0
F	Less prosperous area – people who are older	C2, D, E	3.6
	Better-off housing – council-house residents	C2, D, E	11.6
	Unemployment high – council-house residents	C2, D, E	2.7
	Great hardship – council-house residents	D, E	2.8
	Areas of low income – multi-ethnic communities	D, E	2.1

Source: *CACI Ltd, London.*

4 What are the influences which affect his or her decision to wear a particular item of clothing?

Compare your findings with those of other members of your group.

THE IMPACT OF THE FAMILY BACKGROUND

We learn behaviour patterns in different settings from our experiences within the family. These influences remain very strong throughout our lives. There has been a significant change in the structure of the family, from the 'traditional' nuclear family of husband, wife and two children to an increase in the number of single-person or one-parent family households now to be found.

Families are defined in four ways:

1 *The original family*. Our original family will influence our future buying decisions.
2 *The family by marriage*. Where a family is created, i.e. where two people decide to live together or get married, this new family unit will need to purchase household items, i.e. carpets, curtains, upholstery etc.
3 *The nuclear family*. When children are born, buying decisions are influenced and may include the need to move to a larger property, the need to purchase toys, children's furniture etc.
4 *The extended family*. This includes brothers, sisters, grandparents and other offspring and relatives.

The family is important in making purchasing decisions: it decides what products to purchase on behalf of its members. It is also important to know *which* member of the family makes the final purchasing decision for a variety of prod-

29

ucts/services. Married couples make buying decisions in a number of different ways, i.e.:

1 *Husband dominant* – the husband makes the decision to purchase a specific product. This might be because he has specific knowledge/ expertise, i.e. tools.
2 *Wife dominant* – as above. This case might involve, for example, the decision to purchase a particular steam iron, or kettle etc.
3 *Autonomous decisions* – these are decisions made equally by both partners without consultation with each other.
4 *Joint decisions* – these are decisions made by both partners together.

Other members within the family who can influence the buying decision might include:

- *children* – who might have a preference for a certain type of breakfast cereal
- *teenagers* – who are given a certain amount of freedom to spend money on their preferred type of product, i.e. music, holidays, clothes etc.
- *a young married woman* – who may be influenced by her mother's perspective on what products to purchase, particularly in terms of large household items such as a refrigerator or cooker
- *a new young mother* – who may make her own purchasing decisions if her main role within the family is that of managing the household
- *older members of the family* – who may be able to sway the decision-making process prior to purchasing

The last case is less likely to occur in Western societies, where the opinion of 'elders' does not carry as much weight as it does elsewhere in the world.

STUDENT ACTIVITY

Talk to your parent(s), brother(s), sister(s) and other relatives, and find out what influences their decision to purchase the following types of product:

1 clothes
2 weekly food
3 a new car
4 a new washing machine.

Who in the family makes the final decision to purchase?
Discuss your findings with the rest of your class.

Families evolve and members age, and consequently their patterns of consumption change. This change has an impact on the buying decisions made within the family unit.

The family life cycle is usually identified as progressing through a number of stages, as follows:

- *Bachelor* – a young, single person not living at home
- *Newly married* – a young couple with no children
- *Full Nest 1* – a married couple with dependent young children under the age of six
- *Full Nest 2* – a married couple with dependent children who are six years or older
- *Full Nest 3* – a married couple with dependent older children
- *Empty Nest 1* – a married couple whose children no longer live at home, but the head of the family is still working
- *Empty Nest 2* – a married couple whose children no longer live at home, and the head of the household is retired
- *Solitary Survivor 1* – an older single person who is still working
- *Solitary Survivor 2* – an older single person who is retired

REFERENCE GROUPS

Reference groups are those with which, as individuals, we identify closely in terms of shared norms of behaviour etc. These groups will influence our buying decisions as regards:

- individual taste
- the individual's expectations of the product/service purchased
- the individual's aspirations

Within such groups, one individual may become dominant in terms of the opinions expressed or the point of view put forward. This dominance will have an effect on the buying decisions of other members of the group.

2.3 LIFESTYLE INFLUENCES ON THE BUYING DECISION

Marketeers use the term 'lifestyle' to encompass a variety of topics, which include economics, sociology and psychology. This term, which gives us a picture of how we live, i.e. our leisure activities, interests, aspirations for the future and opinions, combines the individual influences of:

- personality
- attitudes
- culture, and
- social class.

It has been proved that people with the same personality type do not necessarily share the same lifestyle.

STUDENT ACTIVITY

Write down a list of all the groups to which you currently belong.

1 Which members carry the most influence in each group? Why?
2 Having made a decision, have you ever changed your mind because of the influence of one or more individuals within one of the groups?

2.4 WHY DO CONSUMERS BUY?

MODELS OF BUYER BEHAVIOUR

Consumers' behaviour is complex, and the decision to purchase a particular product or service can be influenced by a variety of factors, as has already been demonstrated earlier in this chapter. To recap briefly:

1 Influences specific to the individual might include:

- attitudes and beliefs
- past experience and the motivation to purchase

2 External influences might include:

- how a product/service is promoted and advertised
- whether the product/service is easily available
- whether the product/service is recommended by a friend/colleague/relative.

Consumers buy to meet a perceived need which results from their particular lifestyle. There are several stages in the buying process. These can be explained as follows:

1 The consumer must be **motivated** to take **action** to **purchase** a product/service to meet the **need** which has been identified.
2 The consumer will gather as much information as possible about similar products, and will use a variety of sources, i.e.:

- previous experience (his or her own, and that of both other members of the family and friends)
- sales literature
- other advertising communication materials.

3 The consumer will then acquire information

31

about each of the similar products and compare, perhaps:

- price
- built-in extras etc.

to identify the product/service which is perceived as the 'best value for money' in his or her opinion.

4 The consumer will then decide which product/service to buy.
5 After purchase, the consumer will continue to evaluate the performance of the product against expectations, including after-sales service. Providing that the product proves satisfactory, it is likely that the consumer will return to the same supplier again and again. However, if after-sales service is poor or the product performs badly, it is unlikely that the consumer will return.

This simple model of buyer behaviour might be summarised as follows:

Stages in the consumer buying process

Stage 1   Identify the need
Stage 2   Search for information
Stage 3   Evaluate the options
Stage 4   Decide which product/service to
           purchase
Stage 5   Carry out a continuous evaluation
           following the purchase

STUDENT ACTIVITY

Carry out a survey of several members of your family and close friends. Use the above simple model of buyer behaviour to try to identify the reasons for the purchase of a specific expensive item which they have purchased recently.

1 Did your family/friends follow the above five-stage process? If the answer is Yes, go to Question 2. If the answer is No, go to Question 3.

2 Were your family/friends aware that they had followed this process?
3 How did they go about making the decision to buy?

Produce a short report which presents your findings and offers your conclusions about your findings.

STUDENT ACTIVITY

Look at Table 2.7 on pages 33–5. Decide in which specialist journals you would advertise the following products, and state your reasons:

1 a newly released video about aerobic exercise
2 the latest development in camcorder technology
3 a new game available on CD-ROM
4 a life-insurance policy
5 a new range of camping equipment.

Models are used by marketeers to analyse buyer behaviour and to help in the interpretation and assessment of buying decisions made.

THE 'BLACK BOX' MODEL

Many investigations have taken place which have produced some suggested models of how customers behave, but there has proved to be no consensus. The 'Black Box' (as shown in Figure 2.4 on page 36) refers to the complex thought processes which occur in the buyer's mind that result in the buying decision. How the decision is actually made is impossible to determine, as the information involved in the decision is 'handled' in both an individual's conscious and subconscious minds. However, by observing the environment within which the buying decision is made, the marketeer may be able to identify the likely inputs and influences which the 'Box' is receiving.

If the inputs are compared with the outputs in relation to the buying decision, the impact of a

Table 2.7 Details of some trade, technical, business and professional journals.

	Issue frequency	Circulation (1)	Page rates (2)	
			Mono £	4 colour £
Accountancy				
Accountancy	M	73,161	1,700	2,405
Accountancy Age	W	60,748	2,310	3,210
Financial Director	M	24,970	2,536	3,215
Management Accounting	M	57,686	1,040	1,400
Advertising & Marketing				
Admap	M	–	860	1,390
Campaign	W	16,452	2,525	4,425
Marketing	W	40,186	2,200	4,100
Marketing Week	W	36,887	2,075	3,875
Media Week	W	–	2,200	3,950
Agriculture & Farming				
British Farmer	M	100,564	1,390	2,520
Farmers' Weekly	W	85,240	2,352	4,169
Farming News	W	87,983	4,417	7,112
Architecture & Building				
Architect, Builder, Contractor & Developer	M	24,345	1,480	1,480
The Architects' Journal	W	–	1,345	1,995
Building	W	19,219	1,360	2,130
Business Equipment				
Business Equipment Digest	M	39,767	1,970	2,660
Office Equipment News	M	49,235	3,200	4,010
Office Trade News	M	6,889	1,575	2,205
Business Management				
The Director	M	40,106	3,180	4,380
The Economist	W	284,691[a]	8,150	21,000
Management Today	M	96,157	6,615	8,380
New Scientist	W	86,342	2,835	4,080
Catering				
Caterer & Hotelkeeper	W	40,259	1,820	2,800
Catering	M	44,172	1,600	2,620
Computers				
Computer Shopper	M	127,339	1,655	2,365
Computer Weekly	W	112,022	3,677	4,929
Computing	W	115,421	3,759	5,019
Personal Computer World	M	112,306	2,255	2,955
Confectionery, Tobacco & Newsagents				
Confectioner, Tobacconist, Newsagent	W	16,236	2,965	3,830
Retail Newsagent	W	17,061	928	1,725

ont'd)

	Issue frequency	Circulation (1)	Page rates (2)	
			Mono £	4 colour £
Electrical Appliances				
Electrical & Radio Trading	W	8,005	1,490	2,600
The Independent Electrical Retailer	M	–	1,350	2,100
Electronics				
Electronics Times	W	34,916	2,275	2,885
Electronics Weekly	W	32,764	2,200	2,800
Engineering – General				
The Engineer	W	39,643	1,990	2,990
Engineering	M	21,336	1,750	2,580
Engineering News	M	76,288	2,925	4,200
Finance & Investment				
Financial Adviser	W	40,228	2,775	3,850
Investors Chronicle	W	45,015	3,100	4,300
Footwear				
Shoe & Leather News	M	4,902	675	1,250
Furnishings				
Cabinet Maker	W	8,100	1,185	1,910
Furnishing	M	10,552	1,825	2,350
Grocery Trade				
The Grocer	W	56,274	555	2,315
Independent Grocer	F	40,049	1,325	2,450
Super Marketing	W	18,077	2,100	2,800
Hardware & Ironmongery, DIY				
DIY Week	F	16,258	1,785	2,860
Hardware & Garden Review	M	17,782	2,825	3,805
Jewellery				
British Jeweller	M	–	550	965
Retail Jeweller	F	9,165	2,120	2,520
Medical – General & Nursing				
British Medical Journal	W	–	1,550	2,300
The Lancet	W	27,550	811	1,376
Nursing Times/Nursing Mirror	W	92,101	1,094	1,664
The Practitioner	M	40,619	1,590	2,515
Update	F	33,676	1,964	3,040
Motor Trade				
Autotrade	M	35,073	2,065	3,040
Garage & Automotive Retailer	M	–	1,900	2,400
Garage News	M	16,228	1,420	2,070
Motor Industry Management	M	26,563	850	1,450
Motor Trader	W	25,003	2,075	3,055
Service Station	M	–	1,430	1,980

Table 2.7 (Cont'd)

	Issue frequency	Circulation (1)	Page rates (2)	
			Mono £	4 colour £
Pharmaceutical				
Chemist & Druggist	W	15,541	1,995	2,570
Pharmaceutical Journal	W	42,938	1,995	2,660
Photography				
British Journal of Photography	W	8,492	925	1,285
The Photographer	M	–	995	1,525
Professional Photographer	M	–	772	1,330
Sports & Leisure Trade				
Amenity Management	M	6,124	940	1,320
Sports Trader	M	2,620	705	1,175
Toys				
Toy Trader	M	5,025	880	1,350
Transport (Road)				
Commercial Motor	W	27,503	1,450	2,765
Motor Transport	W	28,766	2,400	3,550
Truck	M	39,686	1,400	2,475
Travel				
Business Traveller	M	47,552	2,590	3,475
Executive Travel	M	38,029	2,660	3,625
Travel Trade Gazette (UK & Ireland)	W	24,596	2,345	3,545
Wine and Spirit Trade				
Licensee	M	31,571	1,500	2,300
Morning Advertiser	D	16,459	2,200	3,050
Off-Licence News	W	25,076	1,810	3,080
Publican	W	32,446	3,199	4,264

Note: The space available allows us to show only a small proportion of existing titles. Inclusion of title does not imply any preference over those not shown.

Sources: (1) ABC data January–December 1992 & July–December 1992. (2) BRAD. August 1993, single insertion rate. [a]Worldwide sales, excl. N. American edition.

variety of influences can be assessed.

More complex models generally seek to explain the relationship between different aspects of the buying decision-making process.

THE HOWARD SHETH MODEL

A comprehensive theoretical model of buying behaviour is the Howard Sheth Model which is illustrated in Figure 2.5 on page 36.

The key factors here are:

1 *Inputs*. These all have an impact on the buying decision. They comprise:

- product information – about price, quality, specification, alternative brands/services etc.
- behaviour – influenced by attitudes, culture and social class

35

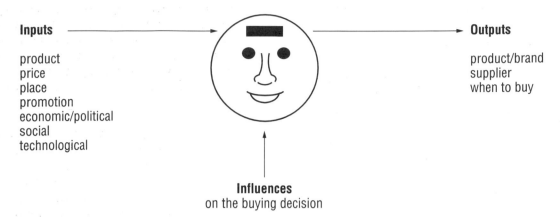

Fig 2.4 The Black Box Model of buyer behaviour.

- perception – this will be influenced by the source of the information. The individual will be selective in the type of information remembered

2 The process. This is determined by:

- the motivation to purchase – there is a potential for satisfaction which might be based on previous experience. This is the criterion on which a product/service is judged

- inhibitors – these are those aspects which might restrain the individual from buying the product/service. They may include:

  – the availability of the product/service
  – whether or not money is available to purchase the product/service at the right time

3 Outputs. These are determined by whether or not the individual decides to make the purchase.

Inputs	Process	Outputs
Product information: Price, specification, image, brand etc.	Motivation to purchase: Satisfiers Past experience Judgements	Purchasing decision: Yes? No?
Behaviour: Attitudes Culture Social class	Inhibitors: Price acceptability Brand Availability Product Price	
Perception: Filtering and selection of information		

Fig 2.5 A simple representation of the Sheth Model of buyer behaviour.

This model confirms a number of points in relation to buyer behaviour:

- how complex the buying decision-making process is
- the need to evaluate customer satisfaction
- the need to understand both the motivation which results in the buyer purchasing the product/service and the external factors which have an impact on the buying decision
- the theory has been used in practical examples and has been proved to work

2.5 ORGANISATIONAL BUYING BEHAVIOUR

Buying decisions in organisations are made by both individuals and groups of individuals, all of whom are influenced by issues similar to those which affect their personal buying decisions. The main aspects of organisational buying are:

- the need to purchase items which help the organisation to meet its corporate objectives
- the fact that the buying process may take longer depending on how many individual groups are involved in the decision-making process

TYPES OF PURCHASING DECISIONS

1 *Re-purchase decisions.* Organisations place repeat purchase orders for items or materials and equipment which they use routinely. In many cases long-term contracts are negotiated and stock is re-ordered when minimum stock levels are reached on stock-control records.

2 *Modified re-purchase decisions.* Purchases of a routine nature may be reviewed from time to time based on the updating of quality standards and the possibility that current suppliers are unable to meet the new standards required by the company. Cost may be a factor, and it may be necessary to seek more cost-effective sources.

3 *New purchase decisions.* These involve the purchase of materials/services related to a new product/service being offered by the company, or to the re-launch of an updated version of an existing product/service. Purchasing which is related to a new product can be risky. Buyers have no previous knowledge of the materials/services required, and there is a need to seek, analyse, evaluate and decide on new sources of supply.

4 *Contracts.* Some industrial purchasing takes place 'under contract'. The products involved are 'standard' ones and are sometimes produced to exact specifications provided by the customer – e.g. components (electrical etc.), paint etc. Such products are offered in a marketplace which generally has only a few large customers – e.g. industrial paint, car manufacturers, government and local authority etc.

Suppliers of these types of product, before they can put in a tender, must be verified as reliable and be able to supply the particular products/services required. Competition in this type of marketplace is usually based purely on price. This forces suppliers to operate cost-effectively in order to remain competitive.

2.6 STAGES IN THE PURCHASE DECISION-MAKING PROCESS

As in consumer purchase decision-making, a number of stages can be identified in the organisational purchase decision-making process:

1 the identification of a product/service need
2 the need for a tight specification for the product/service to be sourced
3 the need to identify possible suppliers of the new product/service
4 requests for samples of costs from shortlisted supplier sources
5 the evaluation of information received and a decision on which supplier source to use, including an agreement on the terms and conditions which relate to the supply and purchase of the goods/services.

Buying decision-making in organisations is not

37

usually the sole responsibility of one individual. An identification of the members of what is termed the Decision-making Unit (the DMU) is essential if marketing to organisations is to be effective.

1 More people will be part of the DMU when complex decisions are to be made.
2 Senior management will be more involved where the buying decision involves quite a large capital outlay.

The DMUs may consist of:

- an individual manager or director who has responsibility for all purchasing decisions
- governing bodies, management committees etc.

Because of the variety of individuals who are likely to be involved in the buying decision with a DMU, potential suppliers must:

- establish how purchase decisions are made
- know which individuals constitute the DMU, and
- identify those individuals within the DMU who wield the most influence

Within the DMU, a number of roles can be identified:

1 *The User* – the individual consumer of the product, i.e. the production manager etc., who will have some influence on the purchasing decision because he or she is the end user. The User may also be:

  – involved in budgeting, and will need to measure value for money
  – the one who is most affected by faulty products, late delivery etc.

2 *The Gatekeeper* – the individual who receives all information regarding potential suppliers and their goods/services. Alternatively, the Gatekeeper may take the form of a purchasing department within the organisation, and its composition is likely to include several members who have specific

technical/operational knowledge which will influence the buying decision. Technical specifications and trade literature are scanned and information is filtered before relevant data is passed on to others.

The Gatekeeper will most likely know as much about suppliers (and their competitors) as is known about its own company's products/services.

3 *The Influencer* – is valued for his or her expertise, e.g. on computer systems, and will be able to influence the buying decision-making process.

The supplier may find it difficult to establish every source of influence within the buying organisation. However, two types of influence can be identified:

- *internal* – including Users and Gatekeepers. However, senior managers/departmental managers and other levels of management will also be involved as the actual purchase gets nearer because the consequences of the purchasing decision will rest ultimately with them.

  Buying decisions within an organisation tend to be conservative, and individuals are unlikely to recommend one supplier in favour of another in case something goes wrong.
- *external* – including:

  – the direct sales team and those from competing suppliers
  – sources of influence within competing companies at senior management level
  – reports in trade newspapers and trade journals

4 *The Decision-maker* – the individual who actually makes the decision to buy. In the case of all new purchases and re-buys, senior managers are those most likely to make the buying decisions. When major capital equipment is to be purchased, i.e. plant and equipment etc., it is likely that directors will make the final buying decision.

5 *The Buyer* – the person who is responsible for actually placing the order and ensuring delivery is made as required. This role is usually housed within the buying department of the company. Senior Buyers will be involved depending on their status within the organisation and the extent to which they are consulted by the decision-makers.

Centralised buying departments tend to carry a great deal more influence.

It is important, therefore, that advertising communication materials be carefully thought through and produced to ensure that they do arrive on the desk of the appropriate Decision-maker/Decision-making Unit within the organisation.

The decision to buy a product/service, whether made by a consumer or by an organisation, is complex, and as described, a variety of influences will have an impact on the final decision.

2.7 CASE STUDY: KELLOGG'S

Kellogg's is the UK's leading manufacturer of breakfast cereal, marketing over 25 different brands. The company's marketing strategy is long-term and continuous – British people have been consuming Kellogg's breakfast cereals for over 60 years.

Kellogg's review their marketing plans annually and collect information from a variety of sources so that all aspects of the brand and markets are understood. They monitor continuously how their own and other brands perform in both the household and retail sectors. In the case of households, trends in types of breakfast food consumed as well as demographic profiles are monitored, and in terms of retail sales, information is gathered on volume, distribution and pricing as well as on 'value-share'. Kellogg's also carry out *ad hoc* research to gather more specific information relative to one aspect of marketing. Objectives for each brand are identified and a marketing plan is then developed.

The company feels that their commitment to advertising over a prolonged period has helped to produce loyalty to their brand – the majority of Kellogg's marketing budget is allocated to advertising. Kellogg's begin an advertising campaign by briefing their advertising agency, stipulating both

the type of consumer behaviour or attitude the company wishes to encourage and the types of media that have been selected. In the case of TV advertising, the agency develops scripts in line with the brief, and when these have been agreed the agency produces the advertisement.

Kellogg's select media in terms of the most cost-effective way of reaching their targeted audience. Television is the main media for Kellogg's major brands. However, other media are also used when there is a benefit to be gained from trying to reach a smaller target audience. Kellogg's have used the press to advertise All-Bran in order to give more information about this product.

In terms of sales promotion, Kellogg's use a variety of approaches:

1 Free sampling, free inserts and bonus packs are used to encourage brand switching.
2 Money-off coupons and offers are used to encourage people to purchase again and again as well as to build brand loyalty.

(Adapted from information supplied by Kellogg's)

2.8 CASE STUDY: PROCTER & GAMBLE

Procter & Gamble, manufacturer of detergents and allied products, feel that marketing is about identifying and satisfying consumer wants and their aim is to produce products which result in consumer satisfaction. P&G recognise that consumers are different, and so they also aim to produce products which meet the needs of different customer profiles.

P&G's marketing/advertising is developed on the basis of a thorough knowledge of the product together with an understanding of which consumers will be the end users. In an effort to market a brand effectively, P&G will:

– develop appropriate advertising
– use sales promotion
– collect information about the market
– analyse information relative to sales and distribution
– develop a long- and short-term budget plan.

P&G do not publish the size of their advertising spend, and the company has no corporate advertising budget – each brand stands alone. The level of spending on each brand is developed on the basis of the expected sales volume and the costs of the product. Advertising is aimed at all potential users – mainly housewives, but for a product like Pampers nappies the profile is tighter. A consumer profile is produced based on age/sex/income/family background, and appropriate media are then identified to reach the specific target group(s).

Although P&G use sales to measure the success of an advertising campaign, the company feels that other factors such as value for money and how well the product does the job can also contribute to the success or failure of a brand. Sales and advertising are dependent upon each other. P&G use sales promotions to increase volume. In-store and point-of-sale materials and displays are used to make the product attractive to the consumer. The advertisement tries to demonstrate the benefits of a specific product to the consumer by using a memorable advertising communication.

The majority of P&G's advertising appears on television. The company uses an agency to create its advertisements. The agency uses the marketing strategy identified by the company and develops ideas which will demonstrate the product's main selling points. The ideas are then presented as 'storyboards' – in the case of television – or as 'layouts' – for other media – to the group within P&G responsible for the brand. The idea(s) are evaluated, and when they are agreed upon, the agency organises the campaign.

(Adapted from information supplied by Procter & Gamble)

STUDENT ACTIVITY

Work in pairs.

1 Scan magazines/newspapers etc. to identify a current advertisement for either a Kellogg's or Procter & Gamble product.
2 Analyse the advertisement and identify which consumer group the advertisement is aimed at.
3 Produce a detailed customer profile of the target audience.

Present your ideas orally to the rest of the group. Ensure that you justify your ideas/explanations fully.

REVIEW YOUR PROGRESS

1 What do you understand by the term 'perception'?
2 What are the influences which have an impact on consumer buying decision-making? Write a paragraph explaining each.
3 Identify and explain the social influences which have an impact on consumer buyer behaviour.
4 What types of influence can lifestyle have on the buying decisions of individuals and families?
5 Explain the Howard Sheth Model of buyer behaviour.
6 Explain the various stages in the purchase decision-making process of organisations.
7 Identify the various elements which make up the Decision-making Unit of an organisation, and explain what you understand by each.

3

Types of advertising

AIMS

- to identify and explain the different approaches
  to advertising for each of the following markets:

  - industrial/trade
  - retail
  - corporate/financial
  - recruitment

UNIT 20 ADVERTISING

- Element 20.1

  - Performance Criteria:
    2 Recommend focus of appeal to be used for target
      audience

It is usual for marketeers to use the same strategy for all
types of market. There are significant differences in what
and how advertising occurs in different sectors of the
marketplace. These sectors include:

  - industrial/trade
  - retail
  - corporate
  - finance
  - recruitment

Consumer behaviour and approaches to advertising are
detailed in Chapters 2, 8 and 9. We will now consider the
other sectors identified above.

3.1 INDUSTRIAL/TRADE ADVERTISING

Industrial advertising offers information about business goods and services – i.e. machine tools, cleaning services, industrial processes etc. – to businesses (business-to-business advertising).

STUDENT ACTIVITY

In teams of three or four, carry out a search in your school/college/local library to identify a variety of trade journals.

1 Choose one journal and analyse the types of advertisement found in it.
2 Choose one other magazine aimed at a different market segment, i.e. women's/ men's magazines etc.
3 What is different about the type and content of the advertisements which appear in the trade journal as compared with the advertisements which appear in the other magazine you have chosen?

Discuss your findings with the larger group.

The purpose of industrial advertising is usually to:

1 raise awareness of the company's products/services to both current and potential customers
2 give specific product and, if applicable, technical information to prospective customers
3 improve sales-force performance and hence effect cost savings as a result of 1 and 2 above.

Industrial markets are very focused, and two difficulties may occur:

1 Is it possible for the advertiser to identify the person who will make the final purchasing decision within the buying organisation? (See Chapter 2.)

2 The purchasing decision-maker may not be easily reached by a direct sales approach, and therefore an alternative approach must be found to enable access to the buyer – i.e. the production of detailed technical product pamphlets, with price lists etc., addressed to the individual concerned. (See Chapter 2.)

3.2 RETAIL ADVERTISING

Advertising within the retail sector aims to draw the attention of customers to products which are available on a particular day at a specific price. The type of advertising found within a retail store is an attempt by the retailer to present a particular kind of image which the customer can relate to. This image helps to draw customers to the store and creates a continuing throughput of customers regardless of the products advertised at any one time.

STUDENT ACTIVITY

Work in small teams and choose a local food store. Visit the store and identify how many posters appear in the windows and around the store.

1 What types of product are being advertised?
2 How many are special offers?
3 Are there any new products?
4 Did any of them appear particularly striking to you?
5 What were the strengths and weaknesses of the poster advertising in the store you visited?

Share the information by giving an oral presentation of your findings.

A good retailer will anticipate customer needs and ensure that the products required are offered at an advantageous price.

If retail advertising is to be successful, it should:

- offer attractive goods at attractive prices to its customers
- ensure that promotional activities in-store are co-ordinated so as to ensure that the products being promoted are available for customers to buy.

CO-OPERATIVE SUPPORT FOR ADVERTISERS

Retailers receive supportive co-operative advertising from manufacturers who usually agree to participate in standard programmes of promotion. These include:

1 events available throughout the year to help sustain product promotion
2 events available to support a specific promotional package
3 point-of-sale materials usually offered by manufacturers during such co-operative campaigns, and usually backed up by a larger national campaign.

STUDENT ACTIVITY

Carry out a survey of a variety of press/ magazine advertisements and see if you can identify six advertisements where two different companies have co-operated and

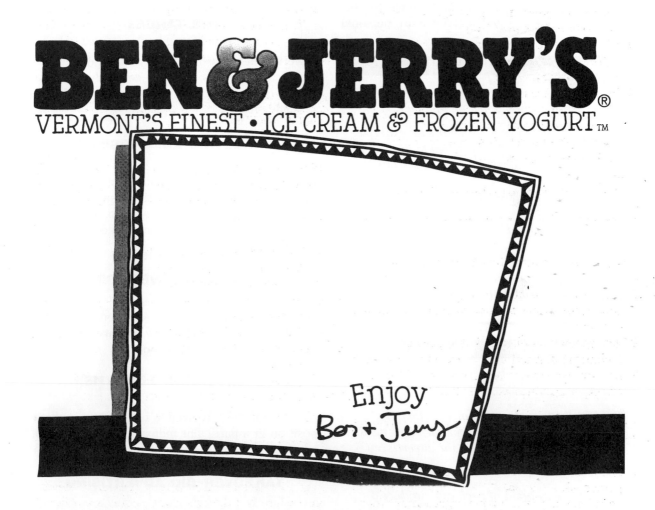

Fig 3.1 An example of point-of-sale materials: a banner for Ben & Jerry's ice cream.

shared the costs of advertising, i.e. where both products are being promoted at the same time within one advertisement. Discuss your findings with the rest of your group and explain what advantage you think there might be for each company in this type of co-operative advertising.

Manufacturers may also provide product materials to assist with illustrations in newspaper campaigns. In addition they might suggest particular themes, and provide copy to support and promote these themes. Shortened versions of television and radio campaign scripts may be provided by the manufacturer so that the retailer can add his or her own 'strapline' or jingle to customise the message and make it more personal and local.

STUDENT ACTIVITY

Figure 3.2 on pages 45–8 shows an example of advertising material supplied to the retail trade by Walkers Smiths Snack Foods Limited.

1 What is the purpose of the advertising material?
2 What are the six steps proposed to improve profits?

Evaluate the document and produce a brief report of your conclusions.

STUDENT ACTIVITY

Look at the four illustrations for Baxters products on pages 49–52. For each one, decide: at which market segment is the advertising aimed?

Evaluate the content of each and produce a brief report of your analysis.

3.3 # CORPORATE/ FINANCIAL ADVERTISING

Corporate advertising usually refers to advertising which is aimed at promoting the financial and business interests of a company. Corporate advertising includes:

- prestige advertising
- advocacy advertising
- diversification advertising
- takeover-bid advertising
- crisis advertising
- financial advertising

THE TARGET

Advertisements usually appear in the business and financial press, and are generally aimed at Socio-economic Group A (the professional class of readership).

PRESTIGE ADVERTISING

Usually termed 'PR' (i.e. public relations), this includes image-building advertisements. This form of advertising space is purchased in order to present a series of controlled messages when and how the company wishes.

ADVOCACY ADVERTISING

A company may have been attacked by another company or other third party, and it will present facts to disprove the criticisms.

DIVERSIFICATION ADVERTISING

If a company is perceived to be in a monopolistic position in a particular industry, it may take out advertising space to try to dispel this impression.

TAKEOVER-BID ADVERTISING

Companies involved in takeovers may become embroiled in a battle to persuade shareholders

Fig 3.2 A Walkers Crisps leaflet circulated to retailers (continued on pages 46–8).

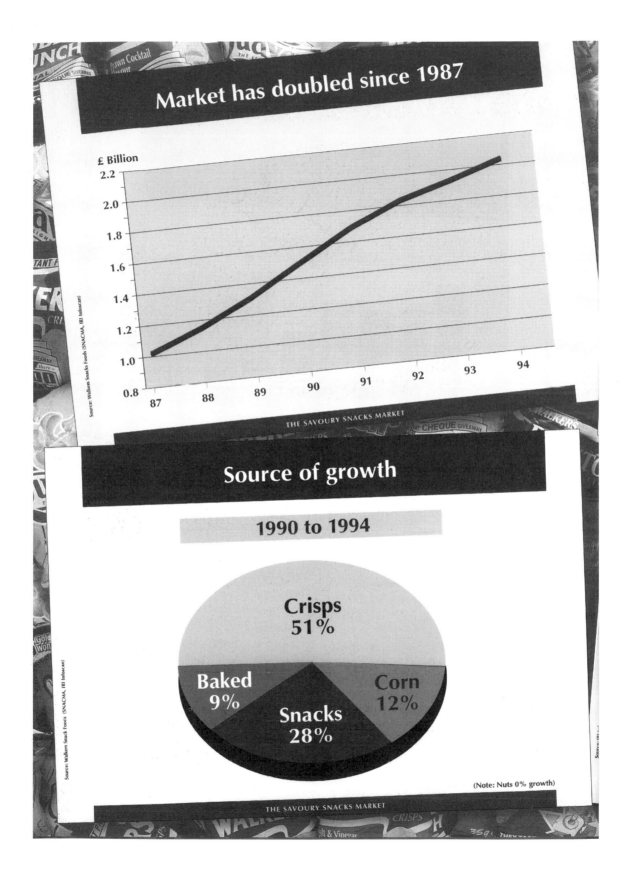

Market has doubled since 1987

£ Billion

Source: Walkers Snacks Foods (SNACMA, IRI Infoscan)

THE SAVOURY SNACKS MARKET

Source of growth

1990 to 1994

Crisps 51%

Baked 9%

Corn 12%

Snacks 28%

(Note: Nuts 0% growth)

Source: Walkers Snack Foods (SNACMA, IRI Infoscan)

THE SAVOURY SNACKS MARKET

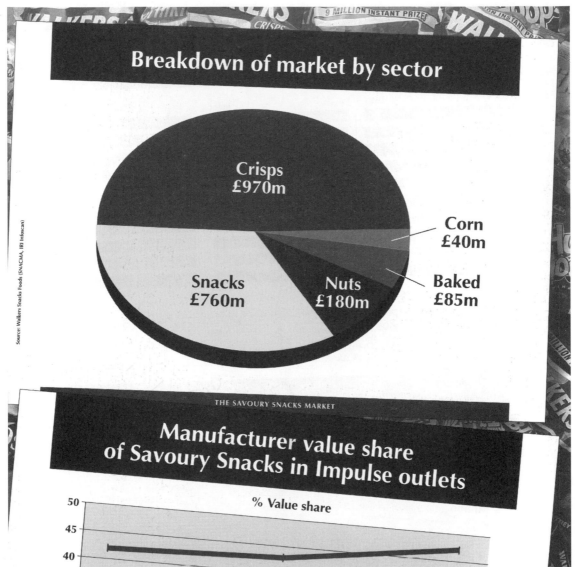

Breakdown of market by sector

Crisps
£970m

Corn
£40m

Baked
£85m

Snacks
£760m

Nuts
£180m

Source: Walkers Snacks Foods (SNACMA, IRI Infoscan)

THE SAVOURY SNACKS MARKET

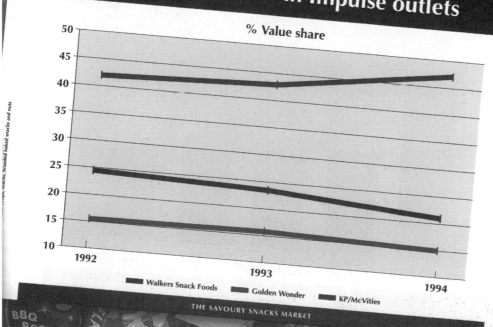

Manufacturer value share
of Savoury Snacks in Impulse outlets

% Value share

(line chart with values 10–50 on y-axis; years 1992, 1993, 1994 on x-axis)

crisps, snacks, branded baked snacks and nuts

Walkers Snack Foods   Golden Wonder   KP/McVities

THE SAVOURY SNACKS MARKET

47

Top-selling packs 1994 – Impulse

#	Pack	Index
1	Walkers C&O Std	100
2	Walkers RS Std	96
3	Walkers S&V Std	60
4	Quavers C Std	50
5	Walkers SB Std	31
6	Walkers B&O Std	29
7	Walkers PC Std	29
8	Wotsits C Std	29
9	Walkers RC Std	27
10	Skips PC Std	25

#	Pack	Index
11	Walkers WS Std	23
12	GW RS Std	22
13	GW C&O Std	22
14	Doritos C Std*	20
15	Hula Hoops RS Std	19
16	Monster Munch PO Std	18
17	Walkers Crinkles CC&C Std	17
18	GW S&V Std	17
19	Nik Naks Spice Std	16
20	Doritos B Std*	16

#	Pack	Index
21	Doritos Original Std*	16
22	Monster Munch B Std	15
23	D/Crunch CS 40g	14
24	Walkers PO Std	13
25	Hula Hoops BBQ Std	13
26	Mini Cheddars 30g	13
27	Frazzles Std	11
28	Monster Munch Mega*	11
29	Snaps (all flavours)	11
30	Walkers TK Std	11

Source: IRI Infoscan value sales 1994 NB excludes private label *Sales Annualised

Walkers Snack Foods

KP/McVities

Golden Wonder

B	Beef	CS	Chargrilled Steak	SB	Smoky Bacon
B&O	Beef & Onion	PC	Prawn Cocktail	SC&O	Sour Cream & Onion
C	Cheese	PO	Pickled Onion	S&V	Salt & Vinegar
CC&C	Cream Cheese & Chives	RC	Roast Chicken	TK	Tomato Ketchup
C&O	Cheese & Onion	RS	Ready Salted	WS	Worcester Sauce

THE SAVOURY SNACKS MARKET

Savoury Snacks has the largest food brand in the UK

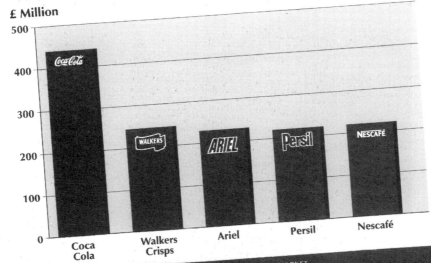

Source: Nielsen/Marketing Top 100 Brands 1994

THE SAVOURY SNACKS MARKET

Baxters Special Soups now come dressed for the occasion.

Impeccably so, may we add.

As befits an occasion. Baxters very special soups are now resplendent in elegant black tie and pinstripes.

There's a newcomer to the range, too; Baxters Beef Consommé, a classic clear soup lovingly created in our family kitchens. Baxters have been making very special soups for well over a 100 years, and always with the same philosophy – only the very best ingredients are good enough for us.

We add a dash of brandy here and a little sherry there to create a range of seven very special soups, now at very reasonable prices.

They aren't just for formal dinners, though. Try these soups as a touch of luxury in your cooking, as exotic sauces and indulgent but inexpensive snacks.

Baxters soups – made to make the occasion really special.

BY APPOINTMENT TO
HER MAJESTY THE QUEEN   FRUIT CANNERS
W. A. BAXTER & SONS LTD

Baxters
REAL SOUP

BAXTERS OF SPEYSIDE LTD., SCOTLAND

Fig 3.3 Two examples of advertising materials for Baxters products aimed at consumers.

Mother is our very own Ena Baxter, and her soup, Baxters Chicken Broth.

Like mothers everywhere, she uses her own special recipe, and nobody else's soup seems quite as good.

Which is why our Chicken Broth is produced to this day in strict accordance with her original methods.

And if it takes a little longer to make, costs a good deal more for the ingredients, then so be it. After all, mother was never one to make soup down to a price, but up to her own impeccable standards.

It's the philosophy right at the heart of Baxters. Indeed, every soup in our Tartan range (with the Baxters name in red) is lovingly

The soup that mother makes.

We take only the finest, freshest vegetables (with the magnificent Spey Valley on our doorstep, there's plenty to choose from), and simmer them in a rich stock with chicken, herbs, and Mrs Baxter's own personal blend of spices. The result is a wholesome, nourishing soup with a splendid flavour.

and carefully prepared in the traditional way.

So too are our sumptuous Special Occasion Soups - now distinguished in black – and our brand new Vegetarian Soups with the Baxters name in crisp, fresh green.

Every can of Baxters is a can of REAL SOUP, soup like your mother used to make.

BY APPOINTMENT TO HER MAJESTY THE QUEEN FRUIT CANNERS W A BAXTER & SONS LTD

Baxters

REAL SOUP

BAXTERS OF SPEYSIDE LTD., SCOTLAND.

Fig 3.4 Two examples of advertising materials for Baxters products aimed at retailers.

Baxters

Britain's No.1 Beetroot brand. Shouldn't you be selling it?

- *Available in packs of six.*
- *Available from your local cash & carry or delivered wholesaler.*
- *You profit from Baxters quality.*

The family of fine foods.

 CERT No. FM 23297   FOR FURTHER INFORMATION CONTACT *Ron Murray* AT *Baxters of Speyside Limited*, FOCHABERS, SCOTLAND IV32 7LD. Tel: 0343 820393.

that the bid is favourable, and each side might take up advertising space in the press in order to present the facts as they see them.

CRISIS ADVERTISING

In crisis situations – i.e. strikes, breakdowns in services – advertisements will appear in the press stating the employer's side of the story or explaining what has happened to the service in question.

FINANCIAL ADVERTISING – SHARE ISSUES

When a private company becomes a public company, shares are sold. Advertisements appear in the press offering shares in, for instance, privatised industries to members of the public.

3.4 RECRUITMENT ADVERTISING

Recruitment advertising, like any other form, is developed within guidelines laid down by a variety of sources. Recruitment advertising must conform to employment law, including Statutes of the Equal Opportunities and Sex Discrimination Acts. The Commission for Racial Equality and the Equal Opportunities Commission have laid down codes of practice which help to regulate job advertisements.

In 1990 the Institute of Personnel Management (now the Institute of Personnel Development) suggested that recruitment advertisements take into account certain criteria:

- the personnel specification should outline specific and relevant information regarding job requirements
- the company should give correct information about itself, and this information should be 'realistic, factual and clear'
- the advertisement should identify:

  - where the job is located
  - the salary being offered

  - details of any additional allowances being offered

- precise instructions should be given regarding the procedure for applications which detail whether an applicant should telephone or write for an application form or whether a letter and CV is the preference
- advertisements should not discriminate against minority groups or on grounds of gender except where detailed in the Sex Discrimination Act or Race Relations Act

Within employment legislation, it is suggested that companies encourage applicants from under-represented groups.

STUDENT ACTIVITY

Choose one of the quality newspapers which include an Appointments Section and scan the pages of job advertisements.

1 How many advertisements encourage applicants from 'underrepresented' groups (those which state, say, 'applications from women are especially welcome as they are underrepresented in the organisation')?
2 Make a list of the types of job where these statements have appeared.
3 Are there specific types of job which attract this type of notice (i.e. are they mostly management or clerical etc.)?
4 Were there any advertisements which stated that a man or woman only should apply?

Present your findings in a brief presentation to the rest of your group.

THE CONTENT OF RECRUITMENT ADVERTISEMENTS

Advertisements may be developed either in-house or by a recruitment agency. If an agency is used, the organisation will discuss requirements, and the agency will usually:

- produce the advertisement

- place the advertisement in an appropriate publication
- filter applications
- carry out preliminary interviews
- shortlist the most appropriate candidates
- arrange with the company dates and times of interviews
- organise psychological testing if required
- carry out a follow-up in terms of applicants who have been unsuccessful.

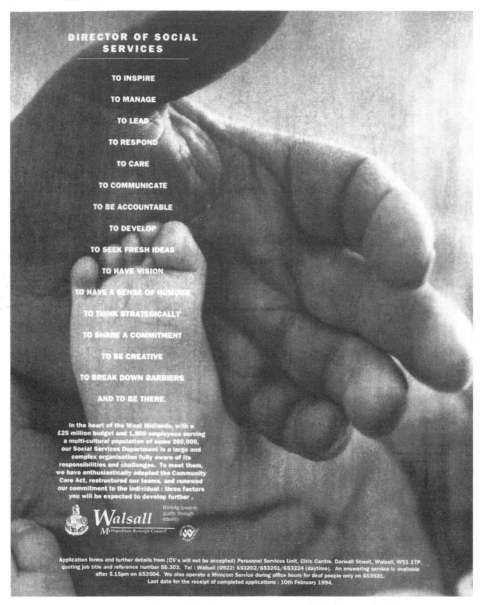

Advertisement of the Year

Client: Walsall Metropolitan Borough Council
Agency: Austin Knight UK Ltd

Fig 3.5 Advertisement of the Year 1994.

THE WORLD IS WATCHING

LLOYD'S
LLOYD'S OF LONDON

NEW AND RECENT GRADUATES

There is no escaping that Lloyd's of London has recently gone through one of the most difficult periods in our 300 years of history. World attention has been focused on how we react. So it is now more important than ever for everyone to see how quickly and effectively we are responding to the lessons we have learned – re-examining the way we do things and undertaking a significant programme of changes and developments that re-establishes the very best in our traditional values and builds new ones for the future. The results will confirm that not only are we the world's most important insurance market, but also the most responsive, innovative and modern.

To succeed we need the very best people. That's why we are currently looking for exceptional graduates (2-1 minimum) who have either recently graduated or already started work. Highly intelligent people with the dedication and determination to immerse themselves in a challenge that is as tough as it is significant. Individuals who are not afraid of the limelight as we achieve our goals. In short, people who are able to make a major contribution to one of the most vital periods of our development.

You'll be employed by a Lloyd's broker, agent or the

Corporation. Whichever, we will provide an unprecedented depth of training in this unique environment. The training provides a direct involvement in the entire workings of the Lloyd's market – underwriting, broking and at the centre. Within this programme everything is geared to your gaining a truly comprehensive knowledge. We will strike the balance between your working on projects that directly tackle real issues backed by structured programmes tailored to your own individual requirements.

The graduate career we can offer will not suit everybody. It was never meant to. Only those confident of their exceptional abilities and prepared to put them on open display, should apply. But with the world watching, your success will be all the more conspicuous. If you meet our stringent requirements and want to participate not watch please apply by sending a Standard Application Form or full CV to Graduate Recruitment, Lloyd's of London, One Lime Street, London EC3M 7HA. If you want more information please call our consultants on 071 580 0522 weekdays during normal office hours. Please quote reference 4566.

Closing date for telephone calls 3rd October 1994.

▸ Financial & Legal

Client: Lloyd's of London
Agency: Moxon Dolphin & Kerby

"This advertisement is highly effective. It is strong typographically with an honest and straightforward approach."

CATEGORY SPONSORED BY THE ROYAL BANK OF SCOTLAND

▾ Senior Management

Client: Walsall Metropolitan Borough Council
Agency: Austin Knight UK Ltd

"Excellent use of copy, breaking with some of the conventions of recruitment copywriting, and it says a lot about the organisation you'd be working for."

CATEGORY SPONSORED BY THE ROYAL BANK OF SCOTLAND

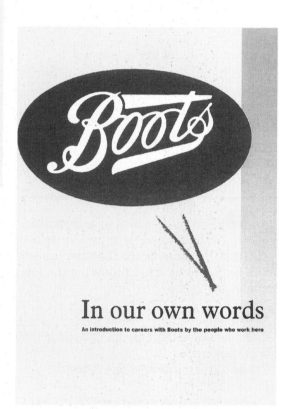

In our own words

An introduction to careers with Boots by the people who work here

▴ Recruitment Brochures

Client: Boots the Chemists
Agency: Media System Ltd

"This brochure is genuine, approachable and very appealing. A clean and simple style combined with excellent photography."

CATEGORY SPONSORED BY THE ROYAL BANK OF SCOTLAND

Fig 3.6 Examples of recruitment advertisements with critical comments.

Work in pairs. *Choose either a national
newspaper or local newspaper which
advertises job vacancies.*

1 Select two advertisements.
2 Critically evaluate both:

- *What do you feel are the strengths and
  weaknesses in each case?*
- *What information is superfluous, if any?*
- *What information is missing, if any?*

*3 Produce what you feel is a strong
recruitment advertisement for one of these
posts.*

*Give a presentation to your group explaining
your analysis of the two advertisements.
Explain also what you feel are the strengths of
the advertisement which you have produced.*

If the personnel professional or an individual responsible for recruitment within an organisation
is handling the vacancy, the following guidelines
should be followed when producing the job advertisement:

- As with all other advertising, the
  communication must be relevant to the group
  being targeted.
- The advertiser will need to consider:

  - what size the advertisement should be (1/4,
    1/2, full page etc.)
  - the costs in terms of size, publication etc.
  - which publications would be most suitable
    for the advertisement to appear in
  - whether to use humour in the
    advertisement
  - whether to include information regarding
    the salary level
  - whether to use the company's name or a
    box number

- Recruitment advertisements must provide

enough information to allow prospective
candidates to decide *not* to apply. They
cannot do this if the information regarding the
skills, knowledge and experience required is
not included in the job advertisement. It is
also important for the advertisement to
encourage individuals to apply who find the
post interesting and who have the potential to
succeed within it.

Produce an appropriate job advertisement for
the following post:

*Wexford Property Company requires a
Personal Assistant. He or she should be
familiar with word-processing packages, and
definitely be familiar with WordPerfect 5.2.
The company needs someone with a bright,
lively personality. The candidate needs to be
tidy in appearance. The job might entail some
driving. Good interpersonal communication
ability is important. The person must be a
good organiser and be able to keep track of a
boss who is always under pressure and who
seems unable to organise himself – help with
this would be appreciated.*

*The office is always very busy, so being able
to work under pressure and to tight deadlines
is important. The individual will need to
liaise with a variety of clients and
organisations.*

*Interested people should reply to Jane
Selman, Wexford Property, 1 Free Lane,
Oxmond, Leicester, in writing. CV and letter
necessary. Closing date? Well, they need to
appoint quickly so the sooner the better!*

3.5 CASE STUDY: MCVITIE'S

McVitie's feel that retailers will stock their
brands if retailers know that these brands will be
supported by consumer advertising. A vital part

of their advertising strategy involves creating consumer awareness.

McVitie's spent £8.5 million on television advertising in 1993 because they feel that this medium has the most impact. Indeed, the bulk of McVitie's advertising appears on television, although the press is also important. McVitie's like to create a personality for key brands with which their consumers can easily identify. Their best known creative theme is 'P-P-P-Pick up a penguin'.

McVitie's joined with Tetley in a 'Link and save' shopping promotion which resulted in a tea and biscuits promotion. Offers like 'Buy 2 get 1 free' and '20% extra free' proved to be popular. 'Mail-in' offers where consumers collected wrappers and sent them in in return for a free gift were also popular, and money-off-next-purchase coupons were used as well, to encourage repeat purchases and to help develop consumer loyalty. In-store 'shelf-talkers' are also now used which take the form of banners or flags to attract consumers to specific products. The sampling of products in-store is becoming more and more popular, and McVitie's demonstrate both new and existing products in this way. The reason existing products are also demonstrated is to show the consumer how good these products are.

The Digestive achieved its centenary in 1992, and McVitie's sponsored sporting competitions and advertised specific events in programmes for trade events in the grocery world.

MCVITIE'S TRADE ADVERTISING

McVitie's serve a variety of trade customers, including:

- co-operatives
- wholesalers and cash-and-carry operations
- the food-service sector, e.g. catering establishments
- confectioners, tobacconists and newsagents
- garage forecourt retail outlets
- the corner shop/independent stores/ convenience stores
- major food retailers, i.e. Tesco, Sainsbury, Safeway etc.

McVitie's subdivide these into 'Direct' and 'Indirect' in terms of receipt of deliveries:

1 *Direct* – receive deliveries from United Biscuits Distribution Service. These direct accounts are serviced by a sales representative or account manager who will highlight new products and promotions to the organisations concerned.

2 *Indirect* – these organisations usually buy direct from wholesalers and cash-and-carry operators. These small organisations may also receive a call from a McVitie's sales representative but will usually rely on information which their local supplier provides.

McVitie's support their products by advertising in trade journals, i.e. *Cash and Carry Management, The Grocer* etc. McVitie's feel that this type of advertising is important if the interest of buyers is to be stimulated. McVitie's also feel that it raises awareness of key brands and new products throughout the trade.

In 1993 McVitie's spent more than £1/4 million on trade advertising. However, the total amount which McVitie's spent on advertising and marketing in 1993 was approximately £42 million, to include:

- press, radio and television advertising
- in-store samples, point-of-sale materials, shelf-talkers and dump bins
- leaflets and other field sales materials
- brochures
- support for dealers
- promotion of new products

(Adapted from information supplied by McVitie's)

REVIEW YOUR PROGRESS

1 What are the three main reasons for industrial/trade advertising?
2 Explain what you understand by the term 'co-operative support for advertisers'.
3 What do you understand by the term 'corporate advertising'?
4 Explain what you understand by each of the following terms in relation to advertising:

- prestige
- advocacy
- diversification
- takeover
- crisis
- financial.

5 What are the specific guidelines offered by the Institute of Personnel Development regarding the content of recruitment advertisements?

6 Why is it necessary to target recruitment advertising very specifically?

Media choice 1 – above-the-line

AIMS

- to explain the different types of above-the-line media
- to identify the advantages and disadvantages of each medium
- to understand the impact of each medium on audiences
- to assess media types and use this information to produce a media plan from a given brief

UNIT 20 ADVERTISING

- Element 20.2

    - Performance Criteria:

        1 Explain media characteristics
        3 Select a suitable media mix to reach target audiences
        4 Produce a media plan within a budget

4.1 WHAT ARE ABOVE-THE-LINE MEDIA?

Above-the-line media are those media which are operated independently, i.e. the advertiser has no control over the media itself but has full control over the content of the advertisement. The following are all above-the-line media:

- television
- radio
- the press
- cinema
- posters (outdoor)

4.2 WHICH TO CHOOSE?

There is a large variety of media available to advertisers, and therefore advertisers must choose the medium which best delivers their message to potential customers in the most cost-effective way. Companies generally use one specific medium, i.e. television, the press etc., to lead their campaign (primary medium), and one or more of the other types to support their initial choice (secondary media).

STUDENT ACTIVITY

Read the article from The Grocer, 2 April 1994, about Budweiser and answer the questions that follow.

BIG PUSH PLANNED FOR BUD

A £14 million marketing campaign led by extensive television advertising will be backing Budweiser this year.

The programme is designed to build on the brand's position in the premium packaged lager sector and will tie in the key sales periods and sponsorship programmes.

The TV ads begin in April and run through until the end of July and there will be a Christmas campaign.

Colour press ads will be used to reach niche audiences and 28 sheet posters will appear in August and September.

Links have also been made with radio stations in London and Scotland.

Promotional emphasis this summer will be on the soccer World Cup taking place in the United States. This will include on-pack incentives, promotions, competitions, sponsorship of media coverage and tactical advertising.

The £1 million three year agreement for the Budweiser Basketball League is also continuing as is its sponsorship of drag racing in the UK.

Peter Jackson, marketing director, Anheuser-Busch European Trade, said: 'The brand is number three in the off-trade and has continued to perform well and such a heavyweight campaign will help ensure it remains at the leading edge of the ppl sector.'

1 In 1994 how much money did Budweiser plan to spend on their marketing campaign?
2 How many different types of media did Budweiser use, and what were they?
3 Which was their primary medium?
4 What was the emphasis of their summer campaign?
5 What promotional incentives were offered to customers to encourage them to buy Budweiser?
6 Which sport does Budweiser sponsor?

4.3 THE PRESS

More money is spent on press advertising than on any other media.

STUDENT ACTIVITY

Working in pairs, visit your nearest library.

Make a list of the companies whose expenditure on press advertising is currently the greatest. Produce a table which displays this information.

Discuss your findings with the rest of your group.

The press, as an advertising medium, is used by many thousands of companies. In contrast, just a small proportion of the larger companies advertise on television. Two of the latter are car manufacturers and soft-drinks manufacturers.

STUDENT ACTIVITY

Working in pairs, choose two national newspapers and obtain one copy of each.

1 Identify how many full-, half- and quarter-page advertisements appear.
2 Who are the advertisers and what product/service are they advertising?
3 Why do you think these companies are advertising in a particular newspaper?

Present your findings in a brief talk to your class.

The cost of press advertising may depend upon a number of factors, including:

* whether the press is national, regional or local
* whether it is a display or a classified advertisement
* the size of the advertisement
* where on the page it appears

Figures 4.1 and 4.2 give examples of display and classified advertisements. One appeared in a national newspaper and the other in a local Somerset newspaper:

Fig 4.1 An example of a display advertisement.

61

classifieds

TOPCOAT — face paintings for birthday parties, fun days, play groups, schools and any event. — Tel. (0823) 254199.   16st42

BOUNCY castle hire, indoor/outdoor, £20, ideal for parties. — Tel. 0823 283724.   16st39

AMAZING Magic for kids/cabaret, fetes/weddings. — Tel. Tim on 0823 288812.   16gstm38

018 PROPERTY FOR SALE

BRIDGWATER, Bower Estate, immaculate semi, uPVC windows throughout, Economy 7 Heating, enclosed south facing garden. Garage. £47,000. — Tel. 0278 425915.   18gmst38p

020 PROPERTY TO LET

TO let, furnished house with garden, off Lisieux Way, £350 per calendar month, no DSS. — Tel. 0823 335312.   20gmst38

TO LET part furnished, modern, two bedroomed house, Wellington centre, gas central heating, available from end of March, usual references, deposit required, no pets, £350 per calendar month. — Tel. Wellington (0823) 662904 evenings.   20gmst38p

021 PROPERTY EXCHANGE

EXCHANGE: Council house, 2 bedroom semi-detached house, large gardens front and rear at Whipton, Exeter, wish to exchange for 2 bedroom house in Taunton area. Cash available. — Tel. (0823) 330357.   21st39

022 ACCOMMODATION

WELLINGTON: Furnished, single room, shared house, central heating, telephone, washing machine. — Tel. 0823 351431 or 0884 841087.   22stgm39

025 PREMISES TO LET

CREWKERNE: Semi-detached rooms, nice house. — Tel. (0460) 76663.   25wyst39

028 MOBILE HOMES

LAKESIDE Park, Bridgwater. Twin unit, 2 bedroom, garden, parking, £20,000 ono. — Tel. Taunton 335084.   28st39

032 COMPUTERS

TRAINING for personal computers/DOS. We come to you so you learn about your computer system. — Tel. (0823) 283724, after 7 p.m. (0823) 286874.   32stgm39

034 ARTICLES FOR SALE

VHS video, £50 needs new head. — Tel. 0278 684762.   34st39

FRIDGES, freezers, cookers, washing machines, reconditioned, guaranteed and delivered; part exchange welcome. — David Disney, Silver Street, Ilminster (0460) 53152.   34wyst43

FAX: New and used from £150 with "on-site warranty" service available for any make; demonstration showroom with the largest display in the West Country. — Adwell (0404) 86591.   34stv43

CARPETS at Bridgwater: All brand new, 15ft. x 12ft from £29, 9ft x 12ft £17; also cheap 12ft x 18ft; could deliver. — Tel. (0278) 685369.   34st43

CARPETS at Taunton, selling now, 15ft. x 12ft. from £29; 9ft. x 12ft., £17 and also 18ft. x 12ft. Can deliver. — Tel. Taunton 321342 up to 9 p.m.   34stgm40p

LAWNMOWER: Qualcast Concorde electric 14in. cylinder, complete with grass-box and long lead, £25. — Tel. 0823 277767.   34st39

Thinking of changing your curtains?
Or have you curtains to sell?
Then consult

THE CURTAIN EXCHANGE

Where a wide range of quality second-hand curtains are on display.

Please phone 0823 326071 for details
34Sg38p

STAIRLIFTS: New and second-hand, bought and sold, fitted and removed by qualified engineers. Free, no obligation assessment, stair lift rental available. — Tel. Ken Mahoney, DMA, (0823) 3355050 (G3).   34wystv41

TWO beige upholstered chairs with chrome swivel base, very good condition, £30 pair. — Tel. 0278 455663 evenings.   34st39

 **BLINDS** TAUNTON **259732** SHADES OF STYLE

FOR PERSONAL SERVICE, QUOTATIONS AND FITTING FREE

VERTICALS — TOP QUALITY BLINDS, WITH NO EXTRA CHARGE FOR COLOURED RAILS 6ft x 4ft (CHOICE OF 30 MATERIALS) FROM **£49**

PLEATED ROOF BLINDS — CHOICE OF 30 MATERIALS, ALSO HEAT REFLECTIVE MATERIALS

VENETIANS & ROLLERS — TOP VALUE FOR SHADING
34st39

WANTED: Fishing equipment, musical instruments, TVs, videos, air guns, music cassettes, recording equipment etc; cash paid. — Contact Fair Deal, 99 Station Road, Taunton. — Tel. (0823) 271680.   34st39

TRICITY electric cooker, double oven, £55. — Tel. 0823 271812.   34st39

MODERN four poster, 5ft. 7in. x 6ft. 8in., mahogany colour, £120. — Tel. 0823 270120▲   34st39

GAS fire, log effect with wooden surround, £80 ono. — Tel. 0278 444129.   34st39p

---

GLASS teak effect unit, 3ft 6in. drawers, cupboards, lights, £60; electric fire, teak surround, coal effect, £15. — Tel. 0278 722185.   3 st39

TABLE (Nathan), solid teak dining table, 5ft x 2ft 6in, extends to 6ft 6in x 2ft 6in, plus four chairs with brown velour seats, all in excellent condition, £165. — Tel. 0278 663811 after 6.30 p.m.   34Sb40p

AGA and Rayburn cookers and wood burning stoves, fully reconditioned, gas and oil conversions available; used models always wanted. — Tel. 0278 691468.   34wystv49

EARLY 1900 chaise longues, one £450; the other, £350 with matching chairs, £100 per pair. — Tel. 0823 259833.   34Sb39

POWERPART hook-up for caravanette or tent, £35 ono; portable mini-loo, ideal for caravanette or tent, £25 ono; girl's or small lday's racing bike, 5-speed, reasonable condition, £30. — Tel. 0823 254572.   34gmst

DAMP? Condensation? Dehumidifier — hire or buy, all sizes. — Tel. Celtic Services 0823 275851.   34Sg39

DRESSING table with mirror and four drawers, teak, £15. — Tel. 0823 254250. 34gmst39

OFFICE furniture, racking, wood/metal filing cabinets, desks, chairs. We've got the lot. — Tel. Chamberlains, Taunton 337491.   34Sg41

OFFICE furniture, new/used, filing cabinets, from £25; desks, chairs, safes, etc. — Tel. 0823 660333.   34Sg38p

SALE: Stone benches, bird baths, statues, pots, etc, up to 50% off retail prices. — Tel. 0823 661430.   34Sg38

CONSERVATORIES Clearance Sale. Now £1,195 (were £3,495). Quality joinery, safety glass. — Freephone 0800-269044.   34Sg38

ADLINE 0823 332233

Fig 4.2 Examples of classified advertisements.

There are specific areas on the page or factors which are thought to be advantageous to advertisers:

- the top right-hand side of the front page
- the right-hand side of subsequent pages
- being the only advertisement to appear on the front page.

Advertisements enjoying these advantages are likely, however, to cost more.

Figure 4.3 shows an advertisement for Vittel which appeared in the *Guardian* 'Weekend' magazine dated 6 July 1996.

Fig 4.3 An advertisement for Vittel.

Half of the Vittel advertisement covered the far left half of a double-page spread. The other half (right) was placed on the far right-hand side of the opposite page. Editorial matter not connected with Vittel filled the space in the centre of this double-page spread.

STUDENT ACTIVITY

Discuss with the person sitting next to you what advantages there might be in placing advertisements in specific places on a page. Share your ideas with the rest of your group.

Readers of newspapers and magazines obtain their copies in a variety of ways:

- by subscription – the magazine being delivered by post
- by purchasing from a newsagent, supermarket or vending machine
- some trade and technical journals are circulated free of charge to specialists who request copies

NATIONAL NEWSPAPERS

There are a large number of national newspapers. Some are published daily and others on Sunday each week. They vary in content and style and therefore attract different kinds of reader.

The readership of British newspapers is broken down into different classes in Table 4.1 on page 65.

STUDENT ACTIVITY

Choose a story which is currently hitting the headlines. Analyse the approach taken by a tabloid, like the Sun, *and a broadsheet, say the* Daily Telegraph.

1 What kind of reader do you think each attracts?

STILL WATER

A natural source of essential minerals,

when you drink it

Table 4.1 British newspaper readership by social grade and status.

Social grade	Social status	Newspaper
A	Upper middle class	The Times, Financial Times
B	Middle Class	Daily Telegraph, Guardian, Independent
C1	Lower middle class	Daily Mail, Daily Express, Today
C2, D, E	Working class	Daily Mirror, Daily Star, Sun

Source: Adtrack.

---

2 Can you identify the socio-economic groups involved?

Discuss your findings with the rest of your group.

ADVANTAGES OF PRESS ADVERTISING

1 It is cheap when compared with the alternative options.
2 It reaches a mass market which can be targeted, e.g. sportswear, cars, mortgage brokers etc.
3 It can be kept and read again and again.
4 It is often used by companies to give detailed information about their products/services (see Figures 4.4 and 4.5).
5 It can be carried around and read anywhere, i.e. in the office, on a train, in a plane, at school/college etc.
6 Its impact can be easily measured.
7 Statistics can be produced which identify the number of copies sold. An analysis of the readership in terms of socio-economic group (see Table 4.2) is also usually published.

Table 4.2 Classification of occupations by socio-economic group.

Grade	Occupation	Example
A	Professional/higher managerial	Solicitor/director
B	Lower managerial/supervisor	Department manager
C1	Non-manual	Invoice clerk
C2	Skilled manual	Plumber
D	Semi-skilled or unskilled manual	Labourer
E	Non-earners/casual workers	Unemployed

Source: Adtrack.

Fig 4.4 A full-page advertisement for National Westminster Bank Plc.

In 1990 the Ford Motor Company launched its 'new' Escort and Orion models. Figure 4.5 shows an extract from its advertising campaign plan:

ADVERTISING

A comprehensive advertising and promotions campaign has been produced, to maximise public awareness of the new Escort and Orion range. Television, press and poster advertising will all be used to support the launch. Comprehensive Dealer advertising treatment has also been developed for local adaptation.

Two separate TV advertisements have been produced, one each for Escort and Orion. The Escort advertisement shows the car in a futuristic fantasy world devoid of any personality. The Escort enters and endows this world with exuberance, personality and life.

The Orion advertisement places the new car in a boring, staid and conventional world, where it stands out in a class of its own. The message is that classical values can also be fashionable and stylish.

The advertising programme will be further reinforced with a press and poster campaign, extending the messages of both the Escort and Orion TV advertisements.

Fig 4.5 Extracts from advertising materials used in Ford's campaign to introduce the 'new' Escort and Orion models.

As can be seen, it was Ford's intention to use television, the press and posters in their campaign for the launch. In the final paragraph is the statement that press and poster advertising will be used to extend the messages for both models.

Observation of different groups within the UK community has led researchers to conclude that members of specific groups tend to have similar values and beliefs and also enjoy similar lifestyles. This information is invaluable to marketeers because it gives an indication of the purchasing behaviour of the individual (see Table 4.2 on page 65).

STUDENT ACTIVITY

Contact the following by telephone:

1 a national newspaper
2 a local newspaper in your area

and ask them to send you a copy of their rate card which details costs of advertising.

STUDENT ACTIVITY

Working in threes, produce a display advertisement for a product of your choice.

1 State the size of your advertisement.
2 In which newspaper would you advertise this product? Give reasons for your choice.
3 How much would the advertisement cost?

Use visuals to illustrate a 10-minute presentation of your ideas to your group.

DISADVANTAGES OF PRESS ADVERTISING

1 Some newspapers are poorly printed due to speed of production, and this may result in a poorly reproduced advertisement. (The development of technology during the past decade has meant there have, however, been vast improvements in quality, as well as some use of colour.)
2 Newspapers have a short life – they last for a day, or even less.
3 Advertisements need to be eye-catching if they are to attract the reader. This is particularly important if a number of advertisements appear on the same page.

REGIONAL/LOCAL NEWSPAPERS

These are published either daily (in the morning or evening) or weekly.

There is evidence to suggest that this type of media has become more popular with advertisers during the past decade. This is particularly true in the case of local retailers and those companies which offer services to both businesses and householders.

FREE NEWSPAPERS

These are usually published weekly and are delivered direct to all homes within a specified area.

This medium is particularly appropriate for local businesses which have a local rather than a national market.

STUDENT ACTIVITY

It may be argued that free newspapers have a wider circulation than local newspapers, the latter having to be purchased. On the other hand, it could also be argued that a proportion of householders who receive free newspapers will throw them away without reading them! Discuss.

STUDENT ACTIVITY

Work in twos or threes. Identify all the newspapers which are delivered free of charge *in your area. Choose one.*

1 *How many pages of advertisements are there?*
2 *Are there more display or more classified advertisements?*
3 *What is being advertised (i.e. product, service, job etc.)?*
4 *What kind of companies are advertising?*
5 *Are they all local companies?*

Discuss your findings with your group.

GENERAL-INTEREST/SPECIALIST MAGAZINES

There is a vast selection of magazines available which caters for every taste and interest: there are 'general interest' magazines – produced specifically for male or female readers – and there are specialist magazines which cover a vast range of leisure and business as well as professional subjects. The majority are purchased through newsagents, although some are available by subscription.

STUDENT ACTIVITY

Visit your nearest library and identify the 10 currently most popular women's magazine titles. Produce a table which lists and gives the circulation figures for each of these titles.

STUDENT ACTIVITY

Working in teams of three or four, carry out a survey of the magazine titles purchased by a particular group within your school or college.

1 *Which three magazines are the most popular?*
2 *How much do they cost?*

3 *Why do people buy these magazines, and what is it they like about them?*
4 *What is the range of subject matter covered by articles in these magazines?*
5 *What subjects are not covered in these magazines which your fellow students would like to see included?*
6 *What kind of advertisements appear in these magazines?*
7 *Are readers persuaded to buy products which are advertised in these magazines?*

Present your findings in an oral presentation to the rest of your group. Produce two visuals to illustrate your talk.

Trade, technical and professional journals are ideal for advertisers whose products or services are offered nationally but whose customers operate within a specialist field.

TRADE JOURNALS

These are produced for specialist retailers – for example, *The Grocer* magazine is aimed at food retailers. Some department stores also publish their own in-house magazine – Sainsbury's and Marks & Spencer are just two examples.

TECHNICAL JOURNALS

These are produced for technicians working in a variety of industries such as petrochemicals, mining etc.

PROFESSIONAL JOURNALS

These are produced specifically for solicitors, architects, accountants, etc.

INSERTS

Inserts are leaflets of one or more pages which are produced by specific companies. They usually give details of products/special offers, and are inserted inside newspapers and magazines (see the examples in Figure 4.6).

69

Littlewoods Pools
Standing Forecast Dept
Liverpool
L70 0AA

URGENT-DATED DOCUMENTS ENCLOSED

POSTAGE PAID — NO STAMP REQUIRED

BUSINESS REPLY SERVICE
Licence No. LV810

2 MINUTES SPENT ON THIS COUPON COULD WIN YOU A £2MILLION JACKPOT

It's so easy to enter - see inside

YOUR CHANCE TO WIN A £2MILLION JACKPOT ON

LITTLE**W**OODS
POOLS

This simple coupon makes it even easier to enter

HERE'S HOW!

By entering Littlewoods Pools, and forecasting the results of football matches, you could win one of many large cash prizes, with a £2 million jackpot from a total weekly payout of up to £4 million! All you have to do is select your matches on the grid on the Entry Coupon and add up the points you get each week. See 'HOW TO ENTER' instructions.

Fig 4.6 Examples of inserts for Littlewoods, SWEB, MFI and Comet. These were included in a variety of newspapers/magazines around the Easter Holiday period in 1994 (continued on pages 71–3).

BEDROOM OFFERS

UP TO 36 CABINETS IN 33 STYLES

UP TO 35% OFF

BEDROOM CABINETS

WHEN YOU BUY 2 OR MORE

FITTED BEDROOM CABINETS **GUARANTEED 20% LESS** THAN ANY OTHER NATIONAL RETAILER'S QUOTE

See page 3 for full details

EXTRA VALUE OFFER!

SPEND £175 OR MORE ON ANY HYGENA OR SCHREIBER BEDROOM AND GET A 12' x 12' BEDROOM CARPET

FOR ONLY £19.99

Current In-Store Price £80

Offer limited to 1 purchase per customer/household and is not transferable to any other product.
(Offer applies to Hygena & Schreiber cabinets and accessories included in the Price List, excluding beds).

MFI

VALID UNTIL JULY 17TH

MFI home works

1 *Abba:*
Gold – Greatest Hits £3.99

2 *Abba:* More Abba Gold £2.99

3 *Ace Of Base:*
Happy Nation £1.99

4 *Bryan Adams:* So Far
So Good £2.99

5 *Aerosmith:* Big Ones £1.99

6 *Joan Armatrading:*
The Very Best Of £1.99

7 *Louis Armstrong:*
The Pure Genius Of £1.99

8 *Michael Ball:*
First Love £2.99

9 *Bangles:* Greatest Hits £1.99

10 *Shirley Bassey:*
Sings The Movies £2.99

11 *The Beach Boys:*
The Best Of £2.99

12 *The Beautiful South:*
Carry On Up The Charts –
The Best Of £4.99

13 *Bee Gees:*
The Very Best Of £2.99

14 *Pat Benatar:*
The Best Of £1.99

15 *Björk:* Debut £2.99

16 *Björk:* Post £4.99

17 *Black Grape:* It's Great When
You're Straight . . .
Yeah £4.99

18 *The Blues Brothers:*
Original Soundtrack £1.99

19 *Blur:* Parklife £3.99

20 *Blur:* The Great Escape £4.99

21 *Mark Bolan & T. Rex:*
The Very Best Of £1.99

22 *Michael Bolton:* Timeless –
The Classics £1.99

23 *Michael Bolton:* Greatest Hits
1985-1995 £3.99

24 *Bon Jovi:*
Keep The Faith £1.99

25 *Bon Jovi:* Cross Road
– The Best Of £3.99

26 *Bon Jovi:* These Days £4.99

27 *Boney M:*
The Greatest Hits £1.99

28 *The Boo Radleys:*
Wake Up! £2.99

29 *David Bowie:* The Singles
Collection £4.99

30 *Boy George & Culture Club:*
At Worst, The Very
Best Of £1.99

269

1

25

12

16

169

90

71

31 *Boyzone:*
Said And Done £3.99

32 *The Brand New Heavies:*
Brother Sister £1.99

33 *Toni Braxton:*
Toni Braxton £2.99

34 *Garth Brooks:*
No Fences £1.99

35 *James Brown:*
Sex Machine 99p

36 *Kate Bush:*
The Whole Story £1.99

37 *The Byrds:*
20 Essential Tracks £1.99

38 *Canto Gregoriano* £1.99

39 *Mariah Carey:*
Emotions £1.99

40 *Mariah Carey:*
Music Box £2.99

41 *Belinda Carlisle:* Best Of
Belinda Vol. 1 99p

42 *Dina Carroll:* So Close £1.99

43 *Johnny Cash:*
The Man In Black £1.99

44 *Cast:* All Change £3.99

45 *Cher:* Cher's Greatest Hits:
1965–1992 £2.99

46 *Christians:* Best Of £1.99

47 *Clannad:* Past Present £1.99

48 *Eric Clapton:*
The Cream Of £2.99

49 *The Clash:* The Singles £2.99

50 *Patsy Cline:* 16 Original Hits
– Dreaming £1.99

51 *Joe Cocker:* The Legend –
The Essential Collection £2.99

52 *Nat King Cole:* The
Unforgettable £1.99

53 *Phil Collins:* Serious
Hits . . . Live! £2.99

54 *The Commitments:*
Soundtrack £2.99

55 *The Commodores:*
The Very Best Of 99p

56 *Harry Connick, Jr.:*
Forever For Now –
The Very Best Of £1.99

57 *The Cranberries:* Everybody
Else Is Doing It, So Why Can't
We? £2.99

58 *The Cranberries:* No Need
To Argue £4.99

59 *Crash Test Dummies:* God
Shuffled His Feet £2.99

60 *Sheryl Crow:* Tuesday Night
Music Club £2.99

23

58

93

155

28

17

76

134 **Cyndi Lauper:**
12 Deadly Cyns . . . And Then
Some £1.99

135 **Annie Lennox:** Diva £2.99

136 **Annie Lennox:** Medusa £3.99

137 **Let Loose:** Let Loose £1.99

138 **Lightning Seeds:**
Jollification £3.99

139 **Andrew Lloyd Webber:**
The Very Best Of £1.99

140 **M People:**
Elegant Slumming £2.99

141 **M People:** Bizarre Fruit £3.99

142 **Madness:**
Divine Madness £2.99

143 **Madonna:** The
Immaculate Collection £2.99

144 **Madonna:** Erotica £1.99

145 **Madonna:**
Bedtime Stories £3.99

146 **The Mamas & Papas:**
Golden Greats 99p

147 **Hank Marvin:**
Hank Plays Cliff £2.99

148 **Massive Attack:**
Protection £2.99

149 **Don McLean:**
The Best Of 99p

150 **Meat Loaf:**
Bat Out Of Hell £2.99

151 **Meat Loaf:** Bat Out Of Hell II
– Back Into Hell £2.99

152 **Freddie Mercury:** The
Freddie Mercury Album £2.99

153 **George Michael:** Faith £1.99

154 **George Michael:** Listen
Without Prejudice Vol. 1 £2.99

155 **Mike & The Mechanics:**
Beggar On A Beach
Of Gold £3.99

156 **Glenn Miller:**
The Ultimate 99p

157 **Kylie Minogue:**
Kylie Minogue £1.99

158 **Monkees:**
16 Smash Hits £1.99

159 **Gary Moore:** Ballads & Blues
1982-1994 £1.99

202

268

196

147

272

138

129

185

160 **Van Morrison:**
Moondance £1.99

161 **Alison Moyet:** Singles £3.99

162 **Jimmy Nail:**
Crocodile Shoes £2.99

163 **New Order:**
The Best Of £2.99

164 **Stevie Nicks:** Timespace,
The Best Of 99p

165 **Nilsson:** Without Her –
Without You, Very Best Of 99p

166 **Nirvana:** Nevermind £1.99

167 **Nirvana:** in Utero £2.99

168 **Nirvana:** Unplugged
In New York £2.99

169 **Oasis:** Definitely Maybe £4.99

170 **Mike Oldfield:**
Tubular Bells £1.99

171 **Roy Orbison:** The All
Time Greatest Hits 99p

278

282

DIRECTORIES

Companies can purchase advertising space in directories such as *Yellow Pages* or the *Thomson Directory*. These directories are split into regions and are circulated to homes and businesses within each region, usually to telephone subscribers.

BRAD (BRITISH RATE & DATA)

This is a reference book which contains a full list of all media which carry advertising. This information is updated each month. It is also possible for subscribers to purchase the BRAD Database, which is updated daily.

4.4 TELEVISION

Television advertising has grown enormously since the ITA (Independent Television Authority) was set up in 1954 by an Act of Parliament – the first 'commercials' appeared in 1955. The ITA later became the IBA (Independent Broadcasting Authority).

One major change that has occurred since the advent of television is that it has replaced radio as the main broadcasting medium. Commercial television, in particular, has expanded very quickly. There are a number of regional commercial television stations, each offering 'slots' of time which can be purchased by prospective advertisers.

STUDENT ACTIVITY

Write a letter to your regional commercial television station and ask them to send you a rate card.

1 How much would it cost you to advertise a product/service if your advertisement lasted for 30 seconds and you wished it to be on air at 7.30 pm on a Saturday evening?

2 How much would the same advert cost you if you wished to advertise:

(a) during the commercial break for News at Ten *on any weekday*

(b) at 12.00 midnight on a weekday evening
(c) during Saturday afternoon soccer?

Produce a table displaying the costs in each case.

The companies which originally used television for advertising were those whose products had a strong brand image and were generally identified as Fast Moving Consumer Goods (FMCG), i.e. washing powder, cereals, sweets, pet foods etc. FMCGs still feature very strongly in television advertising, but there has been a steady growth in advertising by: banks, building societies and other financial institutions; car manufacturers; food and DIY retailers; leisure services/tour operators; and many others.

Table 4.3 details the top 10 television brands in Europe for the years 1992 and 1993. There are some familiar names as well as others which are less well known.

Table 4.3 The top 10 television brands in Europe July 1992 and June 1993.

Rank 1993	Rank 1992	Brand
1	2	*Kellogg's*
2	4	*Renault*
3	Jt 6	*L'Oréal*
4	5	*Kinder*
5	8	*Citroën*
6	Jt 6	*Ariel*
7	9	*Ford*
8	10	*Peugeot*
9	1	*Barilla*
10	3	*Fiat*

Source: *Adtrack.*

Look at Tables 4.4 and 4.5. The top-selling grocery brand in the UK in 1992 was Coca-Cola. In the 'soap wars', Unilever and Procter & Gamble were in first and second places. Nestlé spent £71 million on television advertising, which placed them fourth overall.

Table 4.4 The UK top 10 selling brands 1992.

Rank	Brand
1	Coca-Cola
2	Persil
3	Ariel
4	Nescafé
5	Andrex
6	Silver Spoon Sugar
7	Whiskas
Jt 8	Flora
Jt 8	PG Tips
10	Walkers Crisps

Source: *Nielsen (The Campaign Report, 26 November 1993).*

Table 4.5 The top 10 television advertisers 1992.

Advertiser	Spend (£m)
Unilever	155
Procter & Gamble	128
Nestlé	71
Kellogg's	59
Mars	54
British Telecom	35
Ford	29
Kraft General Foods	25
Cadbury Schweppes	24
Allied Lyons	24

Source: *BARB/Register – MEAL (The Campaign Report, 26 November 1993).*

STUDENT ACTIVITY

Produce a pie chart and a bar chart for the companies featured in Table 4.5, showing the percentage slice of the cake in each case.

Which diagram best illustrates the table to give a true picture?

ADVANTAGES OF TELEVISION ADVERTISING

1 It can project the product or service directly into the home where the audience is comfortable, relaxed and receptive.

2 Sophisticated visuals can be projected which make use of colour, sound and atmosphere. Together these help recall.

3 Famous personalities are often used in 'voice-overs', which may cause audiences to assume that the individual is recommending the product.

4 Repeating the advertisement over and over again adds impact.

5 Advertisers can choose to advertise in one region only, or in a select number of regions, or nationally, in order to reach their target audience.

6 Retailers know that if a brand is advertised on television, demand for that product is likely to increase and the item must be stocked to take advantage of the expected upsurge in demand.

7 Television can be used to launch a new product or raise the profile of an existing product, and it is often linked with other media, i.e. newspapers, magazines, posters etc., to ensure that fuller and more specific information is passed on to potential customers.

STUDENT ACTIVITY

Identify the products for the following jingles/phrases:

1 '_____ Bildz Brits.'
2 'You can with a _____.'
3 'You know when you've been_____.'
4 'Only _____ have the answer.'
5 'A _____ a day helps you work, rest and play.'
6 'Thank _____ it's Friday.'
7 'Have a break, have a _____.'
8 'Now hands that do dishes can feel soft as your face with mild, green ____ _____.'
9 'The mint with the hole!'
10 'Get a little extra help.'

79

STUDENT ACTIVITY

Which products do the following television advertising campaigns relate to:

1 the 'Thank you very much...' series
2 'You can't beat the feeling'
3 'Everything we do is driven by you'
4 'House of people'

Identify five other jingles, phrases or campaign themes for products or services which have been advertised on television recently. Test these on your group to see if they are easily remembered. How many got them right?

DISADVANTAGES OF TELEVISION ADVERTISING

1 It is difficult to target a specific market because television is a mass medium.
2 Viewers have been known to change channels, make a cup of tea or even switch off the television set during the commercial breaks!
3 Because it is a costly form of advertising, it is unlikely that small, specialist companies will be able to afford to use this medium.
4 An advertiser can lose a slot/slots if another advertiser is willing to pay more for the same slot(s) of time.

STUDENT ACTIVITY

Work in pairs. Choose a product with a well-known brand name, i.e. Mars Bar, Kit Kat, Levi's etc. Produce a storyboard of pictures and script for a 20-second slot on television. Present your ideas to your group.

4.5   RADIO

Currently, there are a large number of commercial radio stations. These offer the advertiser an opportunity to sell a product or service by using sound (including special effects) and by creating a particular atmosphere or mood. Some of these commercial stations provide listening for a specialist audience. Classic FM, for example, offers programmes for people who prefer to listen to classical music. W H Smith advertises children's books and classical music tapes on this station.

If a radio message is to have impact, it is important that it be repeated again and again.

STUDENT ACTIVITY

Work in pairs. Read the following two radio scripts which were produced by the Ford Motor Company as part of a campaign to launch the 'new' Escort and Orion models in 1990. One is entitled 'Apology' and the other 'Jake'. These were produced by Ford for the local dealer to adapt in consultation with his or her local radio station.

1 Make a recording of the two scripts and include the name and address of a local Ford dealer. (You should try to create atmosphere and use music or sound effects as appropriate.)
2 Share the result with other members of your group.

ESCORT AND ORION RADIO SCRIPTS

'Apology'

MVO (male voice-over, serious voice): We would like to apologise to all members of the general public who have recently been subjected to being asked 'Where?' all the time. This is because it has become known that

Ford's new model Escorts and Orions are now available.

If you are asked 'Where?' please say 'Sample'.... Yes, Sample, your Ford dealer, 55 Sample Street, Sampleton.

'Jake'

Jake: Hello. This is Jake from Sample, your local Ford dealer.

In the interest of crowd control following the announcement of the availability of Ford's new model Escorts and Orions, I have been asked not to tell everyone that they can get these models at Sample, the local Ford dealers, 55 Sample Street, Sampleton.

Thank you.

The above scripts were one part of a larger national and local campaign which embraced press, television and poster campaigns.

ADVANTAGES OF RADIO ADVERTISING

Local radio is a popular medium with local advertisers, and competes effectively with the local press.

1   Its advertising can be aimed at specific audiences.
2   Its advertising can be timed to be 'on air' when business people are travelling to and from work. Travellers are usually interested in traffic and weather reports and consequently prove to be a captive audience.
3   Radios can be carried and can be listened to on a train, plane or boat. Workers in open-air trades, i.e. builders, decorators etc., also tune in to radios.
4   Radio is a medium which can be enjoyed both by people who do not have access to a television set and by those people who do not purchase or have access to printed media.

STUDENT ACTIVITY

You are working for a local garage which retails new and used cars and offers petrol at discounted prices. The latest model of car for which the garage is the local dealer is just being launched by the manufacturer. The dealership may be for a Ford or Nissan or Renault etc. – the choice is yours.

1   Contact your local radio station and obtain a rate card which details its charges.
2   Produce a script to last 30 seconds to advertise the garage and its products/services.
      The radio campaign will be as follows:

• Weeks 1 & 2: twice between 8 and 9 am and twice between 5 and 6 pm every weekday
• Week 3: once between 8 and 9 am and once between 5 and 6 pm every weekday
• Week 4: once between 5 and 6 pm every weekday

3   Produce a table showing:

(a) cost per slot
(b) cost per week
(c) total cost of campaign.

DISADVANTAGES OF RADIO ADVERTISING

1   It is difficult to create an image of a product, particularly if customers are expected to be able to identify the product on a shelf in a retail unit.
2   The success of radio advertising is difficult to assess. Some radio stations are endeavouring to produce listening figures, although these are not widely available.

4.6   CINEMA

There has been a decline in the popularity of the cinema and a move away from big-screen cinemas to smaller multi-screen facilities. However, multiplex cinemas are beginning to spring up in a variety of locations nationwide in an attempt to woo back audiences.

Cinema advertisers tend to fall into two main categories:

1 local companies which advertise regardless of the film being screened

2 large organisations whose advertisements 'track' a film wherever it is showing nationally, i.e. the advertisement is automatically shown wherever the specific film is being screened.

Targeting the audience is important because the audience profile attending a Disney film such as *Bambi* will be vastly different from that attending a film carrying an 18 (adults only) certificate.

Cinema advertising campaigns tend to be quite long, and generally span a minimum of three months and sometimes even six months in order to achieve the required result.

STUDENT ACTIVITY

Working in small groups, *exchange information regarding the following:*

1 *Which film did you last see at the cinema?*
2 *What advertisements were shown?*
3 *What made you remember this/these particular advertisement(s)?*
4 *Which advertisement, of all those you have seen at a cinema, do you best remember? Why?*

4.7   POSTERS

STREET POSTERS

The number of sites available to advertisers has reduced over time, and consequently such poster advertising is not as popular a medium as in the past. However, a number of large organisations still use it to cement the message of their primary media (see the examples in Figure 4.7). The message needs to be short because people will see it for a short period of time only.

It is possible to purchase advertising 'packages' that vary according to whether the campaign is to focus on a local, regional or national mix.

ADVANTAGES OF POSTER ADVERTISING

Posters:

1 reach a mass market
2 are a relatively cheap media choice
3 are eye-catching because of their size.

DISADVANTAGES OF POSTER ADVERTISING

1 Damage due to weather limits poster durability.
2 Posters are only effective in daylight hours.
3 Popular sites may be difficult to acquire.

Poster sites can be as large as 10ft high by 40ft long. Smaller poster sites can also be found at bus shelters, in bus stations and on litter bins.

Figure 4.7 on pages 83–4 shows examples of press advertisements which were also used as posters. These were part of a campaign for the Halifax Building Society.

STUDENT ACTIVITY

In groups of three or four, carry out a survey of your local area.

1 *How many poster sites are there?*
2 *Where are the sites located?*
3 *What products/services are currently being advertised?*
4 *Which poster, in your opinion, was the most striking? Give your reasons.*
5 *Did anything surprise you about the sites or the advertisements?*

Individually, produce a short formal report which details your findings.

POSTERS ON TRANSPORT

Other small poster advertisements appear on taxis and buses.

BECAUSE THERE'S MORE TO LIFE THAN A MORTGAGE.

We've just introduced some great new mortgage deals, including a cashback of up to £10,000, so you can still afford to soak up the sun this year.
To find out more, just call into your local Halifax branch or phone us free on **0800 10 11 10** for an information pack.

HALIFAX
Get a little extra help.

Fig 4.7 Examples of press advertisements for the Halifax Building Society.

83

YOUR HOME IS AT RISK IF YOU DO NOT KEEP UP REPAYMENTS ON A MORTGAGE OR OTHER LOAN SECURED ON IT.

BECAUSE THERE'S MORE TO LIFE THAN A MORTGAGE.

We've just introduced some great deals, including a new range of discounted variable rate mortgages, so you can still afford your fun and games.
To find out more, just call into your local Halifax branch or phone us free on **0800 10 11 10** for an information pack.

HALIFAX
Get a little extra help.

Working on your own, choose a product and produce an eye-catching poster for use on a hoarding which is 10ft high by 40ft long.

Write a brief explanation of the idea behind the image you have produced and state why you think the poster will be effective. Who is your target market? Which poster site in your locality would you choose for your poster and why?

4.8 WHAT'S THE LATEST?

VIDEO/VIDEOTEXT

1 *Teletext* – transmitted on the television networks. This is still a medium which has not yet been fully exploited. People are slow to change their television sets, and many sets do not have this facility.
2 *Video/video games.* Advertisements are beginning to appear at the beginning of these media. The Midland Bank is one financial institution which uses video to advertise its products/services.

CABLE TELEVISION

Consumers are able to buy a 'package' of programmes of particular interest to them, i.e. a sports channel, film channel etc. Advertising can target specific groups, particularly as the names and addresses of subscribers are recorded. However, the number of subscribers to cable is small at the present time.

SATELLITE TELEVISION

This uses a satellite to receive programmes from earthbound stations and project these anywhere in the world. Subscribers need a 'dish' if they are to receive these transmissions. There are many programme choices for viewers of satellite TV, and it provides an opportunity for companies who operate internationally to advertise their products.

SPONSORSHIP

Sponsorship is a growth area and takes several forms, including the sponsorship of organisations, personalities, events and competitions. Many companies support a variety of sports and television programmes in order to raise awareness of their brand image – Coca-Cola sponsors the 'Movie Premiere' series on commercial television for instance.

Visit your nearest library. Find out as much as you can about which sports are supported by sponsorship and by which companies. Produce a short formal report which details your findings.

At the beginning of the 1990s, trends showed a shift away from the use of above-the-line media, with more companies choosing alternative, more cost-effective below-the-line advertising, such as direct mail and point-of-sale. We take a closer look at below-the-line advertising in Chapter 5.

4.9 CASE STUDY: CADBURY

Read the following extract which is taken from a document produced by Cadbury entitled *Advertising – the Most Visible Element in the Marketing Mix*.

85

ADVERTISING AND THE CONFECTIONERY INDUSTRY

The confectionery market is heavily advertised within the FMCG sector with creative and distinctive advertising campaigns supporting all the strong brands. The fact that over 60% of chocolate purchases are made on impulse emphasises the importance of strong advertising to keep brands in the forefront of consumers' minds.

Cadbury is one of the top 20 UK advertisers in Britain today. Cadbury's Dairy Milk has been advertised since 1905, and in 1928 the 'glass and a half of full cream milk in every half pound' campaign began.

The slogan, which combines the simple message of food value with enjoyable eating, is one of the all-time 'greats' of British advertising and with minor changes, it has admirably served Cadbury's Dairy Milk ever since.

The message has reached consumers in every part of the country on posters, in almost every magazine and newspaper, and on television, and the glass-and-a-half picture remains an integral part of the wrapper design.

WHY ADVERTISE?

Advertisements relate products or services to people. To be effective, they must be appropriate to the product itself and relevant to the target market so that a competitive advantage is sustained. In basic terms, for a company such as Cadbury, the advertising campaign stimulates the demand for the particular brand, thus producing a profit for the company.

ADVERTISING AND BRANDING

In addition to providing information about a product, advertising transforms it into something more appealing to consumers than an object produced in a factory. Strong advertising creates brands, adding an emotional element to the sales proposition, so establishing a brand personality. Branding links a reputation to a name and creates an individual value.

Branding also provides a focus for interest and loyalty, and this is well illustrated with the Cadbury brand itself. The slogan 'The chocolate. The taste' used for Cadbury's Dairy Milk, which is the Cadbury flagship brand, creates interest in the full range of Cadbury's chocolate products.

PLANNING AN ADVERTISING CAMPAIGN

Cadbury works with a number of leading advertising agencies. Since the introduction of commercial television in 1955, television has been the major medium used by Cadbury.

Before a campaign can be planned, the client marketing manager and the agency need to answer the following questions:

- What is the product designed to do?
- Who will buy the product?
- Where will it be sold?
- What is the advertising message?
- What is the best way to reach the target audience?
- What kind of images, language and selling points should be used?
- What is the available budget?

Answer the following questions:

1 What percentage of chocolate purchases are made on impulse?
2 When was Cadbury's Dairy Milk first advertised?
3 What makes advertisements effective?
4 Why does Cadbury think that 'branding' is important?
5 What is the slogan used for Cadbury's Dairy Milk?
6 What is Cadbury's main media choice?

4.10 CASE STUDY: CADBURY'S FLAKE

Read the following extract from a document entitled *Cadbury's Flake Advertising*.

Flake, first introduced in 1920, commands sales of 160 million bars a year and market research shows that over half of these are consumed by women.

Flake has a secondary use as a culinary brand for decoration and to add a special crunch to chocolate recipes. This new role for Flake was established in the late 1970s and early 1980s through the very successful culinary press campaign.

THE ADVERTISING BRIEF

The key objective is usually to stimulate sales.

The decision to buy a chocolate bar is made outside the shop, the choice is made inside. In the confectionery market a large proportion of purchases are made on impulse, so an objective for the Flake advertising is to ensure that Flake is on the list from which the choice is made!

A considerable amount of market research is undertaken to understand the market as a whole – who the competitors are, consumer profile etc. From this, the brand position within the market can be identified, e.g. young and frivolous, romantic or up-market.

TARGET AUDIENCE

Target audiences are usually expressed by age, sex and socio-economic group which is based on occupation and indication of income and lifestyle.

Advertising is developed with the core target audience in mind for Flake. It is women aged 16–20 C2 although many people outside that group enjoy Flake.

THE ADVERTISING MESSAGE

The message is the most discriminating or the most motivating thing to communicate about the product. The core strategy for Flake was established in the early 1950s and still remains 'the ultimate indulgence of eating a Cadbury's Flake means it doesn't matter what's going on around you'. The same strapline has also been used consistently: 'the crumbliest, flakiest milk chocolate in the world'.

MEDIA CHOICE

Choice of media is all about reaching the target audience in the most cost-effective way. Flake is a mass market product and television is the most effective way of reaching a large number of young women, with cinema being used occasionally.

The Flake culinary campaign was run in the women's magazines as they provided the opportunity to include the recipes for readers to try. Sometimes, as part of the overall sales drive, Cadbury runs a trade advertising campaign to encourage the retail trade to stock up at the start of a consumer campaign.

EXECUTION OF THE BRIEF

Flake advertising has maintained its basic escapist style of a young girl 'fantasy' situation indulging in a Flake and 'getting away from it all'. The essential elements are:

1 *The Girl. She is naturally beautiful, youthful, sensuous, but not spoilt, brazen or gratuitously sexy. She often demonstrates female independence, often in a solitary setting. She loses herself in the Flake experience, being carried away by the product so that irritations, inconveniences and hazards are totally disregarded.*

2 **The Setting.** *Added values are created by atmospheric settings that are attractively escapist but not simply extravagant for their own sake. The 'Poppy field of 1973' was the epitome of floaty, soft-focus femininity.*

The 1980s saw the emergence of beautiful strong women, confident in themselves, with deep emotions, and very independent. The nineties woman is at ease with her life, juggling her career and family but allowing time for herself, as the latest Flake advertisement shows.

3 **The Product.** *The Flake product is pivotal to the commercial, and portraying the eating experience is crucial. All the clues in the eating sequence are important: unwrapping; the flakiness of the eat; the way the bite is savoured; the look on her face of wilful abandonment. Nothing else matters!*

4 **Unpredictability.** *Over the past 10 years a sense of excitement fanned by unpredictability has been introduced with film that is spiked with adventure.*

5 **Music.** *This complements the various settings and helps create mood.*

Work in groups of three or four. You are to present the following to the board of Cadbury:

Task 1: produce a storyboard with a script for a new advertisement for Flake which will appear on television
Task 2: decide upon the length of the 'slot'
Task 3: decide upon appropriate secondary media to back up the initial television campaign, and produce visuals and content for each of these
Task 4: produce a media plan indicating a specific launch date and identify the timing of the proposed media mix
Task 5: cost the plan and present this information in visual form
Task 6: carry out a peer- and self-assessment. What contribution to the assignment did you and each member of your group make? What would you do differently next time to ensure an improved result?

Your presentation should last 15 minutes, and you should be prepared to answer questions on your proposals.

Note: before you commence, produce an action plan which details the following: aims; success criteria; information needed; sources; target dates for completion of stages; review dates for progress meetings; a deadline.

REVIEW YOUR PROGRESS

1 What is meant by 'above-the-line'?
2 Which are the major above-the-line media?
3 Which type of media is the most popular?
4 Which media would best suit a local company offering a decorating service to householders?
5 In what year was commercial television born?
6 What impact has commercial television had on radio broadcasting?
7 Which media would best suit advertisers who wish to appeal to a mass market?
8 Which are possible growth areas for the future?

Media choice 2 – below-the-line

AIMS

- to explain the different types of below-the-line media
- to identify the advantages and disadvantages of each medium
- to understand the impact of each medium on audiences
- to assess media types and use this information to produce a media plan from a given brief

UNIT 20 ADVERTISING

- Element 20.2

  - Performance Criteria:
    1 Explain media characteristics
    2 Compare costs of media types
    3 Select a suitable media mix to reach target audiences

- Element 20.3

  - Performance Criteria:
    2 Prepare a suitable style of advertisement for a chosen media

5.1 WHAT ARE BELOW-THE-LINE-MEDIA?

Below-the-line media include those advertising media which are usually paid no commission and do not incur 'percentage costs'. The following are all usually described as 'below-the-line' media:

- direct mail
- direct response
- point-of-sale
- sales literature
- sales promotion
- exhibitions and trade fairs
- aerial advertising

5.2 DIRECT MAIL

Direct mail is a term used to describe all postal advertising which is addressed directly to the customer. A direct mail campaign might wish to:

- inform the customer about the product

LANDMARK EXPRESS

26th December 1994

FOR A FREE QUOTATION PHONE FREE

0500 203015

ANY TIME BETWEEN 8.00 AM AND 8.00 PM MONDAY TO FRIDAY
OR BETWEEN 9.00 A.M AND 1.00 PM SATURDAY

Personal Reference: L328

A motor insurance policy that takes your good driving experience into account

Dear Mr Bunting,

I am pleased to bring you news of a motor insurance policy that has been designed specifically for the experienced driver, providing exceptional cover at a lower cost.

Our policy offers you all the cover you would expect, plus additional cover you wouldn't. The extra cover comes as standard with every comprehensive policy. It includes protection of your no claims bonus where appropriate, cover for legal expenses and a free courtesy car following an accident when you use our recommended repairer.

The one thing your policy won't do is make you pay for the mistakes of careless motorists. So, because you're not subsidising inexperienced or careless drivers, your premiums will be amongst the most competitive available.

The enclosed leaflet outlines the insurance and our unique service level commitments in more detail. So have a look through it, and see for yourself the excellent level of cover and service we can offer. To find out how much your premium would be, just ring FREEPHONE 0500 203015 for your EXPRESS quotation.

If your policy is not due for renewal for some time, you should still telephone on the above FREEPHONE number or return the FREEPOST coupon now. We will be happy to provide you with an immediate quote as an indication of our premium levels and then contact you nearer your current policy renewal date with an up-to-date quote.

We look forward to hearing from you.

Yours sincerely,

Adrian Knight

Adrian Knight
Vice President.

Landmark Express Limited, PO Box 252, Northampton NN4 7DH.

REGISTERED IN ENGLAND NO. 2950357. REGISTERED OFFICE: 500 PAVILION DRIVE, NORTHAMPTON BUSINESS PARK, NORTHAMPTON NN4 7YJ. THE DIRECT INSURANCE DIVISION OF LANDMARK INSURANCE COMPANY LIMITED.

0235749/90321X

Member Companies of American International Group, Inc.

Fig 5.1 An example of a direct mail shot letter from Landmark Express, selling motor insurance.

- offer something to the customer, i.e. special
  offers

Fig 5.2 Two examples of direct mail shots from The Great Universal Stores, highlighting special offers and prize draws (continued on page 92).

- include a follow-up campaign to remind the customer of a previous mailshot

and may also involve free gifts/samples/offers. In addition, direct mail could be used to:

- introduce new products/services to existing customers
- reduce the number of 'cold calls' by the sales force (the telephone might be used to convey the advertising message)
- ensure that prospective customers receive information ahead of a visit from a sales person so that they are prepared prior to his or her visit.

MAILING LISTS

Direct mail can be tailored to a particular target audience and is very versatile. If the mailshot is to be effective, a mailing list will need to be acquired or produced based on very specific criteria which relate to the segment of the market being targeted. Such lists can be obtained from a variety of sources, some of which are detailed below:

1. directories and registers, industry journals and other publications
2. the organisation's in-house information system, which may or may not be stored on a database and might include information regarding:

   - current customers
   - prospective customers (from enquiry lists)

3. the Chamber of Commerce or trade associations
4. companies who are specialists in the area of direct mail advertising

CREATING THE DIRECT MAIL MESSAGE

The envelope

1. The envelope design should be eye-catching and the recipient should *want* to open the envelope to read further.
2. It is a person-to-person communication and should be addressed to a specific, named individual.
3. The message should be presented neatly with an air of 'officialdom', i.e. it should look professional.
4. Sometimes advertisers use textual clues (see Great Universal's mailshot in Figure 5.2), sophisticated design techniques etc.

The communication

The contents of the envelope must:

- *attract* and *hold the attention* of the recipient
- *create interest*
- *persuade* the recipient to be *positive* and *take action*

Repetition is also important to ensure the message is effective. The mailshot may:

- be repeated several times during the period of a wider advertising campaign
- use a variety of approaches, i.e. different appeals/content. These might include:

  - a letter with a leaflet which includes a reply paid portion
  - a folder with a free gift together with a reply-paid portion
  - a letter or other promotional communication which suggests that time is running out to take advantage of the offer

A repetition of the main message, ending with a further message which suggests the consumer will miss out on something special if he or she doesn't respond now, is designed to try to make the consumer take action to purchase the product/service which is being promoted.

The structure/style of the communication

1. The letter/communication should begin with a *heading* which grabs the attention of the reader.
2. The first paragraph should raise curiosity/interest.

3 The content should be personalised as far as is possible.

4 Copy should be relevant and interesting and to the point.

5 The content should include a common *theme* which is supported by a number of points which are made throughout the communication.

6 The final paragraph should remind the recipient of the action to take, including when and how.

7 Graphics/visuals and other devices may be used to highlight key aspects of the message, and a different style of writing would be needed depending on the target audience – anyone from financial managers to anglers.

8 The layout should be logically structured and the text easy to read.

STUDENT ACTIVITY

Over the period of one week, collect as many examples of direct mail items as you can. Analyse the examples you have collected. Which (if any) meet all of the criteria (as defined above) which make a direct mailshot successful?

1 *Did you believe the promises/claims which were made?*

2 *Did you read the item of direct mail to see what was being offered or did you resist the temptation? If you resisted, what were your reasons?*

3 *Did you have to do lots of reading? If so, did this put you off?*

4 *What attracted you – the free gift(s)?*

5 *Did you have to complete little tests/games? If so, did these put you off or were you insulted by their simplicity etc.?*

6 *Were you motivated enough to want to take action and send away for information/the product etc.? If not, what put you off?*

Share your findings with your group.

HOW TO IDENTIFY PROSPECTS

It is important to identify prospective clients carefully. Information may be obtained from a variety of sources. For example:

– a list pulled from a variety of directories, i.e. BRAD, telephone etc.
– a list which is managed/owned by a particular marketing-services organisation
– brokers who will produce a list based on specific criteria given to them by their clients
– lists produced from a company's client list.

The sources mentioned under the heading 'Mailing lists' which appeared earlier in this chapter are also useful for identifying prospects.

Direct mail generally suits businesses which have a small, specialist target market, e.g. motor insurance. It is selective in that it is addressed to specific individuals chosen on a local/national basis, and it is flexible in that the letter can be written, produced and mailed immediately. It is also possible to enclose additional information in the form of price lists, samples etc. The advertisement is totally controllable, being mailed as and when required, and information can be filed by the recipient for future reference if required.

STUDENT ACTIVITY

You are to produce a sales letter with enclosure(s) which will promote a product/service of your choice. Your letter must highlight the most important aspects of the product which you feel should be promoted strongly and persuade your target audience that it is worth their while to respond to your communication. Any further special features of the product should also be highlighted in the letter – rather than in the enclosures. You will need to use 'special effects' to highlight details which you feel are important, so visual impact will play a part. Make sure also that your letter and enclosures conform to accepted standards of grammar and spelling.

Test your letter/promotional materials with

your fellow students. What was their response?

1 Were they interested enough to read all of the letter and enclosures?
2 If not, why not?

Think about the envelope. Will this be plain or will there be some information/visuals etc. on the outside which might draw the recipient's attention to the materials included inside or try to persuade the recipient to open the envelope? Remember, many pieces of direct mail are discarded without even being read by the recipient.

WHAT ARE THE DISADVANTAGES?

Drawbacks to the direct mail approach include:

1 Appropriate lists may be difficult to obtain or costly to produce.
2 Exceptional skills are required if the campaign is to be successful, i.e. good writing and display skills, if the customer is to be 'hooked'.
3 Some direct mail is thrown away immediately by the recipient without being read. This should be overcome by making effective use of design and ensuring that the presentation of the package is eye-catching.

5.3 DIRECT RESPONSE

WHAT IS DIRECT RESPONSE ADVERTISING?

Direct response is a method which is used to advertise a product/service on television, radio or in the press, and which asks the consumer to respond directly by:

– telephoning a given number, or
– writing to a given address, or
– 'clipping' a coupon which appears in the press (or on an 'insert' – see Chapter 4) and returning it to the address given, or

– returning a reply-paid card which is stuck to the page of an advertisement.

It is a form of advertising which appeals directly to the consumer.

STUDENT ACTIVITY

Work in pairs. Look at Figures 5.3 and 5.4. on pages 96–100
Identify the strengths and weaknesses of each coupon-response advert shown. Share your findings with the wider group.

Direct response is often termed 'armchair shopping' because of the methods it uses, and access to the 'armchair shopper' is growing, particularly with the development of 'teleshopping' which is creating new opportunities for the advertiser to reach directly into the home of the consumer.

There are two types of direct response advertising:

1 *One-step advertising.* The communication is designed to complete the sale. This is the most commonly used type.
2 *Two-step advertising.* The communication is designed to 'pave the way' to completion of a sale.

Testing the market provides the opportunity to assess which of these two methods will prove most effective for a specific advertiser.

STUDENT ACTIVITY

In your local press or a magazine of your choice or a colour supplement from one of the Sunday newspapers, there appear a variety of advertisements which offer goods by post. The ads might be offering life insurance or language courses or indeed a wide variety of other goods and services. Choose a local newspaper which is delivered free to your door and identify the following:

Fig 5.3 Examples of inserts and coupon-response advertisements for Next, the AA and Freemans.

Fig 5.4 Three examples of coupon-response advertising which appeared in She *magazine in May 1995, for the Renault Clio (pages 98–9) . . .*

PAPA LOVES TO DO HIS SHOPPING IN THE CHAMPS ELYSÉES.

Ah, the elegance of the Champs Elysées! The special edition Renault Clio Champs Elysées, that is. These days you'll rarely catch Papa popping out to buy a *bouquet* in anything else.

Stroll down its list of attributes and you'll soon see why. With its Pioneer remote control CD player, alloy wheels, power assisted steering and tilt-and-slide sunroof all as standard, the Clio Champs Elysées is chic personified.

Not that more down-to-earth virtues have been ignored. Infra-red remote control door locking, electric front windows, the option of an automatic gearbox — all (and much more besides) make the Champs Elysées functional as well as fun. Renault's Anti-theft Protection system (RAPS) is also in place, to discourage those who like to do their shopping without paying.

Perhaps best of all, however, the whole delightful package costs from just £9790*– and there's a range of finance options available to make payment even easier.† So you see, you can find real value for money in the Champs Elysées. You just need to go via your Renault dealer.

To Renault UK, FREEPOST, PO Box 21, Thame, Oxon OX9 3BR.
For More Information about the Clio from Renault, fill in the coupon or call Renault Freephone **0800 52 51 50.**

Mr/Mrs/Miss (please delete) _____
BLOCK CAPITALS

Address _____

_____ Town and County _____

Postcode _____ Telephone _____

Present car make and model _____ Registration letter
(eg Renault 5). _____ (eg J)

Month/Year you expect to replace / M M Y Y / Age (if under 18) _____
CE/SHE/19K

Tick box if your next car may be diesel. ☐   ◖ For 'Motability' details. ☐

CLIO CHAMPS ELYSÉES

RENAULT
CARS
WITH FLAIR

TRIPLE WORLD CHAMPIONS Williams RENAULT FORMULA 1 · 1992, 1993 & 1994

... the Writers Bureau and various holiday brochures.

1 How many ads of this type appear in that particular issue?
2 What type of products/services are you being invited to find out more about/purchase by post?

Compare your findings with your group.

WHY IS DIRECT MARKETING POPULAR?

There are a number of reasons why direct response advertising has become popular. These are:

- the growth of supermarkets/hypermarkets and the decline in the kind of stores which offer 'personal service'
- the lack of parking facilities for customers in major centres
- the growth in credit sales
- the growth in sales by telephone

DIRECT RESPONSE AND SPECIALIST MARKETS

Direct marketing is becoming popular in a variety of specialist markets – an example being cosmetics. The largest single user of direct response advertising currently is the insurance industry.

DIRECT MARKETING AGENCIES

There are a number of direct marketing agencies, and the demand for these has increased recently because advertisers need to be able to measure the level of response to their advertisements.

COUPON RESPONSE

In both the national and local press, as well as in specialist magazines, advertisements of varying sizes offer a wide variety of goods and services. Coupons which invite completion and return for a purchase using credit cards are becoming more and more common (see Figure 5.5 right and overleaf).

SUBSCRIBE TO SHE
AND WIN A LUXURY WEEKEND
BREAK IN CHESHIRE

Take out a subscription to SHE for yourself or a friend at the special introductory price of £18 for 12 issues (normally £21.60) and you could win a luxury weekend break at Nunsmere Hall in Cheshire. Built around 1900, Nunsmere Hall is a member of the exclusive consortium Grand Heritage Hotels, and has been lovingly restored to its former glory. With its air of luxury and tranquillity, Nunsmere Hall epitomises the elegant English country manor. The 32 individually designed bedrooms have spectacular views, and each has a king-sized bed, breakfast seating and a large marble bathroom. Nunsmere Hall is ideally situated for exploring the Cheshire countryside, and is close to several golf courses. Outdoor sports, such as archery, croquet, riding, tennis and fishing, can also be arranged through the hotel.

We have two first prizes, each worth £1,000, comprising two nights' accommodation for two, Champagne on arrival, full English breakfast and dinner in the superb Garden restaurant on both days. Prizes are subject to availability and must be taken by December 30 1995. For a brochure or information about Grand Heritage Hotels, tel: 0171-376 1777, or call Nunsmere Hall direct on 01606 889100.

HOW TO APPLY To order a subscription and enter the prize draw, tel: 01858 468833, Monday to Friday, 9am-9pm, quoting ref 0899/900-373. Or, post the order coupon with payment to: SHE Subscription May Prize Draw, FREEPOST, Licence No 6313/7, Leicester LE87 4BN. All orders must be received by May 11 1995 to qualify for the prize draw, which will take place on May 12 1995. Winners will be notified by post. After the closing date for the prize draw, you can still order subscriptions at this special price (while the full UK subscription rate remains at £21.60). This offer applies to new subscriptions in the UK and NI only.

SHE SUBSCRIPTION OFFER

Phone our CREDIT CARD HOTLINE on 01858 468833, Mon-Fri, 9am-9pm. Please quote ref 0899/900-373 when ordering.

☐ **Yes**, I would like to order a new introductory **subscription to SHE for myself** at the special price of £18, starting from the next available issue, and be entered for the prize draw

☐ **Yes**, I would like to order a subscription **as a gift for a friend** at £18, starting from the next available issue, and be entered for the prize draw

My name   REF: 0899-373

Title ....Initials ....Surname...

Address ....

....Postcode....................................

Gift recipient   REF: 0900-373

Title ....Initials ....Surname...

Address ....

....Postcode....................................

I wish to order a total of ... new UK subscriptions and I enclose a cheque for £18/£36 (delete as appropriate) made payable to SHE magazine.

Or, debit my Access/American Express/Visa/Diners card for £18/£36 and thereafter annually for the appropriate amount (you'll be notified in advance of renewal and price changes). My number is:

☐☐☐☐ ☐☐☐☐ ☐☐☐☐ ☐☐☐☐

Signature..

Expiry date........................Tel no........................

All orders will be acknowledged and we will advise commencement issue. All information correct at time of going to press.

Data protection: The National Magazine Co Ltd may make names and addresses available to other companies. Tick here if you would prefer not to receive mailings ☐

If you would like to enter the prize draw without taking out a subscription, send your name and address on a postcard to the address opposite by May 11 1995.

SHE–THE MAGAZINE FOR WOMEN WHO JUGGLE THEIR LIVES

Fig 5.5 Examples of coupon-response advertisements from She *magazine, inviting you to use your credit card or pay by cheque to purchase the items advertised.*

CATALOGUES/CLUBS

Many organisations sell by distributing catalogues which offer fashion clothes and household goods, e.g. Freemans, Great Universal etc. Individuals can join these 'clubs' and act as selling agents for the goods offered via these catalogues.

TELEPHONES

'Telemarketing' is one term used to describe the method of direct advertising by telephone. The introduction of BT's latest initiative whereby callers' numbers can be accessed may prove to have a negative impact on this type of advertising.

TELEVISION

Viewdata, Ceefax and Oracle as well as other direct television media are all aspects of direct response advertising. See Chapter 4 for more information on television advertising.

STUDENT ACTIVITY

Do you have Teletext or Ceefax on your television set at home? If not, try to work with a friend or some fellow students. Arrange to review the advertisements which appear on either Ceefax or Teletext during a period of one hour on a chosen day. Make a list of what you think were their good and bad points.

1 How many of them invited you to send away for further details?
2 How many of them invited you to purchase direct by telephoning and using a credit card?

5.4 POINT-OF-SALE

Point-of-sale material is used to attract customers to products displayed in retail outlets.

This can take the form of:

– mobiles
– posters
– displays
– dump bins
– illuminated displays
– display stands
– shelf-edge tickets

STUDENT ACTIVITY

Work in teams of three or four. Visit a local supermarket and carry out a survey, aisle by aisle.

1 How many different kinds of 'point-of-sale' material, i.e. shelf-talkers, overhead posters, dump bins, wire stands etc., are used for different products?
2 Which were the ones which really caught your eye and why?

Present your findings in an oral presentation to the rest of your group.

5.5 SALES LITERATURE

Many companies produce sales literature which gives customers, actual or potential, more information about their products. There are a variety of forms which sales literature can take, i.e.:

– one-page leaflets
– brochures
– catalogues – which usually illustrate and describe the company's products

Sales literature can also take the form of calendars, timetables, hotel stationery, diaries, price lists and order forms, to name but a few.

Baxters ®

BY APPOINTMENT TO
HER MAJESTY THE QUEEN
FRUIT CANNERS
W.A. BAXTER & SONS LTD

VISITOR FACILITIES 1994

OPEN 7 DAYS A WEEK – January to December.
9.30 a.m. – 5 p.m. weekdays.
10.a.m. – 5p.m. weekends.

FACTORY TOURS – Weekdays only.
Guided tours of the factory from 9.30 a.m. - 11.30 a.m. and
12.30 p.m. - 4.00 p.m. (last Factory tour 2.00 p.m. Friday)

Tours subject to availability.

**Parties greater than 10 people, please book
in advance to avoid disappointment - an enquiry
prior to your visit should confirm availability.**

FACTORY TOURS ARE NOT AVAILABLE ON THE
FOLLOWING DATES DUE TO FACTORY HOLIDAYS.

4th to 8th April, 11th April, 2nd May, 20th to 24th June,
27th June to 1st July, 8th to 12th August,
17th & 18th October, 22nd & 23rd December,
26th to 30th December, 2nd & 3rd January 1995.

Baxters ®
Visitors Centre

Baxters of Speyside Ltd. Fochabers, Scotland. IV32 7LD.
Tel: (0343) 820393

*L'histoire Baxter a commencé il y a plus de 125 ans lorsque George Baxter et sa
femme Margaret ouvrirent une épicerie dans le bourg de Fochabers. Les
confitures maison de Margaret se firent sans délai une réputation pour leur
qualité et leur goût exceptionnel. La génération suivante, William et Ethel,
continuait à développer l'entreprise et faisait construire en 1914 une nouvelle
fabrique de confitures. Ethel consacrait son haut talent culinaire à l'élaboration
de recettes de potages dont la plupart sont encore produits de nos jours. Les
principes et les traditions établis par William et Ethel et conservés par leurs fils
Gordon et Ian, ainsi que leurs épouses Ena et Margaret, sont aujourd'hui confiés
à la quatrième génération, les enfants de Gordon et Ena : Audrey, Michael et
Andrew qui gèrent l'affaire avec le dynamisme et l'enthousiasme de toutes les
générations Baxter.*

**Venez découvrir l'univers de Baxters, partie du glorieux
patrimoine de l'Ecosse**

OUVERT 7 JOURS PAR SEMAINE
VISITES D'USINE SUIVANT DISPONIBILITÉ – EN SEMAINE SEULEMENT

*Die Baxter Geschichte begann vor über 125 Jahren, als George Baxter und seine
Frau Margaret in dem kleinen Dorf Fochabers einen Lebensmittelladen
eröffneten. Margarets hausgemachte Marmeladen wurden bald für ihre
erstklassige Qualität und ihren guten Geschmack bekannt. Durch die nächste
Generation, William und Ethel, wurde das Geschäft weiter ausgedehnt, und
1914 wurde eine neue Marmeladenfabrik gebaut. Ethel widmete sich mit großem
kulinarischen Geschick der Erfindung neuer Suppenrezepte, wovon viele auch
heute noch angewandt werden. Die von William und Ethel aufgestellten
Grundsätze und Traditionen wurden von ihren Söhnen, Gordon und Ian, und
deren Frauen, Ena und Margaret, fortgesetzt, und heute wird das Unternehmen
von der vierten Generation, den Kindern von Gordon und Ena – Audrey,
Michael und Andrew – mit der für die Baxters typischen Energie und
Einsatzfreude weitergeführt.*

**Kommen Sie und entdecken Sie die Welt von Baxters, ein
Stück stolze schottische Tradition!**

GEÖFFNET 7 TAGE DIE WOCHE
FABRIKBESICHTIGUNGEN NACH VERFÜGBARKEIT – NUR AN WOCHENTAGEN

*La storia di Baxter ebbe inizio più di 125 anni or sono, cioè quando George
Baxter e sua moglie Margaret aprirono un negozio di alimentari nel paesino di
Fochabers. Le marmellate casalinghe di Margaret divennero presto famose per la
qualità e il sapore superlativi. I loro successori, William ed Ethel, continuarono
ad espandere l'attività, e nel 1914 si costruì un nuovo stabilimento per la
produzione di marmellate. Ethel applicò il suo grandissimo talento culinario allo
sviluppo di nuove ricette per le minestre, molte delle quali vengono prodotte
tuttora. I principi e le tradizioni introdotti da William ed Ethel ci sono stati
tramandati dai loro figli, Gordon e Ian, e signore, rispettivamente Ena e
Margaret. Oggi la quarta generazione, la famiglia di Gordon ed Ena – Audrey,
Michael ed Andrew – prosegue l'attività con l'energia e l'entusiasmo tipici di
Baxter.*

**Venite a scoprire il mondo di Baxters, parte dello
stupendo patrimonio scozzese**

APERTO TUTTI I GIORNI, ANCHE LA DOMENICA
GIRI DELLO STABILIMENTO SE DISPONIBILI – SOLO NEI GIORNI FERIALI

*La historia de Baxter comenzó hace más de 125 años, cuando George Baxter y su
esposa, Margaret, pusieron una tienda de comestibles en la aldea de Fochabers.
Las mermeladas caseras de Margaret se hicieron rápidamente famosas por su
calidad y sabor destacados. La generación siguiente, William y Ethel,
continuaron expandiendo el negocio y, en 1914, se construyó una nueva planta
de elaboración de mermeladas. La destacada habilidad culinaria de Ethel se
concentró en la creación de recetas de sopas, muchas de las cuales continúan
elaborándose hoy día. Los principios y las tradiciones establecidos por William y
Ethel fueron mantenidos por sus hijos, Gordon e Ian, y sus esposas, Ena y
Margaret, y actualmente la cuarta generación, la familia de Gordon y Ena –
Audrey, Michael y Andrew – llevan adelante el negocio con la energía y el
entusiasmo característicos de los Baxter.*

**Venga y descubra el mundo de Baxters, parte del
orgulloso patrimonio de Escocia**

ABIERTO 7 DÍAS A LA SEMANA
LAS VISITAS A LA FÁBRICA ESTÁN SUJETAS A DISPONIBILIDAD – DÍAS DE
SEMANA SOLAMENTE

バクスターストーリーは、125年以上前に、
ジョージ・バクスターとその妻のマーガレットが、
フォチャバーの村に乾物雑貨を開店したことに始まります。
マーガレットの作ったホームメイドのジャムは、まもなく
その並々ならない味質と味とによって有名になりました。
次のウイリアムとエセルの時代に、ビジネスは益々拡大を続けた。
1914年には、新しいジャム製造設備が設置されました。
エセルの優れた料理の腕は、スープのレシピへと向けられて、
そのうちの多くのスープは、今日でも製造されています。
ウイリアムとエセルによって築き上げられた

バクスターの規律どんな伝統は、彼らの息子のゴードンとイアン
及びその妻のエヴァとマーガレットによって受け継がれましたが、
そして、今日、ゴードンとエヴァの家族である4代目の
アンドレー・ヒミイケル、アンドリュー一族が、
その典型的なバクスター家のエネルギーと情熱をもって、
この家族事業を継続しているのです。

**Découvrez l'univers de Baxters
Entdecken Sie die Welt von Baxters!
Scoprite il Mondo di Baxters
Descubra el mundo de Baxters
バクスターズの世界**

スコットランドの誇り高い伝統の一部であるバクスターズの世界を御覧下さい
1週間営業開業、工場ツアーは、受け入れ状態の都合によります。平・金・金のみ。

FRONT COVER: Bronze Stag commissioned by W. A. Baxter & Sons Ltd to commemorate the 125th Anniversary of the company which was founded in 1868.

*Fig 5.6 Two examples of company literature, for Baxters and Kellogg's, produced to give
information about the companies' products (continued on pages 107–9).*
(continued on pages 107–9).

Discover the World of Baxters

The BAXTER STORY

began over 125 years ago when George Baxter and his wife Margaret set up a grocery shop in the village of Fochabers. Margaret's home-made jams soon became famous for their outstanding quality and flavour. The next generation, William and Ethel continued to expand the business and in 1914 a new jam making plant was built. Ethel's outstanding culinary skills were devoted to developing recipes for soups, many of which are still produced today. The principles and traditions established by William and Ethel have been carried forward by their sons Gordon and Ian and their wives Ena and Margaret, and now the fourth generation, Gordon and Ena's family Audrey, Michael and Andrew are taking the business forward with typical Baxter energy and enthusiasm.

George Baxter 1868

'The Old Shop' Fochabers

THE FACTORY

A selection of Baxters quality food products, made here on the banks of the Spey.

GUIDED TOURS

Guided tours of the factory. For full details, see "Visitor Facilities."

THE OLD SHOP

Where it all began—the original shop has been lovingly recreated and is a feature of the Visitors Centre.

NEW FACILITIES FOR '94

- Additional quality retail outlet offering the "Best of Scotland" merchandise.
- New Audio Visual show with enhanced facilities.

GEORGE BAXTER CELLAR

The complete Baxters range along with unusual speciality foods.

VICTORIAN KITCHEN

Quality foods, cookery utensils and an extensive range of international gifts.

SPEY RESTAURANT

Serving delicious Scottish fayre. Be sure to come in during your visit to Baxters.

RIVER SPEY

TO CAR PARK

TO FOCHABERS

TO ABERDEEN

A96

TO INVERNESS

Baxters®

Enjoy the Baxters Experience

- Free admission
- Free car and coach parking with facilities for the disabled
- **NEW FOR '94** New Reception and Auditorium facilities
- **NEW FOR '94** Enhanced Audio Visual show
- Guided factory tour
- The Old Shop Museum - Where the Baxter Story began
- The George Baxter Cellar - speciality foods, wines & spirits
- Mrs Baxter's Victorian Kitchen - extensive international gifts, cookery utensils and quality foods
- **NEW FOR '94** Additional quality retail outlet offering the "Best of Scotland" merchandise
- **NEW FOR '94** Enhanced Restaurant facilities opening mid '94
- Herd of pedigreed Highland cattle
- Landscaped grounds and views of the magnificent River Spey
- Woodland walks and trails
- Family picnic area
- Toilet facilities for the disabled
- Coach parties are requested to book in advance.

All Visitor facilities are suitable for the disabled except for the factory tour.

Come and discover the world of Baxters, part of Scotland's proud heritage

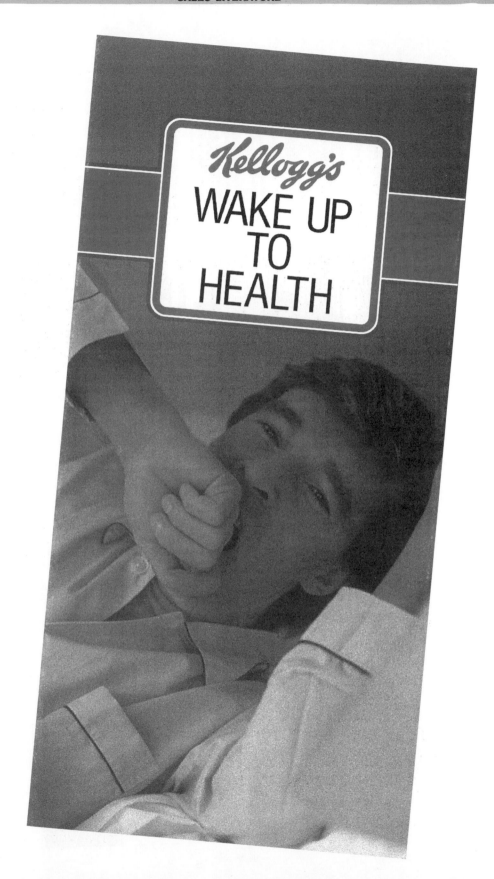

BREAKFAST SETS YOU UP FOR THE DAY

Everybody knows that healthy eating is the key to healthy living. It's important all through our lives. For children, it provides the 'building blocks' essential for proper growth and well-being. For all ages it can reduce the risk of illness, even cancers and heart disease.

There's nothing difficult about eating well. Forget the fancy diets. Instead, aim for a balanced diet, rich in fibre and carbohydrates, low in fats, with adequate amounts of protein, vitamins and minerals.

This leaflet is about the most important meal of the day – breakfast. While many nutritionists recommend eating a good breakfast every morning, a lot of people still do not realise how important it is.

A proper breakfast makes a major contribution to the nutritional quality of a well-balanced diet. It provides the nutrients that are not always made up for in later meals and snacks.

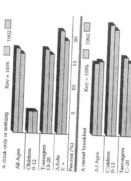

SO WHAT IS BREAKFAST?

Breakfast literally means breaking the fast. And for some people, especially younger children, it breaks an overnight fast that can be as long as 16 hours! That's why breakfast is so important. Missing a proper breakfast means you're not stoking up with enough energy for the day. You'll soon run out of steam, as we explain later.

Breakfast means different things to different people, from croissants for the French to biscuits for the Italians. A large cooked meal of egg, bacon and sausage was once the traditional breakfast here, but over the last 20 years we like the rest of Europe, have moved towards a cereal based breakfast which is a healthier alternative.

This changing pattern of breakfasting is influenced by the availability of tasty, nutritious and value-for-money breakfast cereals of consistently high quality.

Today nearly 45% of people in Britain for example eat cereals for breakfast. The rest have toast and/or a drink, or a cooked meal... and about 5% eat nothing at all!

WHO EATS BREAKFAST?

It's no surprise to find that youngsters are the biggest breakfast cereal eaters. On an average morning up to 66% of children from toddlers up to the age of 12 will be enjoying **Kellogg's Corn Flakes** and other cereals.

Teenagers are great 'meal-skippers', as parents know only too well. Skip breakfast and you year olds start the day with a breakfast cereal.

Cereals are also the most popular breakfast for adults - on average 40% eat them each morning.

This figure varies with age - it's higher among the over-55s, for example. In contrast, 14% of people under 55 start the day with only a drink, compared with just 6% of the over-55s.

Many younger adults say they don't have time to eat a proper breakfast.

This is silly: you can eat a bowl of cereals in minutes... and the benefits last for hours.

Changing breakfast habits.

The following charts graphically illustrate some trends in British breakfasting eating habits over the past 16 years (in an average day).

A drink only or nothing

								Key = 1976 ⬜ 1992 ⬜
All Ages								
Children 0-12								
Teenagers 13-20								
Adults 21+								
Percent (%)	5	10	15	20				

A cereal breakfast

								Key = 1976 ⬜ 1992 ⬜
All Ages								
Children 0-12								
Teenagers 13-20								
Adults 21+								
Percent (%)	10	20	30	40	50	60	70	

With a cooked dish

						Key = 1976 ⬜ 1982 ⬜
All Ages						
Children 0-12						
Teenagers 13-20						
Adults 21+						
Percent (%)	5	10	15	20		

WHY BREAKFAST IS IMPORTANT

Eating a regular breakfast can help to promote good health. A proper breakfast should provide us with about a quarter of our daily intake of energy and nutrients. Skip breakfast and you risk missing out on recommended dietary amounts of vitamins and minerals.

Some people miss breakfast because they don't feel hungry, others because they think they have no time. They believe that if they eat well enough at lunch, dinner and snack time, they won't have to worry about this first meal.

Other people believe that cutting out breakfast will help them to lose weight. It won't! All the evidence suggests that avoiding breakfast makes it harder to lose weight.

Perhaps if more people realised that eating breakfast not only can help to improve their performance during the day but also adds to the nutritional value of their total daily diet, they would think again.

Breakfast is an important meal. Skipping it can contribute to dietary inadequacies.

THE IDEAL BREAKFAST

Ready-to-eat cereals ideally fit the recommendations made by experts for healthy eating...

✱ They are very low in fat.

Fats can make us overweight, and saturated fats have links with heart related diseases. Doctors are constantly warning us to reduce our fat intake.

✱ They are high in complex carbohydrates. This is the healthiest way to get our energy requirements.

✱ They are often high in fibre.

This aids healthy digestion and helps to promote regularity and avoid constipation. Fibre may also be useful for people trying to lose weight: a high fibre cereal can suppress appetite and make it easier to reduce those calorie-rich snacks.

✱ They provide a significant amount of vitamins and minerals.

Cereals can be a particularly important source of vitamins for people eating to reduce weight: indeed, dieters who miss breakfast could suffer from inadequate diets.

✱ Most ready-to-eat cereals are taken with milk. Milk is high in calcium. A poor intake of calcium may affect bones in later years.

The National Food Survey in 1992 showed that ready-to-eat cereals contributed 15% of the average iron intake, and 10% of fibre, but less than 0.5% of average fat intake, and about 3% of sugar.

EVERYBODY BENEFITS

Children benefit.

Breakfast cereals are very good for young children and those on poor diets, who may depend on fewer foods to meet recommended daily intakes of nutrients.

In a recent Department of Health national food survey, 2,705 British schoolchildren aged 10 to 15 were questioned about their dietary habits.

Breakfast cereal eaters had higher intakes of vitamins B1, B2, B6 and niacin, and of calcium and iron. They also got less energy in their diet from fat. Similar results were found in the Irish National Nutritional Survey.

A survey in America showed that nutrients missed at breakfast are not made up in later meals and snacks.

Teenagers and adults benefit.

Low-fat and high fibre diets reduce the risk of heart disease and cancer.

Adults who skip breakfast tend to have significantly higher serum cholesterol levels than breakfast eaters – and as a consequence they have an increased risk of developing heart disease.

More than three-quarters of teenage boys and two-thirds of girls eat ready-to-eat cereals. Compared with non-eaters, they have a greater intake of the B vitamins and lower intakes of fat. And teenagers who eat the most cereals are more likely to receive the recommended intakes of calcium and iron.

In fact, only girls who eat breakfast cereals get the recommended amount of iron – and iron deficiency causes anaemia which results in fatigue, apathy and a general feeling of unhealthiness.

Teenagers have many food fads. Girls who are over-preoccupied with slimness and dieting may purposely miss breakfast. That's a mistake and could lead to an inadequate diet.

Instead, weight-watchers should start the day with a fortified breakfast cereal – high in nutrients relative to its calorie content. Such cereals will also provide these girls with significant amounts of their iron and vitamin needs.

Mothers-to-be benefit.

By eating fortified breakfast cereals pregnant women are more likely to build up good stores of vitamins and minerals, especially folic acid and iron, which are both important for healthy pregnancy and healthy babies.

BREAKFAST... AND PERFORMANCE

Research shows that missing breakfast over an extended period of time can affect behaviour, and affect performance at work and school.

Studies in Britain, America and Sweden show that missing breakfast can result in poorer physical and mental performance in the late morning hours – and a mid-morning snack only partly helps. One study in Sweden looked at the effects of breakfast on the

performance of factory workers. It found that productivity was higher in those eating an adequate breakfast, and the rejected work rate was lower.

Swedish scientists also studied the effects of breakfast on school work. They found that on the days when children had an adequate breakfast, they tended to work faster and make fewer mistakes in tasks requiring concentration, such as maths.

In another study, missing breakfast was found to affect the learning abilities of poorly-nourished children far more than it affected adequately-nourished youngsters. Lower attentiveness and higher irritability in children were found to be associated with missing breakfast.

Skipping breakfast and prolonging the overnight fast can be associated with low blood sugar and insulin levels in the morning. These low levels are thought to be linked to poor problem-solving in the late morning. So hunger may reduce a child's ability to learn.

In contrast, eating breakfast cereal was found to be especially beneficial for children with lower reaction times and problem-solving abilities, when measured in the late morning.

Although it is difficult to assess the effects of hunger on physical and mental performance, these findings generally show that regular breakfast cereal eating makes a positive contribution to work and school performance.

As we said at the start... healthy eating is the key to healthy living.

Kellogg's

Kellogg Company of Great Britain Ltd.
Talbot Road, Manchester M16 0PU
Kellogg Company of Ireland Ltd.
Unit 4, Airways Industrial Estate, Clonshaugh, Dublin 17.
© 1992 KELLOGG COMPANY

For further information please telephone 0800 626066
(Republic of Ireland 1800 626066).
The Kellogg Freephone Helpline is open from 8.00am
to 6.00pm Monday to Friday

5.6 SALES PROMOTIONS

Sales promotions can also take a variety of forms, i.e. money-off coupons, special offers, free samples of the product, competitions etc.

CROSS-BRANDING

Cross-branding refers to 'cross-coupon' offers. Included on product packaging, these offer money off *other* products (not always products which are produced by the same manufacturer).

STUDENT ACTIVITY

Scan the pages of a newspaper/magazine of your choice.

1 How many sales promotions can you identify, i.e. 'win a motor car', a free holiday, cash prizes, money-off coupons etc.?

2 How many of these are schemes which involve 'cross-coupon' offers, i.e. a coupon, which appears on the product packaging, which offers money off another product?

Produce a short report which details your findings and offers your conclusions.

DISADVANTAGES OF POINT-OF-SALE MATERIALS AND SALES LITERATURE AND PROMOTIONS

1 There is a danger that advertising materials may be wasted. For example, point-of-sale materials may never be used, and many retailers dislike accepting 'money off' coupons unless the manufacturer can make the promotion attractive to the retailer.

2 Schemes have a limited life span, and customers may switch to a brand because there is money off but revert back to buying their usual brand when the promotion ends.

3 Judging the level of demand for products which are on promotion is difficult, and there is nothing more annoying to a prospective customer than special offers which are advertised but which are 'out of stock' when the customer wants to buy them.

STUDENT ACTIVITY

You are to produce the copy for an advertisement for a local store which sells a wide range of furniture at affordable prices. The store is called Furnisave. The company wishes to include illustrations of chairs, beds, tables etc., and is offering discounts of 20 per cent off dining suites and 50 per cent off beds. The offers are to last for one month only (the dates to be determined by you).

Produce the copy for the advertisement and show how you would lay out the whole advertisement, including visuals. Remember to use appropriate words like **save, buy** or **look** – or whatever else you feel is appropriate. In addition, use words such as **replace** and **discover** to 'grab the attention' of your audience.

5.7 EXHIBITIONS AND TRADE FAIRS

The popularity of trade exhibitions has grown steadily, and many small companies regularly exhibit at locations such as the National Exhibition Centre in Birmingham, and Earls Court and Olympia in London. Exhibitions can also be held in smaller locations (i.e. hotels, libraries), large venues other than exhibition centres or even in the open air depending on the product and whether there is a need for the product to be demonstrated.

Most exhibitions are run by trade associations. However, some are sponsored by large organis-

PARTY TIME AT ASDA

Permanently Low Prices Throughout the Store

PARTY FOODS

ROUND LETTUCE EACH	**29p**
TURKEY & HAM PIE WITH CHESTNUT STUFFING LOOSE Per qtr	**69p**
ASDA WAFER THIN SMOKED HAM/TURKEY LOOSE Per qtr	**75p**
ASDA FROZEN PARTY SAUSAGE ROLLS 50'S	**99p**
ASDA IN-STORE BAKERY 18 WHITE SOFT ROLLS	**£1.08**
ASDA CRISPY CRUMB VEGETABLES WITH GARLIC DIP 200g	**£1.59**
ASDA FROZEN PARTY PIZZA FINGERS 285g	**£1.79**
ASDA MULTIPACK SALADS 4 X 100g	**£1.89**
ASDA FRESHLY PREPARED TEDDY PIZZA	**£1.99**
ASDA MINI PORK PIES 12's	**£2.69**
ASDA COOKED CHICKEN (HOT & SPICY WINGS/CHINESE WINGS/TIKKA BITES) 581g	**£2.89**
AMOY FROZEN DIM SUM PARTY PACK 12's	**£2.99**
WHOLE CHEESE & ONION QUICHE FROM THE DELI	**£3.99**
ASDA FRESH SMOKED SALMON SIDE (PRE-SLICED) 1lb	**£6.99**

PUDDINGS FOR PARTIES

BRITISH COLUMBIAN RED DELICIOUS APPLES LOOSE PER lb	**49p**
ASDA HO-HO-HO'S NOVELTY CAKES 3 PACK	**99p**
ASDA SNOWMEN NOVELTY CAKES 3 PACK	**99p**
ASDA DEEP FILLED MINCE PIES 12's	**£1.09**
ASDA RUM/BRANDY/COINTREAU CREAM SELECTION PACK 3 X 85ml	**£1.99**
ASDA FROZEN TRIPLE CHOCOLATE GATEAU 10-12 PORTION	**£1.99**
CHRISTMAS STILTON – WHITE STILTON WITH MINCEMEAT LOOSE PER lb	**£2.49**
ASDA FRESH SHERRY TRIFLE 794g	**£2.79**
ASDA WHISKY DUNDEE CAKE 907g	**£4.49**
ASDA LUXURY CONTINENTAL CHEESE SELECTION 630g	**£5.49**

Star Buy ★ Brussels Sprouts 2lb Pack **49p**

THAT'S ASDA PRICE

POCKET THE DIFFERENCE

NOW OPEN EARLIER FOR EASIER SHOPPING

EXTENDED CHRISTMAS OPENING TIMES

THURSDAY 23rd DECEMBER – 8am to 9pm	WEDNESDAY 29th DECEMBER – 8.30am to 9pm
FRIDAY 24th DECEMBER – 8am to 6pm	THURSDAY 30th DECEMBER – 8am to 9pm
SATURDAY 25th DECEMBER – Closed	FRIDAY 31st DECEMBER – 8am to 6pm
SUNDAY 26th DECEMBER – 11am to 5pm	SATURDAY 1st JANUARY '94 – Closed
MONDAY 27th DECEMBER – 9am to 6pm	SUNDAY 2nd JANUARY '94 – Closed
TUESDAY 28th DECEMBER – 9am to 6pm	MONDAY 3rd JANUARY '94 – 10am to 5pm

LINWOOD ROAD, LINWOOD.

OPENING TIMES
Monday to Friday 9am – 8pm.
Saturday 8.30am – 8pm. Sunday 9am – 6pm.

FREE PARKING · COFFEE SHOP · CUSTOMER TOILETS · AUTOCASH DISPENSERS · MAJOR CREDIT & DEBIT CARDS · PETROL AVAILABLE · BAKERY · PIZZA BAR

PRICES APPLY TO THE LISTED STORE(S) ONLY. ALL PRODUCTS ARE AVAILABLE AT MOST ASDA STORES AND ARE SUBJECT TO AVAILABILITY. PLEASE CHECK WITH YOUR LOCAL STORE.

Fig 5.7 Two examples of press advertisements for Asda Stores.

VALENTINE'S DAY IDEAS WITH LOVE FROM ASDA

Permanently Low Prices Throughout the Store

SPECIALLY FOR VALENTINE'S DAY

BENDICKS PRALINE HEARTS	**59p**
ASDA SWEETHEARTS – 3 FUN CAKES	**99p**
FRESHLY PREPARED VALENTINE PIZZA From	**£1.99**
MCVITIE'S FROZEN PASSION CAKE	**£2.59**
FERRERO ROCHER T16	**£2.65**
DEIDESHEIMER HOFSTUCK KABINETT 75cl	**£2.99**

GIFTS FROM THE HEART

VALENTINE CARDS From		**59p**
VALENTINE MUGS Each		**99p**
VALENTINE HIPPO/BEAR/TEDDY Each		**£1.99**
FRESH SINGLE RED ROSE		**£1.99**
VALENTINE CARD & FRESH RED ROSE		**£2.99**
VALENTINE BEAR WITH HEART		**£4.99**
VALENTINE FLOWER BOUQUET		**£4.99**
MENS DAISY SQUARE JERSEY BOXER SHORTS		**£5.50**
ONE DOZEN RED ROSES		**£9.99**
THE VERY BEST OF THAT LOVING FEELING	DOUBLE CASSETTE	**£9.99**
	DOUBLE CD	**£14.99**
CABOCHARD 3 PIECE SET	SRP £17.95	**£11.99**
WHITE/NAVY STRETCH LACE BODY		**£12.99**
CACHAREL AFTERSHAVE 50ml	SRP £19.95	**£16.95**
ANAIS ANAIS 50ml EDT SPRAY	SRP £25.00	**£18.95**

THAT'S ASDA PRICE

POCKET THE DIFFERENCE

THE ASDA DIFFERENCE

MAJOR CREDIT & DEBIT CARDS · CUSTOMER FACILITIES · BAKERY · PIZZA BAR · CLOTHING BY GEORGE · NEWSPAPERS & MAGAZINES · BOTTLE BANK

OPENING TIMES

Monday to Saturday 8.30am – 8pm.
SUNDAY 10am – 4pm*

21 MARKET STREET, BROMSGROVE.

OPEN SUNDAY 10am – 4pm*

ations, including the national press. Some exhibitors prefer to have their own portable exhibition which they take 'on the road' to visit towns, cities, schools, libraries, etc.

Exhibitions provide personal contact with prospective clients and offer the customer a chance to test the product or see a demonstration of how it works. Exhibitions are also used to help boost sales, and they are an effective way of distributing catalogues direct to the client group. Furthermore, an exhibition can help to enhance a company's reputation in the trade and keep its name in the public eye.

On the other hand, exhibitions can prove costly in terms of resources required, both material and human. In addition, competitors are gathered together at the same time, and this can distract prospective clients. Smaller venues can also prove disappointing in terms of attendance figures.

TIPS FOR SUCCESSFUL EXHIBITING

If success is to be achieved, a number of factors must be considered:

1 *Which trade exhibitions to choose?* The following criteria might be used to select an appropriate venue:

   - a venue which has been previously used and has proved successful
   - personal experience of an exhibition which has been successful in terms of visitor numbers
   - advice obtained from a variety of reliable sources such as agents, other distributors etc.
   - which media covered the event previously – did the exhibition have a high profile?

It is difficult to assess how successful a new venue might be. Approaching the organisers will allow brief information to be gathered, upon which a decision can be made.

2 *How much to spend?* The budget for an exhibition should be based on previous experience as far as is possible. A good design company or an in-house designer should be able to provide a reasonably accurate projection of likely costs. Costings may be

obtained for some or all of the following:

   - display materials
   - space to be rented
   - catalogues/advertising materials/sales literature
   - direct marketing, i.e. mail and telephones
   - activities associated with public relations
   - promotional gifts
   - invitations and tickets to existing customers
   - the cost of photographs/illustrations/ displays etc.

3 *The stand.* Where should the stand be placed in terms of customer flow? This is an important factor if the organisation is to gain maximum exposure. In addition:

   - the stand should be inviting
   - an *island* or *corner* site will increase frontage and allow easier access to prospective customers
   - where are the stands of the company's competitors sited? If too close, these can distract prospective customers to competitors' products/services.

Getting people to the stand is imperative, and many gimmicks are used to achieve this aim. Displays/demonstrations should not be placed so that they block the stand and prevent prospective customers from entering. Famous personalities can be used, but these might attract a large number of people for the wrong reasons. Celebrities do not sell products.

4 *Planning a schedule.* A plan should be produced which identifies what needs to be done and by when. This will ensure that all materials, sales literature, displays etc. are ready when required.

5 *Effectiveness.* After the event, it will be necessary for a company to measure how successful the exhibition has been in terms of targets and criteria identified prior to commencement. A variety of methods might be used, and a cost per enquiry or cost per sale might then be calculated (see Chapter 11 for more details).

STUDENT ACTIVITY

Work in small teams of four or five. Design an exhibition stand which will be one of a number to be part of a local exhibition whose theme is 'Educational opportunities for you'. Produce leaflets and other advertising materials which will 'decorate' your stand and explain the kind of educational opportunities which your school/college can offer to the local community. Build a model mock-up of the design of the stand and show where displays, tables, chairs etc. will be placed.

Note: all visual materials and contents of leaflets/posters must be produced to a professional standard. You will be competing with other groups of students to gain the contract for designing and developing an appropriate display stand for your school/college, so make it memorable!

STUDENT ACTIVITY

ALTERNATIVE ADVERTISING MEDIA

Consult statistics regarding the use of a variety of below-the-line media, i.e. aerial etc. From the information you have obtained, decide the following:

1 You are in a seaside location and are hosting a special fun-spots event in aid of charity. You wish to draw the attention of day visitors to the event. Which media would you suggest? What would be the cost?
2 You are a local company that wishes to raise awareness of its financial expertise. Where might you advertise and why?
3 You are a recruitment agency that would like a cost-effective way of advertising its services all year round. Which type of media would you choose and why?

5.8 AERIAL ADVERTISING

Aerial advertising is restricted depending upon the country in which it is being used. Restrictions exist to ban low-flying aircraft over urban areas in some countries. However, flying low over the sea to attract the attention of holiday-makers on the seashore is permissible.

Again, aerial advertising takes several forms:

– *banners*, which are trailed behind the aircraft
– *writing*, using the smoke trail from the aircraft to write a message in the sky
– *airships*, which carry advertising on their structure (an example would be the Goodyear airship)
– *lasers*, which have been used to project advertisements into the night sky
– *balloons*, which, secured to the ground with a line, are often used to attract travellers to the location of an event, e.g. a special sale.

Some aspects of below-the-line marketing are gaining in popularity. However, the skills, knowledge and experience required to ensure that the advertising message is communicated effectively are vast, and the price of specialist companies is costly. What is the future for this type of advertising? If commentators are to be believed, the future is bright, particularly in terms of direct marketing. Now look at the case study below and decide for yourself the strengths and weaknesses of a below-the-line approach.

5.9 CASE STUDY: WHAT DOES THE DIRECT MAIL ASSOCIATION'S FIRST STUDY TELL US ABOUT DIRECT MARKETING

The DMA's survey – to be carried out once a year in future – suggests that the direct market is worth £4.5 billion. The report includes within the term 'direct marketing' not only direct mail, inserts, telemarketing and door-to-door selling but also direct response broadcasting, i.e. TV and radio. Direct mail represents 25 per cent of this type of advertising.

Figures provided by the Royal Mail identify that £1 billion was spent on direct mail in 1994, which is an increase of 12 per cent on 1993. This increase is set against the reduced costs of producing direct mail, which have fallen by 25 per cent since 1990. Telemarketing is proving a close second to direct mail.

During one month the DMA identified that 78 per cent of display advertising which appeared in the national press invited the reader to take advantage of a form of direct response. Split further, the survey identified that direct response was included in 50 per cent of local press advertising and 25 per cent of national press advertising, and that magazines average 59 per cent. The DMA's calculation for total spend on direct response advertising across a year was £1.52 billion.

The spend on direct response for radio averaged 32 per cent, although percentages varied widely across local stations. This represents a spend of £79.16 million. Of cinema advertisements, 2.5 per cent include a form of direct response, representing a spend of £1.89 million.

Direct response advertising on television has replaced the traditional forms of direct response identified earlier. It is estimated that 23 per cent of TV advertising includes a telephone number. This figure has increased from 17.7 per cent in 1993.

Inserts account for a spend of £213 million, and door-to-door selling for £180 million. Other outdoor advertising represents 7 per cent – i.e. a £23.7 million spend.

The reader should note one or two shortfalls in the research: the seasonal nature of the medium is not taken into account in some instances, and there are no historical figures to check against in others, in addition to which only a small number of media owners were prepared to participate in the survey.

(The above was prepared from an article which appeared in *Marketing*, 6 April 1995, pp. 20–21)

Now answer the following questions:

1 What is the DMA?
2 What is the total spend on direct marketing identified by the DMA?
3 Which aspect of direct marketing is proving to be a close second to direct mail?
4 What percentage of advertising includes direct response in:

  (a) the local press
  (b) the national press?

5 What are the drawbacks of the research?

REVIEW YOUR PROGRESS

1 What do you understand by the term 'direct marketing'?
2 What are the main differences between direct mail and direct response?
3 What is the role of direct marketing agencies?
4 Identify as many types of media which are used for direct response as you can think of.
5 Identify as many types of point-of-sale material as you can remember.
6 What is the difference between sales literature and sales promotions?
7 Identify the strengths and weaknesses of trade exhibitions.
8 Identify as many types of aerial advertising as you can.

6

Advertising research – pre-campaign, during campaign, post-campaign

AIMS

- **to identify and explain the terms primary and secondary research**
- **to look at types of research used before, during and after the advertising campaign**
- **to explain sampling – in particular, quota sampling techniques**
- **to understand how to test the effectiveness of the advertising campaign by measuring the impact and recall rate of the campaign**
- **to assess the effectiveness of the advertising campaign**

UNIT 20 ADVERTISING

- **Element 20.3**

  - **Performance Criteria:**
    4 Describe appropriate methods to pre-test the advertisment

6.1 RESEARCH

Advertising research affords advertisers the opportunity to test an idea before committing money resources to a campaign which could prove ineffective. Prior to incurring costs relative to expensive artwork or the production of television commercials or the purchase of 'air time', research may be carried out to test creativity in terms of:

– theme
– presentation
– copy
– selling points.

There are a number of specialist organisations which offer a variety of services for carrying out research, providing specific information etc as shown in Figure 6.1 below and overleaf.

PRIMARY RESEARCH

Primary research is that which is carried out by an individual or a company to gather information for a specific purpose. The main sources of primary data are:

1 interviews, which are carried out either:

– face to face, or
– on the telephone

2 questionnaires sent by post
3 panel research – consumers are invited to join a panel. Members use the product over a period of time and report back on their opinions/findings
4 group interviews – individuals are invited to join in a discussion during which the researchers will lead the proceedings by asking specific questions

117

Fig 6.1 Examples of advertisements for two companies which offer research services – Business & Market Research and Research International.

5 retail audits, involving the ongoing audit of both stocks and sales levels to determine brand share

6 attitude surveys

7 specialised primary research, which may include 'mystery shoppers'. These are used by retailers or other service industries to identify the level of service which customers experience. Employees are unaware that a survey is taking place.

First-hand data is usually collected using one or more of the following methods:

1 *Observation*. The researcher will normally:

   – watch what is taking place
   – produce accurate information based on his or her observations.

2 *Experiment*. The researcher will create a situation and measure results which occur as a direct result of the experiment.

   An organisation may decide to test-market a product in a specific region of the market in order to test the reaction of the target audience prior to making a decision to launch the product on a national basis. The profile of the market segment tested will usually reflect the profile of the whole market.

3 *Questioning*. Most research uses a form of questionnaire to ask questions for which the company needs answers. Questioning might take place:

   – face-to-face in an interview situation, or
   – via a telephone-questioning session, or
   – by sending a questionnaire by post.

If questionnaires are to be effective, they must be developed with a specific purpose in mind, and their use must be carefully planned. A *pilot* questionnaire should be used first to allow errors in data collection to be eliminated and to ensure that the design of the questions is relevant to their purpose, i.e. that correct information is being gathered which will assist the company in its future decision-making.

Errors usually occur during surveys because:

- information is interpreted incorrectly either by the respondents or by interviewers carrying out the survey, or
- respondents deliberately give false information because they try to give the answers they think are required.

QUESTIONNAIRE DESIGN

The following are points which need to be observed when a questionnaire is being constructed.

1 The first question should always be one which acts as an *eliminator*. There is no point in wasting time and resources interviewing people who do not fall within your target profile.

2 Use *closed questions* when a simple Yes or No answer is required, for example:

Do you use X brand of
washing powder?   Yes   No
Do you drive a car?   Yes   No

3 Use *open questions* to obtain a *personal* response to a question. (Responses from each member of the sample will vary, however, and are therefore difficult to quantify.) An example is:

What do you think about the local council's decision to make the high street a pedestrianised area?

4 Do not ask *multiple questions*, for example:

Do you like the style, colour and make of this garment?

It would be difficult to evaluate which aspect of the sample is favourable or not.

5 Questions may require respondents to prioritise their preferences by *ranking* choices so that their responses can be analysed numerically. For example:

Please place, in order of priority, the following special features of the car of your choice, where 1 is the most important and 5 is least important:

    Radio
    Tape deck
    Audible warnings
    Air-conditioning
    Power steering

6 Questions may be *scaled* to allow respondents to make a choice from intervals along a continuum. For example:

Indicate what you think about the library facilities in your school/college:

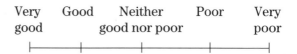

| Very good | Good | Neither good nor poor | Poor | Very poor |

STUDENT ACTIVITY

Work *in pairs. Conduct a survey with students within your school/college. The topic can be one of your choice but it must be agreed with your tutor. It may be that you wish to find out:*

– *whether the facilities within your school/college are adequate or whether other facilities would prove advantageous, or*
– *whether there is much support for developing a youth group within the school /college.*

Construct an appropriate questionnaire and carry out the survey. Collate the results, and present your findings to the rest of your group in an oral presentation which should last about 15 minutes.

SECONDARY RESEARCH

Secondary research, also termed 'desk research', makes use of data which has already been collected for some other purpose, and it is thus a cheaper method of collecting information than that involved in primary research. Secondary data may contain many different types of information, usually in the form of facts and figures which may be used for a variety of purposes. Data may be held on databases or be produced in hard copy.

There are three main problems with secondary data:

1 it may not be relevant to the company's needs
2 it may be too old to be useful
3 its accuracy is difficult to confirm.

Only information that is relevant and that comes from reliable sources should therefore be used.

STUDENT ACTIVITY

Work in small teams and carry out a 'sweep' of your school/college library.

1 How many different sources of data can you identify?
2 What type of data is available?
3 Where might you find information regarding the latest employment trends?
4 Where might you get up-to-date information on the activities of a particular trade association?

Discuss your findings with other members of your group.

When carrying out research, it is cost effective to carry out 'desk research' first and then fill in any gaps with primary research. This is particularly important if resources are limited. Researches on secondary data can be carried out quickly, and there is no need to employ qualified market researchers: the task can be handled by individuals within the company, where costs are absorbed in day-to-day operations.

Sources of secondary data

1 External sources. The most reliable sources outside a company are:

- government-published statistics and other information
- data banks held within universities, which tend to specialise in an area of particular interest
- chambers of commerce
- data held by research organisations
- large advertising agencies and media companies

In addition, trade journals, newspapers and magazines as well as the Central Statistical Office produce a vast range of information in article and statistical form which could be useful to an organisation, i.e. numbers and types of readers etc.

STUDENT ACTIVITY

READERSHIP PROFILES OF PRESS/MAGAZINES

Look at the information contained in Table 6.1.

1 Which is the most popular magazine for people who fall into the AB and C1 socioeconomic groups?
2 Which is the most popular magazine read by men?
3 Which is the most popular television magazine read by the 35/54 age group?
4 How many colour pages does the Readers Digest *contain on average?*

Table 6.1 Readership, circulation and page-rate details of general and listings magazines.

	Circulation (1) '000	Adult readership (2) '000	Adult readership (2) %	Men %	Women %	15/34 %	35/54 %	55+ %	ABC1 %	C2DE %	Mono £	4 colour £
Population profile				48	52	37	32	32	45	56		
Weeklies												
Country Life	42	471	1	49	51	24	44	32	68	32	1,870	3,060
Exchange & Mart	136	1,772	4	74	26	48	39	13	41	59	3,360	3,820
Time Out	108	487	1	57	43	68	28	3	76	24	2,410	2,860
The Weekly News	374	1,015	2	34	66	20	31	48	26	74	4,630	6,825
Fortnightlies												
Private Eye	201	834	2	70	30	50	41	10	78	22	3,600	–
Smash Hits	350	1,208	3	33	67	73	25	2	38	62	7,780	13,300
Monthlies												
BBC Wildlife	132	1,147	3	52	48	33	37	30	51	49	1,830	3,080
Esquire	75	261	1	70	30	78	17	5	72	28	–	3,400
The Field	31*	358	1	56	44	17	42	41	68	31	1,580	2,290
Geographical Magazine	28	318	1	65	35	36	33	31	68	32	1,200	1,875
Readers' Digest	1,652	6,138	14	49	51	24	38	38	53	46	14,200	19,500
The Scots Magazine	72	363	1	52	48	11	38	50	57	42	590	900
TV Listings												
Radio Times	1,503	5,433	12	50	50	37	33	30	61	39	12,700	16,100
TV Quick	700*	2,903	6	39	61	53	30	18	37	63	7,000	8,000
TV Times	1,018	4,946	11	46	54	40	31	28	40	60	9,600	14,400
What's on TV	1,530	3,067	7	42	58	51	27	23	36	64	–	14,500

Note: *July–December 1992.
Sources: (1) ABC date January–June 1993. (2) NRS July 1992–June 1993. (3) BRAD. August 1993, single insertion rate.

121

2 *Internal sources.* There are many sources within companies, which might include:

- sales figures
- distribution figures
- data for departmental cost analyses, i.e. labour, packaging, selling etc.
- financial information, i.e. cash flows, budgets etc.

Data collected internally could be useful, as a secondary data source, to other departments within organisations if those departments are aware of its existence.

STUDENT ACTIVITY

Read the passage below and answer the questions which follow.

WHAT IS 'GEODEMOGRAPHICS'?

Geodemographics uses demographic data such as age, class and family background to classify individuals in terms of specific geographical areas – hence the 'geo-' in 'geodemographics'. We can use a customer profile based on neighbourhood to:

1 identify the type of house an individual occupies, and by using other sources, identify the types of product/service they are typically likely to purchase
2 target the advertising accurately by the use of postcodes
3 carry out similar research as in (1) to identify usage of and opinions about products/services purchased.

During the 1980s there was a growth in companies holding information, on databases, about the lifestyles of populations within specific neighbourhoods. Several companies developed such systems – CCN rewrote their MOSAIC system and ACORN developed a database called Insite, to name but two. Retailers have used this type of information extensively when deciding on new site development, and its use in this respect

continues to grow at a fast pace. The local and regional press too find geodemographics useful – as does local radio.

If geodemographic systems are to be even more accurate and useful in terms of profiling, it is suggested that annual updates on population profiles will need to be implemented.

1 What do you understand by the term 'geodemographics'?
2 To whom might the information be useful?
3 How are retailers using this type of information?
4 What are the likely developments in the future?

Discuss the issues with the rest of your group.

SAMPLING

There are many techniques of sampling but the one most often used is the **quota sample**. Quota sampling is carried out by selecting a sample that is representative of the whole. If the population for a survey is made up of 30/70 per cent male/female, and the socio-economic split is known, the quota sample may be a total of 100 interviews, which may be made up as shown below:

Socio-economic group	Male	Female
AB	13	15
C1	9	35
C2	4	10
D	4	10

The interviewer uses personal judgement and some introductory questions to confirm that each individual interviewed meets the quota criteria. When 13 AB men have been interviewed, no other males in the AB category need to be interviewed as the quota for that category is complete. The 'hunt' will then continue to interview individuals who fit the other groups of the quota.

Quota-sampling techniques are used extensively in market research because they are a cost-effective method of gathering primary data. However, it is possible to produce biased results because of the kind of individuals which interviewers will encounter in the street. It is unlikely that an interviewer will encounter many of the working population if the survey is carried out during the daytime for instance.

IN WHAT FORM ARE RESEARCH FINDINGS TO BE FOUND?

Research findings are published in many different forms, some of which may involve statistics. The latter can include a wide range of information and be displayed in a variety of forms:

1 audience viewing figures
2 newspaper circulation figures (including a breakdown of the lifestyle of the readership, socio-economic group etc.)
3 the level of sales of magazines etc.

Having defined the target audience, the advertisement can then be aimed specifically, using a variety of research information.

STUDENT ACTIVITY

Look at the statistics in Table 6.2 on page 124 which relate to expenditure on advertising in a variety of media between the years 1987 and 1992.
Work in small teams of three or four and make decisions regarding the following:

1 Which media would you use to advertise each of the following products:

(a) a 'top of the range' luxury motor vehicle, i.e. Rolls Royce, Bentley etc.
(b) a new brand of toothpaste
(c) a village fête which is a charity fund raiser for a local hospice
(d) a short course for managers, offered nationally
(e) a new range of educational toys for the 3–5 age group?

2 What are the reasons for your media choice in each case, and what are the advantages of these media in each case?

Discuss your suggestions with other members of the wider group.

STUDENT ACTIVITY

Look at the statistics in Figure 6.2 on page 125 and answer the following:

1 What do the figures in the charts tell you about display advertising?
2 How can consumer behaviour explain the predictions in Chart 3 in your opinion?
3 Has consumer expenditure grown or reduced during 1993 and 1994 according to these statistics?

6.2 PRE-CAMPAIGN RESEARCH

Before advertising appears, it is useful to:

• decide on a theme and produce copy
• pre-test the advertisement
• produce a media schedule

THE THEME

A decision must be made regarding the theme to be used to sell the product. Will the product be sold on its quality, price, aesthetics or some other criteria decided upon by the marketing team, and based on sound research?

The marketeers may decide to carry out research based on what motivates consumers to buy. The theory behind this approach was covered in Chapter 2.

FOCUS GROUPS

Alternatively, the marketeers may decide to use focus groups. Focus groups comprise individuals who are invited to take part in a discussion based

Table 6.2 Total advertising expenditure by medium and by type 1987–92.

	£m						Percentage of total					
	1987	1988	1989	1990	1991	1992	1987	1988	1989	1990	1991	1992
By medium												
National newspapers, incl. col. suppl.	959	1,099	1,222	1,187	1,121	1,155	15.8	15.6	15.6	15.1	14.8	14.8
Regional newspapers, incl. free sheets	1,280	1,544	1,707	1,715	1,628	1,640	21.1	21.9	21.8	21.7	21.5	21.0
Consumer magazines	378	440	482	480	438	432	6.2	6.2	6.2	6.1	5.8	5.5
Business & professional magazines	602	703	838	790	708	688	9.9	10.0	10.7	10.0	9.3	8.8
Directories	310	365	439	492	504	523	5.1	5.2	5.6	6.2	6.6	6.7
Press production costs	305	357	389	412	417	427	5.0	5.1	5.0	5.2	5.5	5.5
Total press	3,834	4,507	5,077	5,076	4,816	4,864	63.3	64.0	64.9	64.4	63.5	62.2
Television, incl. prod. costs	1,872	2,127	2,286	2,325	2,313	2,478	30.9	30.2	29.2	29.5	30.5	31.7
Poster & transport, incl. prod. costs	216	244	271	282	267	284	3.6	3.5	3.5	3.6	3.5	3.6
Cinema, incl. prod. costs	22	27	35	39	42	45	0.4	0.4	0.4	0.5	0.6	0.6
Radio, incl. prod. costs	111	139	159	163	149	154	1.8	2.0	2.0	2.1	2.0	2.0
Total	6,055	7,044	7,827	7,885	7,587	7,825	100	100	100	100	100	100
By type												
Display advertising												
Press [a]	2,370	2,680	2,983	2,964	2,893	2,938	39.1	38.0	38.1	37.6	38.1	37.5
Television	1,872	2,127	2,286	2,325	2,313	2,478	30.9	30.2	29.2	29.5	30.5	31.7
Other media [b]	349	410	465	484	458	483	5.8	5.8	5.9	6.1	6.0	6.2
Total display	4,591	5,217	5,734	5,773	5,664	5,899	75.8	74.1	73.3	73.2	74.7	75.4
Classified advertising [c]	1,464	1,827	2,093	2,113	1,923	1,926	24.2	25.9	26.7	26.8	25.3	24.6
Total	6,055	7,044	7,827	7,885	7,587	7,825	100	100	100	100	100	100

[a] Including financial notices and display advertising in business and professional journals, but not advertising in directories.
[b] Poster and transport, cinema and radio.
[c] Including all directory advertising.
Source: The Advertising Association's Advertising Statistics Yearbook 1993, NTC Publications Ltd, tables 3.1.1, 3.1.3, 4.2.1 and 4.2.2. Please see this source for definitions.

Advertising business indicators

Outlook is for steady unspectacular growth

THE RECENT SLOWING of UK economic growth has caused most forecasts of advertising expenditure to be revised downwards slightly. The two charts at the foot of the page show that the growth (although not the level) of display advertising is expected to peak in the first quarter of 1995, classified a little later.

Consumer behaviour goes a long way to explain these projections: the chart on the right illustrates the close relationship between consumers' expenditure and display advertising. For example, when consumers' expenditure growth peaks, as it did in 1983, 1986 and 1988, display growth was soon to turn downwards.

Consumers' expenditure has grown only slowly over the past two years (less than half its rate in the late 1980s) and appears to be slowing – probably due to high levels of personal debt, higher taxes and the plateauing of house prices – therefore suggesting that display adspend growth will soon peak.

Some encouragement has been derived from recent output figures which suggest that the consumer sector may have picked up, leading some to believe that consumer confidence may be recovering, thus boosting advertising. However, this is not borne out by the leading indicators which provide the first signs of a peak in growth (detailed at the top of this page) and which continue to signal slower growth in the consumer sector. The NTC Indicator, a 'summary picture' from these indicators, continues its descent, its growth stunted largely by a fall in retail sales in January, higher interest rates and slower growth of job vacancies. The Index of Publications Demand also provides evidence of a gradual deceleration.

The good news, however, is that a slower rate of growth should be more sustainable. Barring the possibility of a politically inspired pre-election boom to ignite consumer demand, the next few years should bring solid growth with rising levels of adspend. ∎

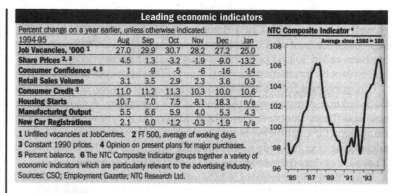

Leading economic indicators

Percent change on a year earlier, unless otherwise indicated.

1994-95	Aug	Sep	Oct	Nov	Dec	Jan
Job Vacancies, '000 [1]	27.0	29.9	30.7	28.2	27.2	25.0
Share Prices [2,3]	4.5	1.3	-3.2	-1.9	-9.0	-13.2
Consumer Confidence [4,5]	1	-9	-5	-6	-16	-14
Retail Sales Volume	3.1	3.5	2.9	2.3	3.6	0.3
Consumer Credit [3]	11.0	11.2	11.3	10.3	10.0	10.6
Housing Starts	10.7	7.0	7.5	-8.1	18.3	n/a
Manufacturing Output	5.5	6.6	5.9	4.0	5.3	4.3
New Car Registrations	2.1	6.0	-1.2	-0.3	-1.9	n/a

1 Unfilled vacancies at JobCentres. 2 FT 500, average of working days.
3 Constant 1990 prices. 4 Opinion on present plans for major purchases.
5 Percent balance. 6 The NTC Composite Indicator groups together a variety of economic indicators which are particularly relevant to the advertising industry.
Sources: CSO; Employment Gazette; NTC Research Ltd.

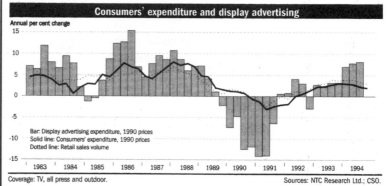

Consumers' expenditure and display advertising

Annual per cent change

Bar: Display advertising expenditure, 1990 prices
Solid line: Consumers' expenditure, 1990 prices
Dotted line: Retail sales volume

Coverage: TV, all press and outdoor. Sources: NTC Research Ltd.; CSO.

Index of publications demand (pages x circulation): UK printed

LAST MONTH'S FIGURES IN BRACKETS	NOVEMBER 1994	12 MONTH MOVING AVERAGE	YEAR ON YEAR % CHANGE NOVEMBER '94	YEAR-TO-DATE
National Newspapers	136.0 (133.9)	123.8 (122.8)	+9.5 (+11.2)	+14.6 (+15.2)
Regional Newspapers	110.5 (108.7)	105.1 (104.6)	+6.4 (+3.6)	+5.2 (+5.1)
Total Newspapers	125.9 (123.8)	116.4 (115.6)	+8.3 (+8.4)	+11.0 (+11.3)
Colour Supplements	130.7 (134.2)	107.3 (102.9)	+29.2 (+32.2)	+12.7 (+11.0)
Consumer Magazines	127.7 (121.2)	107.9 (106.9)	+10.6 (+3.1)	+5.8 (+5.2)
Business Magazines	109.5 (129.8)	105.6 (105.1)	+5.6 (+9.2)	+7.5 (+7.7)
Total Magazines	124.5 (125.3)	107.2 (106.1)	+12.6 (+9.0)	+7.3 (+6.7)
Total Publications	125.5 (124.2)	114.0 (113.1)	+9.4 (+8.6)	+10.1 (+10.2)

Indices are based on average 1992 = 100. Source: Paper Market Digest.

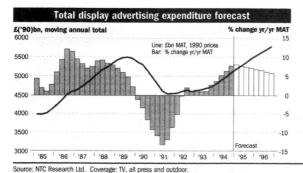

Total display advertising expenditure forecast

£('90)bn, moving annual total   % change yr/yr MAT

Line: £bn MAT, 1990 prices
Bar: % change yr/yr MAT

Forecast

Source: NTC Research Ltd. Coverage: TV, all press and outdoor.

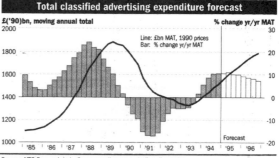

Total classified advertising expenditure forecast

£('90)bn, moving annual total   % change yr/yr MAT

Line: £bn MAT, 1990 prices
Bar: % change yr/yr MAT

Forecast

Source: NTC Research Ltd. Coverage: all press excluding directories.

Fig 6.2 An article from **Admap** *March 1995 on consumer and advertising expenditure.*

on questions posed by the market researchers. Notes are taken of comments made, and a report is produced. From comments contained in the report, it is likely that a theme will be identified.

RECALL STUDIES

Recall studies are usually associated with television, radio and press advertising.

Television and radio

Once a theme has been decided, a 'mock-up' of the radio or TV script must be produced and tested on a small quota sample representative of the wider audience.

The press

Similarly, if press advertisements are to be used, copy must be produced and shown to potential customers for comment and subsequent adjustment as necessary. Tests may continue until the target response rate is achieved.

STUDENT ACTIVITY

Work in pairs. Choose a popular advertisement which has appeared on television recently which you feel might have been of interest to your fellow students. Produce a questionnaire which you are to use to carry out a survey as follows:

1 Identify a sample of three or four students who saw the advertisement in question.
2 Arrange to meet with them and discuss aspects of the advertisement.

Individually, produce a written report of your findings.

RECALL TESTS

An advertisement may be placed in a regional edition of a national newspaper, with research taking place the following day.

Researchers are sent out into the street to ask people if they:

1 read the newspaper, and
2 saw the advertisement.

Of those who did see the advertisement, a sample are invited to take part in a study where they are questioned on every aspect of the content of the advertisement. The aim is to see which parts of the advertisement were best remembered. The weaknesses are eliminated from the advertisement and the final version of the advertisement produced and used in the proposed campaign.

STUDENT ACTIVITY

Work in small teams of three or four and carry out a recall study based on a newspaper/magazine advertisement of your choice. You are to organise the study, collate results and deliver a 15-minute oral presentation which details your findings and in which your group draws conclusions in terms of:

1 the content of the advertisement, i.e. script, visuals, layout etc.
2 any refinements you feel appropriate.

Produce the suggested visual to enhance the advertisement and use it during your presentation to illustrate the points you wish to make.

STUDENT ACTIVITY

In the following excerpts from 'Advertisement pre-testing works – or does it?', an article by Wendy Gordon (Chairman of The Research Business Group) which appeared in Admap *magazine dated March 1995, Wendy suggests that all methods used for advertisement pre-testing are artificial and are variations of short-term-memory tests.*

Fig 6.3 A map of UK regional daily and Sunday newspapers.
Source: **Marketing Pocket Book 1996, NTC Publications Ltd.**

WHAT IS ACCEPTED PRE-TESTING WISDOM TODAY?

Pre-testing is controversial. *Most people who have been involved in several pre-tests over a number of campaigns will know that it is often a political minefield, since by its name it 'tests' the advertisement or campaign...*

No single measure predicts effectiveness. *This has been the greatest change in advertising research over the past few years. There is no longer a belief in a single measure; instead a combination of measures are used and interpreted in different ways. Of the 22 systems of pre-testing listed in the December 1994 edition of* Admap, *some 13 claim to use norms for an interpretation of the ad's performance. The remainder claim to interpret the results against the advertising objectives.*

The most common measures are:

– Recall: *impact, stand out, branding;*
– Communication: *central message;*
– Emotional response: *(i) message, and (ii) execution;*
– Likeability;
– Association: *image, attributes;*
– Persuasion: *preference/attitude skills...*

...there are a number of critical facts concerned with what has been termed the 'information society' – characterised by the generation, distribution and consumption of information of all types. This concept forms the foundations of an awesome book recently written by Giep Franzen called Advertising Effectiveness – Findings From Empirical Research ...

The facts on which this article is based are drawn from this book but the consequences and implications for pre-testing are my own responsibility and not Professor Franzen's.

- Fact 1: we are overloaded with communication ... *The quantity of mass media communication has octupled since 1960 excluding all the junk mail that falls on our carpets and desks. Advertising TV minutes have increased by 255 per cent and the number of pages of print ads have increased by 34 per cent over a ten-year period...*
- Fact 2: we are becoming increasingly selective about what we attend to. *Studies show that an average reader gives two seconds of attention to an advertisement in a newspaper or magazine irrespective of colour or black and white, 1.5 seconds' attention being focused on the visual and 0.5 seconds on the copy...*
- Fact 3: attention and processing is stimulated by relevance. *Interest in the product, the product category or the brand is the most important factor influencing attention...*
- Fact 4: attention and processing can be enhanced or adversely affected. *The nature of the communication stimulates attention and processing too. Physical factors for press advertisements such as colour (more important than size), front of publication (likely to receive more attention than the back) and location alongside editorial (effective if the editorial is relevant), and, for TV commercial, length (longer ones are more likely to be established in the memory) and number of commercials in the break (the greater the number the greater the decrease in spontaneous recall) – all of these affect attention...*
- Fact 5: 30 per cent of the meanings of commercials are miscomprehended. *A shocking series of studies show that people miscomprehend the meaning of both press and TV ads (as much as 30 per cent to 54 per cent of the meanings) – not because people are stupid, but because perception is not objective.*

EXPOSURE ISSUES

...there is no evidence that short-term memory (as measured by recall, stand out or brand name playback) and advertising effectiveness in terms of real market performance are correlated...

ATTENTION ISSUES

If most advertisements, whether print or TV, only warrant an average of less than four seconds' attention, what are we achieving in a 25-minute interview or a one-and-a-half-hour group discussion?...

ROUGH STIMULUS ISSUES

Studies show that there are many creative devices, well known in the UK, which enhance attention, memorability and the building of associations around a brand. These include humour, mood, cuteness, famous personalities, unique visuals, music, advertising properties and emotional rewards. All of these are difficult (if not impossible) to simulate before the film is produced since so much relies on final production and direction...

COMMUNICATION ISSUES

The fact that the main message is played back in response to a direct question does not mean that the meaning has been integrated into the individual's perception (current baggage of attitudes, beliefs and behaviour) about the brand ... The issue of miscomprehension should not be ignored, particularly in advertising that is conveying facts of some kind...

TARGETING AND RECRUITMENT ISSUES

Relevance is the main theme ... the sample for both a qualitative and quantitative pre-test needs to be recruited against this overall criterion ... The most important discriminator is the closeness or distance of the individuals to the brand and this needs to be defined far more carefully than is usually the case ... Recruitment of respondents needs to be reviewed against criteria of relevance ... If a relevant sample is interviewed for a pre-test and analysed sensitively, the interpretation can be far more powerful.

QUALITATIVE PRE-TESTING ISSUES

...Group discussions at any point other than early strategy development lead to cynicism from respondents, agency and client alike ... Far better to use individual depth interviews, carefully recruited against brand relevance as discussed above, to provide an understanding of how the advertisement is being integrated into an individual's perceptual framework of the brand...

DISCUSSION POINT

Is there any real benefit to the advertiser in carrying out pre-testing of his or her advertising communications?

6.3 DURING-THE-CAMPAIGN RESEARCH

During the course of the advertising campaign, further recall studies will be carried out to test which details of the advertisement readers best remember. Information regarding the number of responses to advertisements will give a measure of the effectiveness of the campaign.

If the advertisement includes a coupon response, the effectiveness of the media used can also be assessed by monitoring the codes which are included on coupons (different codes for different publications). The company can then assess which newspaper/magazine advertisements reached their target audience most effectively.

If the cost of the advertising space is divided by the number of respondents, the cost per enquiry can be obtained.

6.4 POST-CAMPAIGN RESEARCH

Before the organisation can evaluate its success, it must first decide its criteria for success – i.e. does the organisation wish to:

– maintain its market share, or
– increase its market share, or
– raise awareness, or
– a mixture of some or all of the above?

Some of the methods covered in 6.1 and 6.2 can be used to assess the effectiveness of the campaign. Whatever the criteria set for success prior to the start of the campaign, the final results can be measured against these to assess performance.

COST PER ENQUIRY AND COST PER SALE

The success of direct response advertising is easier to assess. The coupon included in the advertisement is coded and will usually identify:

– the publication in which the advertisement appeared
– the actual advertisement
– when the advertisement appeared.

By sorting the coupons received by code number, it is possible to identify how successful the advertisement has been in a specific newspaper/magazine, and thus to calculate the cost per enquiry and, subsequently, the cost per sale, i.e.:

$$\frac{\text{total cost of advertising}}{\text{number of enquiries received}} = \text{cost per enquiry}$$

IMPACT STUDIES

Tracking studies

Tracking studies concentrate on testing the *impact* of the advertisement on audiences rather than the level of recall. The service is offered by Tracking, Advertising and Brand Strength (TABS), which is an independent market-research company. TABS uses computer technology and a questionnaire to gather and sort/store information. These together keep track of the level of reaction to advertised brands. TABS analyses the advertising and is able to identify weaknesses in areas such as creativity and the media used.

Gallup polls are used to carry out 'reading and rating' sampling. Readers are asked to scan each page, and are questioned about every page. They will be asked if they:

– looked at the advertisement or not
– read some of it or all of it.

This research will also usually be applied to other advertisements which appear in the same publication.

The results of the research are generally presented as a series of measures, i.e.:

- *page traffic* – the percentage of people who looked at a specific page
- *rating* – the percentage of people who saw the advertisement.

AWARENESS STUDIES

A method more generally used in some areas is that of *awareness* studies. After a campaign has run for a period of time, a sample survey is carried out. Questions are asked about brands which are in the same market. A company may wish to find out information about activities which are occurring in a particular market of which they have a share. The researcher may gather information by asking questions such as:

- What brands have you heard of?
- What offers have been available?
- From the list presented, which of these brands do you recognise?
- Which brands have you seen advertised locally?

in order to establish which media have been used by competitors and what was contained within the advertisement. The information helps to provide a guide which shows the development of the recognition of a product, and it also helps to identify what has been achieved by the advertisement.

MAKING COMPARISONS

All advertisements should be viewed critically and evaluated qualitatively to see if improvements can be made. Organisations should analyse each advertisement to identify whether:

– it meets the brief
– the target market was attracted by the advertisement
– the advertisement grabbed people's attention
– the message was believable and persuasive.

When comparing media, advertisers need to look at whether:

– the contents of the advertisements are different
– the advertisement appeared at different times in different publications
– reproduction was the same
– the advertisement appeared in colour in one publication and in black and white in another.

Minor differences can have an impact on how successful an advertisement is.

The variety of approaches to research on the relevance and effectiveness of advertising is vast and can prove expensive. Companies tend to use those sources which best supply their particular information needs.

6.5 CASE STUDY: FAIRY LIQUID/EXCEL – THE STORY OF A WASHING UP LIQUID!

RESEARCH AND DEVELOPMENT

Procter & Gamble undertook research in the 1950s to develop a washing-up liquid which would meet consumers' needs. Criteria identified were that the brand should perform exceptionally well and that it should be one which consumers wished to purchase. Many 'formulations' were developed until the product reached performance requirements. It was then necessary to ensure that there were no harmful substances in the product. Packaging was developed, and the product was ready for testing.

CONSUMER TESTS

Testing took place on the product's performance, mildness, perfume, colour and packaging, and feedback was then used to adjust the product accordingly. The product was launched in Birmingham in 1959 on television.

THE LAUNCH

Fairy Liquid had undergone 100,000 dishwashing tests. Consumers liked the product, and at that time just 17 per cent of consumers used a liquid – others used soap powders or left-over pieces of soap bar.

The product was launched nationally in 1960. At this time the average consumer's hands were in washing-up water 25 times a week. Between 1960 and 1980, Fairy Liquid doubled its market share, and by this latter date more than 1,000 million bottles had been sold.

FAIRY LIQUID ADVERTISING

P&G suggest that the reason for the brand's success was that it was mild, performed well and was economical to use. The product was under continual development, and advertising continued to ram home the message of mildness and value for money. Fairy Liquid's theme song: 'Now hands that do dishes can be soft as your face, with mild, green Fairy Liquid' was, however, the subject of much joking!

CONSUMER RESEARCH

Research was carried out continually, and can be mapped as follows:

1981: it was the product most 'desired', but the need for the product to last longer was identified.
1984/85: Ulster was chosen to test the lemon Fairy Liquid, which retained its original green colour. When asked which washing-up liquid had the nicest smell, consumers identified the lemon liquid.

131

1987/88: the need was revealed to persuade people who occasionally used Fairy Liquid that it was value for money all the time.

1988: users still wanted better economy from the product, as well as improved performance in removing grease from crockery and a reduction in 'mess' on the bottle after use.

1992: Fairy Excel was launched in August 1992 on a national scale, and research suggested that the product delivers improved performance on greasy dishes, coupled with less effort, and is kinder to hands. The packaging for Fairy Excel was preferred by consumers.

1993: Fairy Excel Plus was launched in October 1993, and research testing identified both that the product performs 'outstandingly' in terms of tackling greasy dishes and that it lasts longer, and is milder on hands, than any other product.

(Adapted from information provided by Procter & Gamble)

1 Why is consumer research so important to Procter & Gamble, the makers of Fairy Excel Plus?

2 Research the market for dishwasher products. How is the market split between manufacturers?

3 Why is the product so successful?

Discuss the issues you have identified with other members of your group.

1 What are the two main types of advertising research called?

2 Identify the major sources of published data.

3 What are the main points to remember when constructing a questionnaire for research purposes?

4 What do you understand by the term 'quota sample'?

5 Which types of research are most appropriate in each of the following instances:

   (a) pre-campaign
   (b) during the campaign
   (c) post-campaign?

6 What type of information can be provided by tracking studies?

Legal constraints and ethics

AIMS

- to examine the role of the Advertising Standards Authority, the BCAP and the ITC
- to identify the impact of equal opportunities on advertising
- to discuss environmental considerations in relation to advertising

UNIT 20 ADVERTISING

- Element 20.3

  - Performance Criteria:
    3 Conform with legal and voluntary advertising constraints

7.1 LAW AND ETHICS

The National Vigilance Committee was set up in 1926 in an effort to set up voluntary regulation of advertising; and the UK government, on its part, has also sought to control advertising, by legislation: more than 100 statutes currently exist which seek to regulate the sector. Both voluntary and compulsory regulations can be effective for a variety of reasons:

1 *Voluntary controls* seek to set out *recommendations* in writing which are felt to be 'in the public interest'. The risks involved for organisations which ignore these recommendations are loss of status and loss of commission for the agency (if one is involved) as well as the risk of damaging the reputation of the company concerned if the complaint is taken to the Advertising Standards Authority (ASA). In addition to these penalties, the company will be required to change or withdraw the offending advertisement.

   Voluntary controls seek to be self-regulating – the media acting as the censor. It is not in the interests of the media to receive complaints, nor do agents wish to lose commission. Complaints received by the ASA from the public are investigated. Should the complaint be upheld, this could result in the advertisement being withdrawn quickly.

   It is generally felt that voluntary self-regulation is more effective than legislation.

2 *Legal controls* seek to:

   - set down, in writing, regulations to which the advertisement must conform to safeguard 'the public interest'. Organisations which do not conform face a fine or imprisonment if they are found guilty
   - identify illegalities which are meant to act as a preventative measure (legal procedures are lengthy and costly)

7.2 VOLUNTARY CONTROLS

Controls are imposed on advertising in a variety of ways, depending on the media being used.

THE BRITISH CODE OF ADVERTISING PRACTICE (BCAP)

The British Code of Practice is looked after by the BCAP, a self-regulating body which exerts a preventative influence on advertisers. Included in the Code is an explanation of:

1 its aims and origins
2 how the code is administered
3 the code's scope
4 how the code is to be interpreted.

The BCAP also includes some 'general rules' which are divided into three main sections under the following headings:

- Decency – the content should not cause offence
- Truthfulness
- Health Claims – covering advertisements which offer health benefits

The BCAP states that advertisements should be honest, truthful and legal, should be prepared responsibly and should conform to the principles of fair competition. An emphasis is currently placed on proof of claims which are made on behalf of products. Companies may be required to furnish such proof if requested to do so.

The Code of Advertising Practice Committee updates the Code. Members of the Committee include representatives from a variety of organisations, including media owners and agencies. Amendments to the Code are issued as required, and advertising copy can be submitted to the Committee for examination should there be any doubt as to the specific approach which has been adopted.

Advertising & Sponsorship
on Commercial Television

iTc

THE INDEPENDENT TELEVISION COMMISSION (ITC)

The ITC licenses and regulates commercial television in the UK. It was set up by law under the Broadcasting Act 1990 to:

- issue licences that allow commercial television companies to broadcast in and from the UK
- monitor broadcasters' ouput
- set and monitor detailed requirements concerning the amount, quality and range of output for ITV, Channel 4 and the teletext service on these channels.

The ITC is also required to draw up and enforce a Code of Advertising Standards and Practice, and to consider complaints about television advertisements which are alleged to be misleading.

Advertising & Sponsorship on Commercial Television

ADVERTISING

The Broadcasting Act 1990 requires the ITC to draw up and enforce a Code of Advertising Standards and Practice. The ITC also has a duty under the Control of Misleading Advertisements Regulations 1988 to consider complaints about television advertisements which are alleged to be misleading.

These regulatory tasks are achieved by the ITC in three ways:
- setting standards;
- ensuring compliance;
- investigating complaints.

Setting standards

The ITC's Code of Advertising Standards and Practice was adopted after wide public consultation and is kept under regular review with the help of an independent advisory committee comprising representatives of both consumer and advertising interests.

The main objectives of the Code are to ensure that television advertising:
- is not misleading;
- does not encourage or condone harmful behaviour;
- does not cause widespread or exceptional offence.

The Code also includes certain requirements laid down by Parliament (notably a prohibition on political advertising) and others derived from the European Community Directive on Television Broadcasting and the Council of Europe Convention on Transfrontier Television. The ITC also has a duty to act upon any Government directions concerning categories of products or services which may or may not be advertised.

In addition to general rules which relate to all advertising, the Code contains more detailed rules on particular categories, for example alcoholic drinks, financial services, medical products, advertising to children and advertising by religious or charitable groups.

Ensuring compliance

The ITC requires the television companies which it licenses to comply with the Code. They are expected to have adequate procedures to check carefully all advertising proposals before accepting them for transmission. In particular, they should satisfy themselves that any claims, whether explicit or implicit, are true, if necessary by inspecting documentary evidence or seeking the advice of independent consultants. Where there is any doubt about how a rule should be interpreted, licensees are free to seek advice from the ITC.

These requirements, which are more rigorous than those applied to any other advertising medium, help to ensure that, as far as possible, commercials which appear on television meet the necessary standards.

The ITC monitors the finished output closely and, if necessary, can require the amendment or withdrawal of any advertisement which does not comply with the rules. Any direction to withdraw an advertisement has mandatory and immediate effect, and the ITC can impose severe penalties on the television companies for failure to comply.

Amount of advertising

On Channel 3 (ITV) and Channel 4, advertising is limited to an average of seven minutes per hour throughout the day (although an average of seven-and-a-half minutes per hour is permitted in the peak evening viewing period). On satellite and cable channels, the limit is an average of nine minutes per hour over the day

except on 'home shopping' channels which carry no conventional programming. There are also strict limits on the frequency and length of advertising breaks in different types of programmes. There are some categories of programme in which no advertising at all is permitted as in, for example, religious services.

Fig 7.1 A leaflet which explains the role of the Independent Television Commission (ITC).

The AIRC performs a similar vetting process for radio. Certain categories of advertisement are banned from commercial television and radio.

THE ADVERTISING STANDARDS AUTHORITY (ASA)

The ASA is financed indirectly via a levy on published advertisements. It:

- monitors advertisements and ensures they comply with the British Codes of Advertising and Sales Promotion
- responds to requests from advertisers, agencies and the media for guidance on advertisements prior to publication
- investigates complaints about advertisements from the public and from competitors or pressure groups
- can have misleading or offensive advertisements withdrawn.

Complaints

The ASA publishes advertisements in the press inviting the public to complain. It administers the Code, investigates any complaints received and publishes reports each month.

STUDENT ACTIVITY

'It's not all sex, sex, sex . . .'

This was the headline of a poster advertisement which appeared in 1994 for Club 18–30 holidays. The agency responsible was Saatchi & Saatchi, who were ordered to withdraw the advert because it promoted casual sex and drunken behaviour and was offensive. The ASA upheld 432 complaints against this advertisement. Saatchi must also clear any future copy for Club 18–30 advertisements with the ASA prior to publication.
    The advertising campaign included a variety of slogans:

- *'Discover your erogenous zones' using a map of Europe as a backdrop*
- *'You get two weeks for being drunk and disorderly'*

- *'Girls. Can we interest you in a package holiday?'*
- *'It's not all sex, sex, sex, sex . . . there's a bit of sun and sea as well'*

Club 18–30 had apparently requested a shocking campaign, and it was suggested that the campaign had increased sales by 30 per cent and that the company, moreover, were pleased with the campaign.
    The ASA stated that the campaign had caused widespread offence.

Debate the issues surrounding this type of advertisement in terms of the intended audience.

Other bodies which handle complaints include:

1 the television companies
2 the Broadcasting Complaints Commission (BCC)
3 the Broadcasting Standards Council (BSC).

THE PRESS

It would be impossible for the ASA to scan all advertisements which appear in the press due to sheer volume, and it is therefore the responsibility of agencies and advertisers to make sure that their advertisements conform to the Code of Practice and are also legal.

The Newspaper Proprietors Association (NPA)

The NPA carries out pre-censoring of direct response mail-order advertisements , scrutinising copy before the advertisements can appear in any aspect of the press. The current system was agreed after discussions with the Office of Fair Trading, following worries about the number of fraudulent advertisements.

The Periodical Publishers Association

This runs a similar operation.

A guarantee fund exists which receives contributions from all advertisers and this guarantees pay

WHEN THE ASA RECEIVES A COMPLAINT ABOUT AN ADVERTISEMENT, WHAT DO WE DO ABOUT IT?

The Advertising Standards Authority is the independent self-regulatory body responsible for supervising the content of non-broadcast advertisements in the UK. The Authority is recognised by the Office of Fair Trading as an established means of consumer protection.

One of the ASA's tasks is to investigate complaints that advertisements break the rules in the British Codes of Advertising and Sales Promotion.

The ASA's complaints procedure is designed to ensure a balance between speed and fairness.

Receiving a complaint

When a complaint is received the first decision to be made is whether it should be pursued and, if so, in what way.

The ASA pursues complaints that indicate advertisements may have broken the Codes. If we ask advertisers for their comments on the allegations made against them, this does not necessarily imply that there has been a breach.

Complaints from members of the public are investigated without their identity being revealed. Complaints from those with a commercial interest in the outcome are investigated on a named basis.

The ASA does not investigate complaints about TV or radio advertisements. Nor do we intervene in contractual disputes or when claims are subject to legal action.

When the ASA decides to pursue a complaint, a letter is sent to the advertisers and, if appropriate, their advertising agency. This letter sets out the nature of the complaint and asks for their comment. At this point, we inform the relevant media organisations and publishers that a complaint has been received and tell them how it is to be pursued.

If the case seems to be particularly grave, the advertisers may be asked to stop making the disputed claim until the investigation has been completed and a decision reached.

Response required: substantiation

The advertisers or their agency must now reply in writing to the complaint. This should be sent to the ASA promptly. Where substantiation is relevant, the Codes require advertisers to not only have evidence of the truth of their claims but also make it available without delay.

If the advertisers delay the investigation, they may be asked to withdraw the advertisement until the complaint has been resolved.

Evaluation

Once the ASA has received the advertisers' response, the next stage is to evaluate their comments in light of the complaint.

The ASA will continue to press for information, which might include seeking independent expert advice, so that there is adequate material on which to base a judgement.

At the end of an investigation, a recommendation goes to the ASA's Council.

Decision

The Council is solely responsible for the final decision and will now consider the recommendation; there is no obligation to accept it. The parties concerned are informed of the final outcome.

QUICK GUIDE

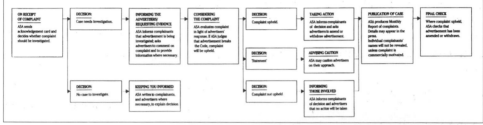

Action

If it is decided that the advertisers have contravened the Codes, they are asked to undertake not to repeat the breach and to amend or withdraw the advertisement.

If they refuse to give this undertaking, the ASA informs media organisations on the Committee of Advertising Practice (which represents all sides of the advertising industry) that the advertisement contravenes the Codes.

As well as being denied advertising space, the advertisers may lose financial discounts or commission until the advertisement is changed.

Publicity

The results of complaint investigations and the names of advertisers and their agencies are published in the ASA's Monthly Reports. With the exception of complaints from those with a commercial interest, who are named, complainants are identified by their local area only. Their identity is not revealed during the complaint investigation without their express prior permission.

Monthly Reports are circulated to the press, government departments and agencies, consumer organisations, the advertising industry and individual members of the public who wish to know about our work.

Advice Service

For advertisers and agencies who are in doubt about the Codes' requirements or would like guidance for future advertisements, we provide a fast, free and confidential pre-publication advice service. This has direct telephone and fax numbers: telephone 0171-580 4100 and fax 0171-580 4072.

COMPLAINTS PROCEDURE

ASA

The Advertising Standards Authority
2 Torrington Place London WC1E 7HW
Telephone: 0171-580 5555
Fax: 0171-631 3051

Fig 7.2 A leaflet from the Advertising Standards Authority (ASA) which explains the procedure for complaints.

should legal action be taken against contributors. The size of a particular company's contribution depends upon the size of that company's spend on media advertising.

THE EUROPEAN COMMISSION

In America and most of Europe, laws exist which identify specific 'penalties' for advertisers and agencies which break regulations. The British Code of Practice covers these statutes in a voluntary capacity. The European Commission, when drawing up its own initial directive relative to advertising, wished to invoke its legal system throughout the whole of the European Union. Voluntary controls set up by the Commission help to minimise the use of legal proceedings which can be extremely expensive and very long winded.

The Commission's Code of Practice is similarly subject to constant revision.

STUDENT ACTIVITY

TANGO

Read *the following article which appeared in* Marketing *magazine dated April 1995:*

The Advertising Standards Authority has upheld complaints that a recent Tango campaign appearing on bus shelters in London was insensitive and frightening.

The poster, a still from a TV commercial featuring the Tango character Napoleon, showed an alarmed man with bulging eyes and an orange hand. It claimed:

'You won't see him coming behind you. But by God you'll feel him. You're about to be "Tango'd".'

'It was not meant to cause offence,' said a spokeswoman for Britvic. 'It is a standard format for posters often used for film ads.'

What was the main reason for the ASA upholding the complaint?

7.3 OTHER VOLUNTARY ARRANGEMENTS

THE ASSOCIATION OF MAIL ORDER PUBLISHERS

Mail Order Protection Scheme (MOPS)

MOPS was set up by the Association of Mail Order Publishers to protect the consumer against traders making fraudulent use of direct response advertising, i.e. money is sent and then nothing is heard. To place this type of advertisement, creditworthiness will be checked and an indemnity will need to be furnished, i.e. a deposit of a specified sum of money.

The BCAP states that direct response advertisers must:

1 hold adequate stocks of product prior to advertising
2 fulfil orders within 28 days normally
3 accept returns of damaged goods within seven days.

The MOPS conforms to the BCAP, as does the Proprietory Association of Great Britain.

BRITISH CODE OF SALES PROMOTION PRACTICE (BCSPP)

The BCSPP controls sales-promotion schemes, i.e. offers, competitions etc. The Code requires any such scheme to be fair and honest. Specific requirements cover the wording of promotions and conduct of competitions. The ASA should be contacted to seek acceptance for ideas initially.

7.4

LAWS WHICH IMPACT ON ADVERTISING

STATUTES

There are a number of statutes which have an impact on advertising practice. The following is a list of some for reference, but this is by no means complete:

- Advertisers (Hire Purchase) Act 1967
- Data Protection Act 1986
- Consumer Protection Act 1987
- Consumer Credit Act 1976
- Control of Misleading Advertisement Regulations 1988
- Copyright, Designs and Patents Act 1988
- European Communities Act 1972
- Food Act 1984
- Trade Descriptions Act 1968
- Supply of Goods (Implied Terms) Act 1973
- Restrictive Trade Practices Act 1976
- Fair Trading Act 1973
- Trade Marks Act 1994
- Unfair Contract Terms Act 1977
- Unsolicited Goods and Services Act 1971 and 1975

STUDENT ACTIVITY

TRADE MARKS ACT 1994

This Act allows the trade mark belonging to a third party to be used in advertisements to identify a proprietor's goods/services providing that:

1 the use does not take unfair advantage of the trade mark
2 the use is not detrimental to the trade mark or its reputation
3 it is used 'in accordance with honest practices in industrial or commercial matters'.

It is therefore permitted that a company's registered trade mark can be used in some cases of comparative advertising.

Carry out a search of a periodical of your choice. Are there any advertisements which are using another company's trade mark to promote their own? Extract the details and share these with the rest of your group.

STUDENT ACTIVITY

COMPARATIVE ADVERTISING

Read *the following extracts from an article which appeared in* Admap *magazine in March 1995 entitled 'How does your advertising compare?', written by David Rickard who is a Trade Mark Attorney with Boult Wade Tennant.*

The paper discusses the 1994 Trade Marks Act and its implications for comparative advertising. The new Act allows trade marks belonging to a third party to be used to identify goods and services. Comparative advertising using another person's registered trade mark is, therefore, now permitted ... In the United States, most comparative advertising has concentrated on making a direct comparison of competing products, and advertisements have tended to be far more aggressive than similar advertisements in Europe. Comparative advertising is considered a valuable tool in the United States and is said to stimulate competition...

Historically, comparative advertising has been a dangerous game to play in Europe ... With the recent changes in law in the UK and possibly elsewhere in Europe, many advertisers are likely to be tempted to engage in this form of advertising by the desire for increased sales...

Advertisements which compare one product with the product of a competitor can take

139

a number of forms. The most basic form is the so-called 'knocking copy'. This form is rare, but still exists. Typically, the comparison will be made with the brand leader and will include a statement such as 'our product is as good as/better than/cheaper than X's.'

Alternatively, an advertisement may imply that a product is better than that of a competitor, but may leave it to the public to make the direct comparison and to reach a conclusion of superiority.

In other cases, advertisements compare specifications such as size, weight or facilities.

Some well-known illustrations of comparative advertising include:

- a British Knights' advertisement of its own trainers with the caption 'your mother wears Nike'.
- Ever Ready's use of a black and white picture of Duracell's battery with the caption 'in tests ... the gold seal LR20 battery outlasted the equivalent sold by Duracell Batteries Ltd in every single appliance'.

TRADE MARKS ACT 1994

The new UK Trade Marks Act allows trade marks belonging to a third party to be used in advertisements to identify goods and services.

It provides that a trade mark may be used by any person to identify a proprietor's goods provided:

- the use is 'in accordance with honest practices in industrial or commercial matters'
- it does not take unfair advantage of the trade mark
- it is not detrimental to the distinctive character of the trade mark
- it is not detrimental to the repute of the mark.

TAKING UNFAIR ADVANTAGE

Whether or not unfair advantage is seen to have been taken will again depend on particular facts. Clearly, advertising a cola flavoured soft drink using the distinctive Coke can and style alongside a similarly coloured product would be taking unfair advantage. However, simply showing two cans of cola soft drink side by side with the different prices underneath would not generally be so.

DETRIMENTAL TO REPUTATION OR REPUTE

... each case will be decided on the specific facts.

CHALLENGING USE

... it is likely that the courts will be called upon frequently, at least in the early days, to determine whether honest and fair comparisons have been made ...

OTHER CONCERNS

When engaging in comparative advertising, account must be taken not only of the Trade Marks Act 1994, but also of:

- copyright
- passing off
- trade libel or malicious falsehood
- Trade Descriptions Act
- Consumer Protection Act, and
- codes of advertising practice.

DRAFT EU DIRECTIVE

The other piece of legislation which may affect comparative advertising in the future is a Draft EU Directive on Comparative Advertising. However, the EU States remain unable to reach agreement and it is unlikely that the Directive will be implemented for some considerable time.

CONCLUSION

As comparative advertising becomes more prevalent, the amount of regulation relating to its various forms is likely to increase. For *the advertiser and the advertising agency the 1994 Trade Marks Act means that within certain limits, products and services can now be advertised with reference to the registered trade marks of a competitor. A new form of advertising is now available in the UK, but it should be noted that despite the new Statute, the use of comparisons is not totally without risk.*

DISCUSSION POINT

What are the major problems with comparative advertising, and what are the advantages to companies who use this method to communicate their advertising message?

CONTRACT LAW

The law of contract impacts on advertising in a variety of ways:

– when hiring exhibition space/outdoor advertising space/space in the press or on television or radio
– when engaging the services of professional consultants, i.e. advertising agencies, copywriters, photographers etc.

A contract is legally binding on both parties. Consumers may sue if claims made about a product prove to be false. In the famous case of *Cahill* v. *The Carbolic Smoke Ball Company*, Mrs Cahill sued when she was refused the reward of £100 offered in the advertisement if the product did not cure the flu. She won – which proved to be a legal breakthrough. A purchase has to be made for the law of contract to apply.

7.5 ETHICS

ETHICS AND SOCIETY

It is generally accepted that marketeers should act with honesty and social responsibility and should follow good practice. Ethics usually refers to a set of standards which are generally learned and connected to moral principles but which may be adjusted depending on circumstances.

Ethical issues which relate to advertising include:

– the argument about advertising tobacco and tobacco products
– misleading advertisements
– sexism in terms of expectations
– shock tactics or offensive advertisements.

THE COMMUNITY

Businesses are now expected to help to solve social problems, mainly by being seen to agree with policies in terms of discrimination but also by educating the population and providing leisure facilities and health care.

GREEN ISSUES/THE ENVIRONMENT

An increasing concern for the environment is being expressed by the public, i.e. about the greenhouse effect, acid rain and the depletion of the ozone layer. Because of consumer pressure to live in a healthy environment, businesses are being forced to conform to a variety of policies such as the banning of chlorofluorocarbons (CFCs), leaded petrol and excess packaging and the promotion of biodegradable products. These are all movements towards a reduction in pollution. Some organisations use the 'green' issue as a unique selling proposition.

SOCIETY

In *Marketing Management – Analysis, Planning, Implementation and Control*, Kotler put forward the idea that marketing should take into account the wider ethical and environmental issues which affect both society and business and that business should try to make amends for unethical practices. These proposals put a different type of pressure on companies in respect of forfeiting short-term gains to help long-term survival. This approach also expects businesses to educate the

141

target audience so that the two parties can work together for the 'greater good'.

THE ADVERTISERS

Advertisers wish to produce advertisements which make people want to buy their products/services – in other words, advertisers are trying to *sell* their products – and people in turn have needs which can only be met by buying certain goods/services. In order for people to be able to buy, they will initially seek information, and advertisers are one of those sources of information.

It may be argued that advertisers are seducers who *make* people buy items which they do not necessarily need and in some cases can ill afford. It may be further argued that some people will resort to crime to attain goods which they cannot afford to purchase. However, it is easy to lay the blame at the advertiser's door when perhaps the *user* is the one who is at fault.

Children are vulnerable, and the Code of Practice has a lengthy section which deals with advertising aimed at children. Children 'pester' parents to buy things – 'I want … etc.' – and advertisers use comic books and slots on TV which appear during children's programmes specifically to target this audience.

Some advertisers may set out intentionally to misuse advertising, hence the need for both the voluntary controls and the statutes covered earlier in this chapter.

STUDENT ACTIVITY

UNILEVER – SOCIAL RESPONSIBILITY

In meeting the needs of consumers across the world, Unilever takes care to respect the physical, economic and social environments of the communities in which it operates. It has a strong tradition of commitment to good citizenship, believing that the success of the company and the welfare of the community go hand in hand.

Minimising the use of raw materials and the production of waste in both products and packaging so as to reduce their impact on the environment is an important element in Unilever's business strategy. Recent product advances include the introduction of a fabric conditioner formulation based on a new active ingredient with an excellent environmental profile, being easily and completely biodegradable. Unilever has expressed its commitment to the goal of sustainable development by signing the International Chamber of Commerce Business Charter for Sustainable Development, and takes a leading role in efforts to promote responsible environmental initiatives, such as those on packaging and recycling.

Unilever is committed to maintaining the highest standards of fairness and integrity in all its dealings with consumers, customers, suppliers, employees and other stakeholders.

(Adapted from information, supplied by Unilever)

1 *What is Unilever doing to reduce waste?*
2 *What is Unilever doing to protect the environment?*
3 *What is Unilever's intention relative to its interactions with external groups, i.e. consumers, suppliers etc.?*

Discuss the issues raised by the extract with fellow students. What, if anything, could Unilever do to improve its performance in terms of social responsibility?

7.6 ENVIRONMENTAL ISSUES

Let us first of all consider a few facts which relate to the environment generally before we consider how these impact on advertising.

SOME KEY FACTS ABOUT THE ENVIRONMENT

1 In the Antarctic, a hole approximately 18 million square kilometres in size has appeared in the ozone layer. As the hole disappears, the density of ozone around the world reduces. Early in 1994 the ozone density above Europe was between 10 per cent and 20 per cent below the norm. Such a reduction in ozone will increase cases of skin cancer in humans.

2 Current levels of carbon dioxide and other 'greenhouse' gases in the atmosphere will increase global temperatures by between 1.5 and 4.5° C during the 21st century.

3 There are estimated to be approximately 30 million species inhabiting the world. The number of species lost per day is estimated to be between 10 and 100 plus, which can be paralleled to the conditions which led to the extinction of dinosaurs millions of years ago.

4 Seashores are polluted. Approximately 70 per cent of the world's population lives by the seashore, and it provides 50 per cent of the fish we eat. PCBs (polychlorinated biphenyl) have been blamed for the deaths of large numbers of dolphins in the Mediterranean in the three years between 1990 and 1993.

5 Soil erosion reduces land availability by between 6 and 7 million hectares each year (UN 1990), which limits the land available for cultivation.

6 Water is polluted in many areas, and unless there is an improvement in the quality of water supplies, this will impact on economic and population growth.

7 Rainforests have been depleted by more than 50 per cent, although they house half of the world's species and are necessary for maintaining the balance in the world's ecosystem.

8 Land is also becoming more polluted.

THE ENVIRONMENT AND MARKETING

1 *The 1960s/1970s.* The 'counterculture' which grew out of this era challenged the approach of the industrial world. Rivers were so badly polluted with toxins that it was possible to set them alight. It was suggested that the world could not continue to grow in terms of its population, and that economic growth too would exhaust the planet's natural resources.

2 *The 1980s.* Oil prices were rising. This slowed down economic growth and brought into stark reality the need to become more 'energy efficient', which in turn resulted in reduced pollution.

3 *The late 1980s.* Many analyses which related to the environment were published. The Organization for Economic Cooperation and Development's (OECD's) State of the Environment Report and the second report of the UN Environment Programme were just two which identified that the environment was being placed under increasing pressure.

The depletion of the ozone, the unstable climate which was linked to global warming and the rainforest reduction became the subject of media attention. Concern began to increase, and it was widely believed that environmental deterioration would result in poor public health.

Economic and technological development cannot be sustained at its current rate for ever. There are limited physical resources which can absorb only a limited amount of pollution, and thus there is a need to incorporate *physical* and *social* needs alongside the economic and technical aspects of business.

The 'STEP' approach to marketing attempts to present a more balanced business approach:

1 *Social* – concerned with consumer and social welfare; cultural values; standards of living; levels of population; employment and health.

2 *Technological* – concerned with the performance of products; production systems and quality standards; technology and technical progress.

3 *Economic* – concerned with meeting customer needs; generating profit; capital growth and investment.

4 *Physical* – concerned with resource consumption; waste and pollution; the protection of species and ecosystems; the quality of life.

'GREEN' ADVERTISING

The objectives of green advertising will most likely be to inform the target audience about the company's green products and to state both the advantages of the product and how these relate to the preservation of the environment. If an advertisement is to attract 'green' audiences, the company will need to profile the customer segment very specifically to achieve its aims. One difficulty which might be encountered could be that of a lack of awareness and understanding of environmental issues in the first place.

All advertising promotions use a theme, and green advertising is no exception, so the use of emotional, moral issues etc. will be explored.

The advertising message will need to include:

– product claims relative to green issues
– claims regarding technology, methods of production, process techniques and the disposal of waste
– the possibility of aligning the product with a 'green' cause
– claims based on facts which help to educate the consumer

As with all other types of advertising, the tone and style of the message is important, and issues relating to the use of different types of media are as described throughout this text.

POLLUTION OF ANOTHER KIND?

It is argued that there are many different forms of pollution, including those of aural and visual pollution. Because of the volume of advertisements which appear in all aspects of the media, it is proving difficult to invent new ideas which will grab the attention of the consumer. Increasingly, advertisements are becoming more risqué or noisy so that the audience sits up and takes notice. (It has also been argued that the television advertisements can sometimes, as a result, be more entertaining than the programmes themselves.)

In terms of written media, the revenue from advertisements is certainly a crucial aspect of economic survival.

The arguments are many and varied depending on your point of view. Who has the right to say that advertisements are good or evil?

7.7 CASE STUDY: ASDA AND THE ENVIRONMENT

Read the extract below.

ASDA IN THE ATMOSPHERE

Asda was the first food retailer to remove CFCs from all its own Brand aerosols by June 1988.

Asda heats the sales area of some of its stores with heat reclaimed from the refrigeration plant, thus reducing energy usage dramatically. Refrigeration systems at all new Asda stores are installed to utilise Government approved refrigerant gas. Systems at old stores are currently being replaced – the gases are removed safely by qualified engineers and returned to the manufacturers for safe disposal.

Asda does not allow the discharge of refrigerant gases into the atmosphere during the repair and maintenance of equipment.

Asda zinc chloride batteries are mercury free and have no added cadmium. The majority of Asda's company car fleet uses unleaded petrol.

Some Asda stores offer free bus services providing the area with a 'community friendly' form of transport – shoppers are transported to and from stores on set routes thus reducing the need for cars.

ASDA IN THE COMMUNITY

Asda stores are located, designed and built in sympathy with the very best in local architecture.

Asda develops its stores almost exclusively in adopted urban areas and does not pursue proposals in green belt land.

Asda stores are built using products conforming to Friends of the Earth recommendations to contain minimum CFC gas and be of a renewable resource, i.e. tropical forest hardwood products are not permitted.

RECYCLING AT ASDA

Asda has appointed SWAP Recycling – Save Waste and Prosper Ltd, Leeds, to manage its recycling facilities nationwide. They are required to ensure the maximum facilities at as many stores as is possible. In less than two years they have provided 83 per cent of Asda stores with facilities.

Asda leads the way in glass, paper and can recycling.

- *7 Asda stores have Aluminium Foil banks*
- *168 stores now have bottle banks*
- *108 stores have paper banks*
- *222 have can banks:*
  - *96 Aluminium*
  - *80 Sava Can*
  - *46 Aluminium Cash Back*
- *27 stores currently have plastic bottle banks*
- *69 have Textile banks*
  - *2 Used Engine Oil banks*

These are constantly being added to with the opening of new stores and additions to those which currently have no facilities.

At Asda House, the Company's Head Office, glass and plastic bottle banks, paper banks and can banks are located to encourage colleagues to play a personal part in this important issue.

Waste card and plastic in store is compacted for collection and re-use. Asda stocks a range of household products made from recycled paper. Asda stocks a range of recycled stationery, together with recycled paper products for children's use, i.e. scrapbooks, writing pads and notebooks, in selected stores.

FOOD AND WINE AT ASDA

Asda sells its own brand barn eggs and free range eggs in all stores along with a range of branded battery eggs.

Asda offers free range eggs packed in pulp-fibre board cartons at all stores. Asda was the first retailer to sell organic milk in all its stores under the exclusive Green Pastures pack.

Freshly baked in-store organic flour bread, baps and rolls are now available in 34 stores.

Asda has a range of organic wines which are available exclusively at licensed Asda stores.

ENVIRONMENTALLY RESPONSIBLE PRODUCTS AT ASDA

These products can be easily identified by Asda's environmentally responsible logo.

Asda does not undertake animal testing on any Asda Brand product. All detergents used in Asda Brand products are biodegradable, these include:

- *foam baths*
- *shampoos*
- *conditioners*
- *liquid soaps.*

Plus a full range of household cleaners from Ecover.

(Adapted from information supplied by Asda)

What steps is Asda taking regarding the following:

1 the atmosphere
2 the community
3 recycling
4 food and wine
5 products?

REVIEW YOUR PROGRESS

1 What is the role of the BCAP?

2 What is the role of the ASA?

3 Which body controls the content of advertisements which appear on our television screens?

4 Which bodies control the press, and what is their role?

5 List six of the main statutes which impact on advertising.

6 What are the main concerns in terms of ethics?

7 What are the main issues in terms of the environment?

8

Creating the message

AIMS

- to identify, evaluate and assess the impact of different types of appeals including strategies
- to explore different types of creative strategy and attempt to put some of these into practice
- to observe some rules for producing advertisements for the press

UNIT 20 ADVERTISING

- Element 20.3

  - Performance Criteria:
    1 Identify, from an advertising brief, product features and benefits to be communicated

8.1 THE CONTENT OF THE ADVERTISEMENT

What should appear in the advertisement? How should the company create a message?

TYPES OF APPEAL

Advertising is about trying to persuade people that there is something special about a company's goods/services. It is an attempt to persuade the consumer that the product/service which is being offered has features which cannot be enjoyed by purchasing an alternative product/service, i.e. that is unique.

STRATEGIES

Companies develop strategies to assist them in meeting their objectives. The types of strategy which might be identified in terms of advertising could include:

- identifying the *benefit* being offered to the consumer by the organisation or its products/services
- putting forward an *argument* to help to sell the product
- identifying *to whom* the argument is being aimed
- being able to convince the target 'audience' to *believe* the message

PRODUCT-ORIENTED STRATEGIES

These strategies relate specifically to the product itself, i.e.:

1 **Generic strategies** sell the *category* of product, e.g. baked beans, slimming biscuit, 'trainers'. They do not sell the actual brand, e.g. Heinz Baked Beans. Generic claims relate to the highlighting of a particular benefit of a product, i.e. quick effective relief from indigestion, clean clothes etc. Some advertisers highlight this kind of generic claim and then relate their particular brand to that claim to gain a cumulative benefit.

2 **Features of the product** are highlighted in an attempt to appeal to the individual's reason. The advertiser attempts to suggest that the logical choice would be their particular brand in preference to others. This is an effective approach if the advertiser is attempting to gain distinction for his or her brand.

3 **Positioning strategies** attempt to carve out a desired and very distinct market niche. The idea of 'positioning' was developed in 1972 by Trout & Ries. Consumers tend to place products into a hierarchy, and positioning is about where in that hierarchy the advertiser's brand appears. Coca Cola's campaigns 'Coke is it' and 'The real thing' were an attempt to position *the* product as the authentic cola drink. Pepsi on the other hand attempted to reposition Coca Cola by suggesting that it was a drink for older people, with the campaign 'The choice of a new generation'. This type of strategy works well for new products.

Questions which need to be addressed in terms of positioning are:

- What is the brand's present position in the market?
- Where are your competitors placed in the market?
- Does the company wish to reposition its brand or adjust its present position in some way?
- What type of advertising approach could we use?

4 The **unique selling proposition** will depend upon the culture of the company and its approach to advertising. Every company's ultimate aim is to create an idea which will result in the sale of the company's products/service, and every advertisement should incorporate one reason why the customer should buy a particular product/service.

The unique selling proposition was a philosophy developed by Rosser Reeves in the USA. It suggests that every product/ service has characteristics which make it *unique at its level*. Preferably, these characteristics should be a major feature of the product, thereby making the brand superior to others. A slogan like 'Guinness is good for you' is a unique-selling-proposition statement.

A unique selling proposition based on a *physical* characteristic limits potential, however, and could run into difficulty with the strict advertising codes which now exist. The claim by Persil that it 'washes whiter' is an example of just such a proposition.

All advertisements should, nevertheless, promote one specific benefit to the consumer (see Figures 8.1–4).

In fact, anything the Rowenta Revo' picks up it does with all the power of a full size cleaner.

Yet it's only half the size and less than half the weight.

The new Rowenta Revo's exceptional power will pick up this cotton just as easily.

Although being small and light enough to pick up with a length of household cotton, it'll handle the toughest cleaning jobs.

The dusting brush and crevice tool are integrated into the handle, so you won't find yourself searching for lost tools.

Rowenta

And by turning the power control to 'Eco', it'll handle the most delicate cleaning tasks.

There's even a shoulder strap to make lighter work of stairs.

So, pick up dust with more ease. Pick up the Rowenta Revo'.

STOCKISTS: ALLDERS, HARRODS, HOMEPOWER, HOMEWORLD, JOHN LEWIS, LIVING, MILLER BROS, POWERSTORES LTD, SAVACENTRE, TEMPO, SELECTED CO-OP, COMET, FENWICK AND POWERHOUSE STORES, EMPIRE, FREEMANS AND GRATTANS CATALOGUES, ALL GOOD ELECTRICAL RETAILERS AND IN IRELAND FROM POWERCITY.
FOR FURTHER INFORMATION CONTACT ROWENTA (UK) LTD. ON 01372 277511.

Fig 8.1 This advertisement for the Rowenta Revo promotes the **power** *of the machine.*

Fig 8.2 This advertisement for Safeway promotes value for money.

BUY ONE PAIR OF SPECTACLES

GET ANOTHER PAIR FREE

Right now at Dollond & Aitchison when you buy a pair of spectacles from the wide range of styles on display, you can get a second pair worth up to £69.99 absolutely free. All we ask is that you pay at least £69.99 for the first pair*.

Then simply choose your free spectacles fitted with standard reading or distance lenses from a special selection within our unique Nice 'n' Easy complete price range.

But hurry, this offer is available for a limited period only. So to get your free pair of spectacles call into your local branch of Dollond & Aitchison right now.

DOLLOND & AITCHISON

THE OPTICIANS

See Yellow Pages for details of your nearest branch.

*Both pairs of spectacles must be for the same person to the same prescription and purchased at the same time. Offer available in selected branches whilst stocks last. This offer cannot be used in conjunction with any other offer. Bifocals and varifocals available at a small extra charge.

Fig 8.3 This advertisement for Dollond & Aitchison promotes an extra, free pair of specs.

Fig 8.4 This advertisement for the Loyd Grossman sauces promotes speed of preparation.

CONSUMER-ORIENTED STRATEGIES

These strategies are specifically aimed at the consumer, i.e.:

1 **Brand image strategies** attempt to give the brand a personality, and that personality – instead of any 'built-in' or intrinsic features of the product – is what is being sold. David Ogilvy is credited with developing the idea of a brand image in the 1950s for products like Schweppes.

With Coca Cola and Pepsi we have two similar products which are differentiated by the way each brand is portrayed and communicated through advertising. This approach works well in a competitive market environment or where the product might be classed as a commodity, i.e. soap, beer etc.

This type of advertising also works well for products which have obvious social identities, i.e. cars. Products which are invisible, i.e. cleaning products or food products stored in cupboards, are also sold by using the brand image approach.

Finally, this approach works well for personal-hygiene type products which relate to an individual's esteem in a social sense.

2 **Lifestyle strategies** draw parallels between the product and a particular way of life. Fuller information regarding lifestyle and its impact on advertising appears in Chapter 2.

3 **Attitude strategies** try to relate the product to a particular state of mind. This approach attempts to sell the idea of what it would be like to own a particular product rather than the actual brand. It is an attempt by the purchaser to buy a particular 'feeling'. Attitude strategies offer a *mood* or *emotion*, for instance (see Figure 8.5 below and on pages 154–5).

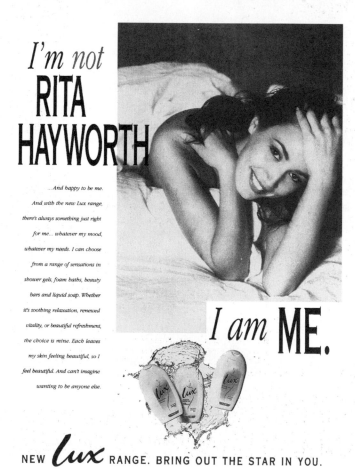

I'm not **RITA HAYWORTH**

...And happy to be me. And with the new Lux range, there's always something just right for me... whatever my mood, whatever my needs. I can choose from a range of sensations in shower gels, foam baths, beauty bars and liquid soap. Whether it's soothing relaxation, renewed vitality, or beautiful refreshment, the choice is mine. Each leaves my skin feeling beautiful, so I feel beautiful. And can't imagine wanting to be anyone else.

I am **ME.**

NEW *lux* RANGE. BRING OUT THE STAR IN YOU.

Late night *smoothie*

(AND JOOLS HOLLAND)

JAMESON

Triple distilled for exceptional smoothness.

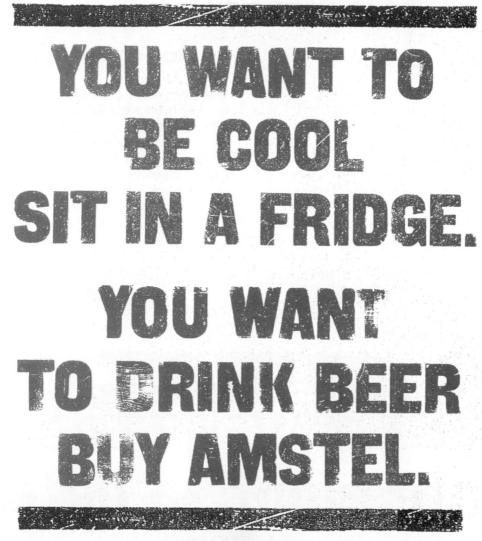

Fig 8.5 Examples of advertisements for the Lux range, Jameson and Amstel which suggest mood, attitude and emotion.

STUDENT ACTIVITY

8.2 THE MESSAGE

Answer the following questions:

1 What is a Volvo?
2 What is a Nike?
3 What is a Ryvita?
4 What is a Mars?

Work in pairs and try to produce a list of questions similar to those above, using brand names for products which you feel will be instantly recognisable. Test these out on your friends or other students. What makes these brands so memorable?

Discuss the issues with your group.

KEEP THE MESSAGE BRIEF

This rule generally applies to press advertising but also works exceedingly well with posters. Advertisers such as David Ogilvy (Ogilvy and Mather) argued that as much detail as possible should be included which offers as much information as possible about the product. This latter approach is more appropriately used, however, in direct response and direct mail advertising, though it does work well when selling cars.

Fig 8.6 An example of a car advertisement, for the Citroën Xantia, which gives a good deal of information.

Ultimately, the following aspects of an advertisement will have an impact on how many words are used:

1 its size

2 the time available

3 the type of message to be conveyed.

HUMOUR

Humour has been used with success in advertising, as in the Cadbury's Cream Egg advertisement showing how the different characters of people born under different Zodiac signs might eat the product. Weetabix recently decided to change its advertising approach and used cartoon visuals and humour in its 'Pirate' advertisement.

STUDENT ACTIVITY

Read the article on page 158 by Grainne Bell, which appeared in the Today newspaper dated Saturday, 4 February 1995:

1 What are the main features of the advertisement?

2 What type of approach is being used by Weetabix?

3 The advertisement appeared on Saturday evenings in January 1995. Who is the advertisement aimed at?

Critically analyse the various components of the advertisement, i.e. visuals, storyline, type of appeal, etc. Discuss your ideas with your fellow students.

Whether to include humour is a difficult decision, as humour simply either works or doesn't!

YOUR AUDIENCE ARE NOT 'IDIOTS'

Credit your audience with some intelligence. People realise when they are being 'spoken down to' and tend to resent the implication. It is unlikely that the consumer will buy the product/service being advertised if this proves to be the case.

In addition, insulting your audience is another 'tabu'. The implication that people do not know how to handle their money or run their home properly will result in their rejection of a product/service.

STEREOTYPING

Stereotyping females as the 'little woman who belongs at home in the kitchen looking after husband and family' will be resented, particularly in the current economic climate where such women are also often tackling part-time work in order to keep the 'wolf from the door'.

MAKE IT ORIGINAL

Advertisements must be *original* and unique and must grab attention. Devices which have been used successfully are:

– drum rolls
– large headlines
– unusual sounds etc.

The style of the advertisement should fit with the brand. The attention-grabbing trick could be done with visuals or music or a mixture of both, depending on the media being used.

8.3 CREATIVE STRATEGIES

How can you be creative?

USE BASIC THINKING TECHNIQUES

When trying to create the content, it is useful to use one or more of the following approaches:

1 **Brainstorm** ideas, particularly if you are working in a team. Write down any ideas which come to mind. It doesn't matter if they seem

AD OF THE WEEK / TODAY

Thirty different model heads were needed to shoot just one scene of the sailors eating their favourite breakfast. Filming took a team of 20 more than five painstaking weeks

Ahoy me hearty breakfast

GRAINNE BELL of advertising agency GBH gives you the inside track on the ads you see on TV

WHAT IT'S SELLING

WEETABIX, the breakfast cereal sought by pirates and children alike.

WHAT IT COST

AROUND £250,000.

HOW IT WORKS

THE latest ad for Weetabix bears more than a passing resemblance to Captain Pugwash, the kiddies' cartoon favourite from the seventies.

This, insist the creators of the ad, is purely coincidental.

For it was designed by Rachel Moore, a 21-year-old student from Bristol University – and she is too young to remember the teatime series.

The ad features the famous Marie Celeste which is manned by the meanest, cruellest pirates in the world. They are so mean that they never ever write to their poor mum.

However, when they encounter the good ship Weetabix, they abandon ship rather than go into battle with them.

Oscar

To make the ad, creative team Neil Sullivan and Gordon Graham hired Aardman Animation, the company behind classics such as Creature Comforts and the Oscar-winning The Wrong Trousers.

A model of the captain was made first using latex and wire and the production

team experimented with paint effects to decide the final overall look and feel.

The final 3-D model of the captain determined the style for all the other characters and the ship.

To decide on the facial expressions a 2-D animator filmed the movements and reactions needed for each character before the final models were made.

This was a lengthy process but it meant they could closely control the expressions on each of the characters' faces. The captain had

Director Richard and assistant Chris Sadler create the pirate set

seven heads just to say "Abandon Ship!". In total 70 heads were sculpted for the 6ft high main pirate characters. Thirty heads were used for just one scene of the sailors eating their Weetabix.

Moved

The commercial was filmed using stop-frame animation, a painstaking technique in which the models are moved bit by bit and filmed frame by frame.

The shoot, which lasted five weeks, involved a ded-

icated crew of 20 people. Director Richard Goleszowski loved adding little props and background information that are not immediately obvious. Top marks to anyone who can spot the cow, a pair of Y-fronts and the rubber duck around the waist of the pirate captain.

The music track is a real hoot. The swash-buckling song was based on My Brudder Sylveste, a German wartime propaganda song.

Judging by the feedback

The pirates approach

to the client and the agency, the ad has gone down equally well with kids and adults.

In my opinion this ad is a classic. It is hard to fault it as it is funny, cute and interesting. Along with the Umbro ad featured here a few weeks ago, this is the best ad I have seen in the last six months.

● *Agency: Lowe Howard Spink, creative team: Neil Sullivan/Grambh Gordon. Production: Aardman Animation, director: Richard Goleszowski.*

The Marie Celeste pirates are looking for trouble

RATINGS: Creativity ✪✪✪✪ Sellability ✪✪✪ Value for money ✪✪✪✪

silly or irrelevant – get them down on paper. It is easy to eliminate those which prove useless later.

2 By using **free association** it is possible that one idea will suggest another or that one work or image will develop into others.

3 **Make lists.** Different types of list will help to produce some ideas for content to be included in the advertisement. See below.

RESAYINGS

Having identified your strategy, make a list of different ways of saying the same thing.

STUDENT ACTIVITY

BEING CREATIVE: 1

Work in small teams. Take the example: 'Butter is healthier for you than margarine.' Make a list of as many different ways of making this statement as you can think of. Lists might be produced by thinking in terms of the following for example:

- *what might be the health benefits of eating butter*
- *reasons why butter is felt to be unhealthy*
- *how many different uses there are for butter*

DATA

Use data which has been collected in market research and split this down into key lists.

STUDENT ACTIVITY

BEING CREATIVE: 2

Using the various statements that you produced in 'Being creative – student activity 1', develop a sublist for each of the statements.

LISTS WHICH REFLECT A VARIETY OF APPROACHES

Lists can be compiled on, for example:

- health issues
- saturated fats *vs* polyunsaturated fats
- associated products
- kitchen utensils
- emotions.

One of the lists produced should identify different types of strategy.

STUDENT ACTIVITY

BEING CREATIVE: 3

Produce a variety of lists using the information identified above.

STUDENT ACTIVITY

BEING CREATIVE: 4

Produce an advertisement for butter based on the lists you have produced in Activities 1 to 3 above. Draw the visuals and produce the content. Present this information in an oral presentation and explain your strategy.

8.4 RULES FOR PRINTED ADVERTISEMENTS

1 *Use appropriate words in the headline.* Certain words are used more often than others in headlines, e.g. 'new', 'win', 'best', 'save'. However, a headline should be produced which is appropriate to the product/service, not one produced deliberately in order to include words such as these.

2 *Include a promise in the headline.* If a promise or proposition is included in the headline, it invites the reader to read all of the advertisement to find out more.

3 *Headlines should be short.* The headline should attract the reader and put the message across quickly.

4 *The advertisement layout should be logical.* The advertisement should run down from the headline to the bottom right of the advertisement. We tend to read from top to bottom and left to right, so to get too creative with the layout can confuse the message and make the advertisement difficult to read.

5 *The size of the advertisement.* Difficulties can be encountered with double-page advertisements in losing parts of the headline in the fall between the two pages. Dividing the advertisement between two pages is difficult. Usually, a one-page advertisement will do the job better.

  Small spaces can work well providing that the space is used to the full.

6 *Photographs/pictures/illustrations.* Photographs are more believable, whereas illustrations are more flexible and images can be manoeuvred to produce the effect required. Photographs work better for most products because the product is then seen as it is.

7 *The brand name.* It is a generally accepted rule that the brand name should appear in the advertisement as early as possible and be repeated several times during the run of the advertisements.

  There is a trend currently to run a series of advertisements to build up suspense about a product or service before the company is identified. This approach was used in a campaign to launch the brand name of Orange, a telecommunications company, in Britain. A danger here, however, is that the consumer may lose interest before the brand is identified, and that the advertising spend will thus have been wasted.

8 *Consumers identify with the advertise-ment.* Consumers like to be able to draw parallels between their own lifestyle and the lifestyle featured in a particular advertisement. The idea is to make the advertisement credible.

8.5 CASE STUDY: THE ANDREX PUPPY

THE PUPPY

The advertising of Andrex scores highly in recall studies, even though the company's advertising spend is less than that of the other top ten toilet-roll advertisers. The puppy has been an integral part of the television advertising of Andrex since 1972. The advertisements are well liked and are effective in raising awareness of the brand. The puppy, in addition to its role as a metaphor and demonstrator of the product's quality, has served as a 'guard dog' for the brand.

HOW DOES THE ADVERTISING WORK?

One in three purchasers of toilet paper buy Andrex, and more and more cosumers are attracted to the brand. In addition, 57 per cent of those people who buy an alternative brand recognise that Andrex is the best-quality toilet paper.

WHO IS THE MAIN COMPETITOR?

Kleenex Velvet is a high-quality product which, at its launch, was identified as the preferred brand in a blind test. Andrex has, however, kept the challenge at bay, and its market share has barely been affected.

THE NEW CHALLENGE

In the late 1980s 'green' products were introduced which were made from recycled paper. These toilet papers captured 5 per cent of the total market within a two-year period. Andrex suffered initial losses but is now retaking market share from the recycled-toilet-tissue sector of the market.

SOME INTERESTING FACTS ABOUT ANDREX

1 It is the UK's second brand leader currently.
2 Half a million rolls are sold every single day!
3 A case sales growth of 900 per cent has been

achieved since the puppy adverts first appeared in 1972.

4 It is the most expensive brand in its market, and manages to maintain a price premium of approximately 30 per cent above the market average.

5 It is the fastest selling brand in its market.

6 Consumers prefer Andrex.

And now a quote from Paul Duncanson, Marketing Manager at Scott Limited, the producers of Andrex:

Winning the Charles Channon Award for Longer and Broader Effects was effectively a vindication of something we at Scott already know and hold dear – that advertising has made, and continues to make, a huge and valued contribution to Andrex's success. The confidence we have always had in the sales effectiveness of our advertising has now received important recognition. Our consistent commitment to advertising is undiminished. Only brands supported in this way build the kind of enduring consumer franchise that has been so critical to Andrex's long-term success.

(Adapted from information supplied by Scott Limited)

DISCUSSION POINT

What is the type of appeal which the puppy advertisements engender? Speculate on the outcome if the puppy were to be dropped from the Andrex advertisements in the future. Could anything else replace the puppy image for this product?

REVIEW YOUR PROGRESS

1 Identify and briefly explain each of the product-oriented strategies.

2 Identify and briefly explain each of the consumer-oriented strategies.

3 Explain the various creative strategies identified in this chapter.

4 Identify and explain as many of the rules for printed advertisements as you can.

9

Deciding the visual/script/layout

AIMS

- to put into practice the use of types of appeal, i.e. a unique selling proposition, emotional appeals etc.
- to look at ways of creating awareness
- to analyse the content of advertisements, including: 'straplines', the tone and style of the message and the impact of words and music
- to observe some rules for producing advertisements for three media types, i.e. cinema, television and radio
- to create advertisements using a variety of approaches

UNIT 20 ADVERTISING

- Element 20.1

  - Performance Criteria:
    1 Identify objectives from a given brief for a target audience
    2 Recommend focus of appeal to be used for target audience
    3 Select appropriate media for reaching target audience

- Element 20.3

  - Performance Criteria:
    1 Identify, from an advertising brief, product features and benefits to be communicated
    2 Prepare a suitable style of advertisment for a chosen media
    3 Conform with legal and voluntary advertising constraints

9.1 HEADLINES AND VISUALS

HEADLINES

Headlines should always be unique and use 'typescript' only – no visuals.

Headlines should be specific and eye-catching, and could include:

- information about the target audience – e.g. 'interested in fishing?'
- information about prices or special offers
- the offer of more than one benefit
- simple wording

However, headlines should not include puns or drawings which might insult or embarrass the intended audience.

Headlines may take a variety of forms:

1 *Offer invitations.* For example:

'Come and stay with us at our country house hotel – log fires, good food and all the comforts of home.'

2 *Make comparisons.* For example:

'We offer products you like at a cheaper price than...'

3 *Make a statement.* For example:

'Buy two and get a third one free.'
'Two for the price of one.'

When NatWest fixes a mortgage, it stays fixed.

There's nothing like a bit of security with your mortgage. And there's nothing like NatWest's range of fixed rates – simply the widest and most competitive selection we've ever offered.

You can choose to nail down your interest rate for just a couple of years, or well into the next century.

Consider our 5 year figure, for example 7.99% **8.3% APR**. Like many others, it's rather good value, and compares well with an average variable rate of 10.1%* over the last 5 years.

Needless to say, you can still move home as often as you like'. Fixing your mortgage won't mean getting stuck with the same property.

However, please remember that this is a limited special offer. So we strongly recommend you hammer out a deal as quickly as possible, particularly as you also get a £400 Cashback".

Just fill in the coupon, or call us on 0800 400 999. Our lines are open Monday to Friday 8am to 8pm and weekends 9am to 4pm.

BEST Overall Lender

NatWest

Call 0800 400 999

Please complete and return to: The Manager, National Westminster Home Loans Limited, FREEPOST, Hounslow, Middlesex TW4 5BR.

Title: Mr/Mrs/Miss/Ms_____ Initial(s)_____ Surname_____ Address_____

_____ Postcode |__|__|__| |__|__|__| Telephone: (including STD code)_____ Please tick where appropriate

and we will send you the correct details. I am a first time buyer ☐ I am moving home ☐ I am looking to transfer my existing mortgage ☐ Most convenient branch_____

For NatWest account holders only) Account Number: |__|__|__|__|__|__|__|__| Sort Code: |__|__| - |__|__| - |__|__| Ref No. **8817**

Customer Information Programme. NatWest supplies customers with a wide range of services. From time to time, we may use any of your personal details to decide whether to tell you about them. If you do not wish to receive this information, please tick this box. ☐

YOUR HOME IS AT RISK IF YOU DO NOT KEEP UP REPAYMENTS ON A MORTGAGE OR OTHER LOAN SECURED ON IT.

Fig 9.1 Examples of advertisements – for Safeway, NatWest, the RAC and Mr Lucky Bags – which make a statement.

RAC

IT SAYS WE'LL CHECK YOUR CAR OUT BEFORE YOU BUY IT

It goes without saying that the RAC will come to your assistance promptly at the roadside. But to make sure that you don't get in to that position in the first place we also offer the RAC Vehicle Examination Service. A service that examines more used cars than any other motoring organisation, and can be used by absolutely anyone (member or not) who wants to buy a used car but doesn't want to buy a lemon. The examination is carried out by an RAC Examining Engineer who knows all the dodges and how to spot them. Firstly, he'll carry out 166 visual checks, then he'll take it for a road test. You'll receive a detailed written report which highlights problems you might otherwise only discover as you drive away with your 'bargain'.

IT SAYS YOU'VE ARRIVED

For more information on this and other RAC Services, or if you'd like to become a member, call 0800 550 550.

4 *Ask questions.* Headlines which ask questions are inviting people to take part:

'Need to get away?'
'Want to pay less?'
'Where do you want to be in five years' time?'

5 *Issue a command.* For example:

'Visit our showroom tomorrow.'
'Join the Army today.'
'Try it now.'

This type of headline provokes a response from the audience. It encourages them to take action immediately.

6 *Aim at specific readers.* If the advertisement is to be aimed at a specific target audience, say golfers, then include the word 'golfers' in the headline. David Ogilvy first put forward this idea back in the 1960s.

7 *Include the brand name.*

McVITIE'S PUTS MILLIONS BEHIND BARS

Following hot on the heels of the Penguin relaunch, McVitie's is now supporting two more delicious chocolate biscuit bars with a multi-million pound investment.

Not one, not two but three syrups make the caramel in new Taxi the smoothest ever. And 10 million homes will get the opportunity to sample just how good it is.

While a more chocolatey chocolate, packed with moist currants and roasted hazelnuts, makes new Fruit and Nut United a chunky chocolate biscuit bar that's too tempting to resist.

Both brands will receive significant TV support breaking in May.

You have to go a long long way to find a better biscuit

Fig 9.2 Two examples of advertisements – for Green Giant and McVitie's Taxi and United – which include the brand name.

8 *Use the words 'How' and 'Why'.* For example:

'Why get an education?'
'How to protect your house against burglars.'

Companies have evolved which offer specialist services to advertisers to ensure that the headline produced for a specific advertising communication is the 'world's best'.

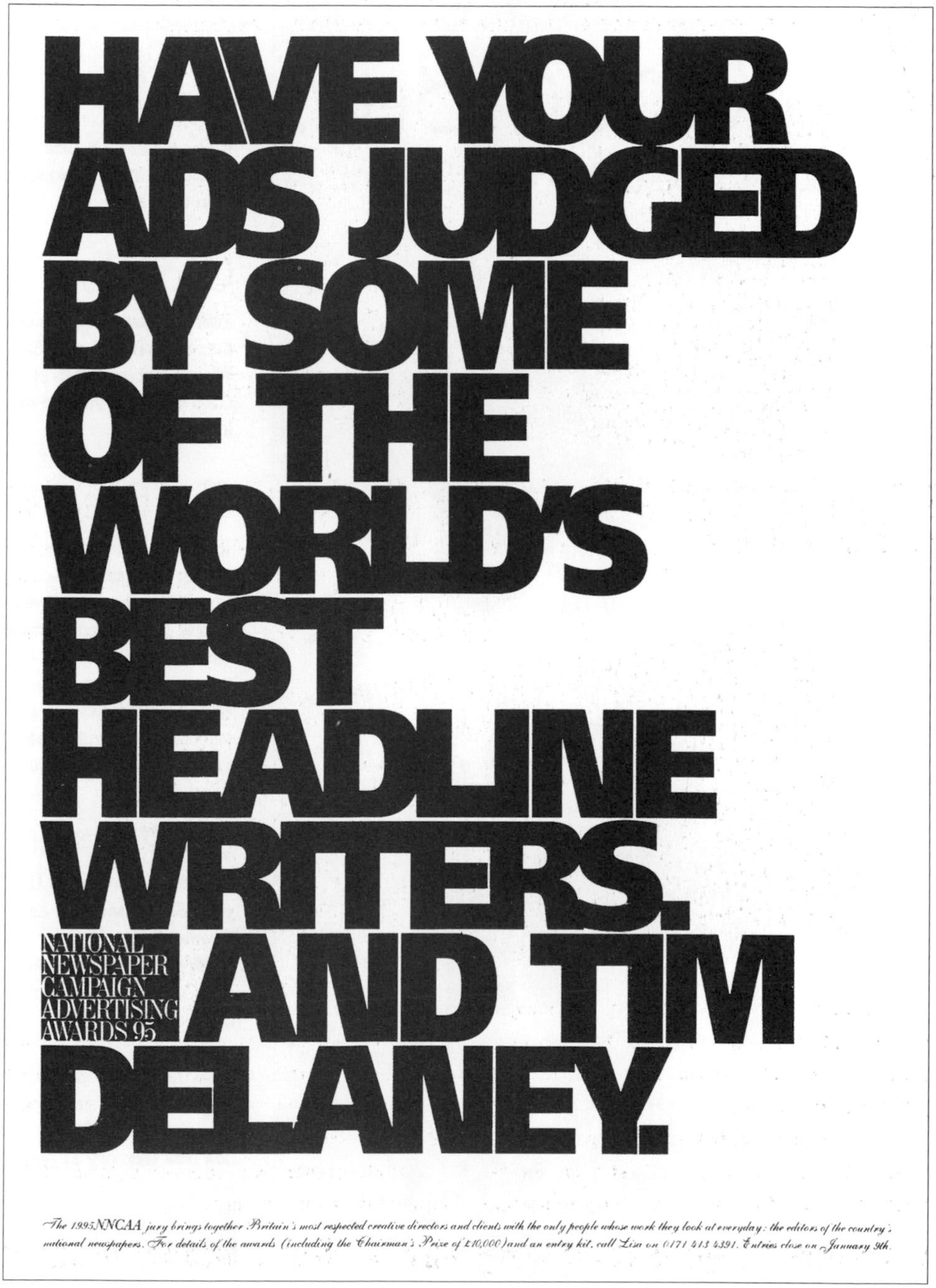

HAVE YOUR ADS JUDGED BY SOME OF THE WORLD'S BEST HEADLINE WRITERS. AND TIM DELANEY.

NATIONAL NEWSPAPER CAMPAIGN ADVERTISING AWARDS 95

The 1995 NNCAA jury brings together Britain's most respected creative directors and clients with the only people whose work they look at everyday: the editors of the country's national newspapers. For details of the awards (including the Chairman's Prize of £10,000) and an entry kit, call Lisa on 0171 413 4391. Entries close on January 9th.

Fig 9.3 An advertisement for the National Newspaper Campaign Advertising Awards drawing attention to the competition for the best headline writer for 1995.

How long should the headline be?

Headlines should say what you wish them to say, therefore, length is not always important.

Use standard punctuation in the headline just as you would in the rest of the text.

WITH THE VOLVO 440 YOU WON'T BURN UP ON RE-ENTRY.

This Volvo 440 has its very own heat shield. It's called air conditioning. Turn it on and in a matter of seconds your microwave on wheels becomes as cool as the proverbial cucumber. But now the burning question: how much? We'll replace the sunroof with alloy wheels and air conditioning for an extra £100. For more information call us on 0800 400 430. The Volvo 440Si, with alloy wheels and air conditioning for a cool £13,025. **THE VOLVO 440. A CAR YOU CAN BELIEVE IN.**

Fig 9.4 Two advertisements – for Clinique and the Volvo 440 – which use standard punctuation in the headline.

The tone of the headline

A balance should be struck between the written message and the visual which will illustrate the theme. If the visual is colourfully 'loud', the text should be calmer, and vice versa.

Some hints on headline development

1 First try writing down the 'benefit' you are selling.
2 What type of appeal have you decided upon?
3 What is the selling argument? Try writing this down in several ways.
4 Now produce a headline for the advertisement and make it as interesting as you can.
5 Keep changing the headline until it makes you stop and take notice.
6 Try thinking laterally.
7 Use word association.
8 Play with words until a strong, attention-grabbing headline is produced.

STUDENT ACTIVITY

Choose a product which has a lower profile than those of its major competitors in this market. When you have:

– researched the product
– researched the market
– decided on the selling strategy
– identified the advertising objective
– decided on the argument you will put forward, to whom and why
– examined the strategies available

you are to produce:

1 the headline for the advertisement which will appear in the press
2 a slogan

**WHEN YOUR CAR NEEDS A SERVICE,
WE GIVE YOU A NEW ONE.**

How would you like a courtesy car every time yours is in for a service? How would you like the option of having it delivered to your doorstep, (or wherever you want for that matter) and yours picked up at the same time? You wouldn't say no, would you? What about a phone call to tell you when your Daewoo is due for a service? Or a phone call from the mechanic before the service to make sure any minor details are not forgotten? And, after your car is brought back, another call to make sure everything's okay? Well you can. And this is the best bit. None of it will cost you a penny, you pay for the car and that's it. (Even that's not a lot. The prices start at £8,295 for the Nexia, to £12,195 for the top of the range Espero.) How come? Firstly, we sell direct through Daewoo Motor Shows, Car Centres and Support Centres, cutting out the middlemen. This means we don't use commissioned salesmen. It also means we can afford to give you more as standard. Just read the list.

DAEWOO

1). Free courtesy car.
2). Pick up and return of your car for service if needed.
3). Direct contact with the mechanic who services your car.
4). 3 year/60,000 mile free servicing including parts and labour.
5). 3 year/60,000 mile comprehensive warranty.
6). 3 year Daewoo Total AA Cover.

7). 6 year anti-corrosion warranty.
8). 30 day/1,000 mile money back or exchange guarantee.
9). Fixed purchase price with no hidden extras.
10). Delivery included.
11). Number plates included.
12). 12 months road tax included.
13). Full tank of fuel.
14). Metallic paint included.
15). Electronic ABS.
16). Driver's airbag.
17). Side impact protection.
18). Power steering.
19). Engine immobiliser.
20). Security glass etching.
21). Mobile phone.
22). Free customer helpline.
All in all, quite a number of reasons to choose Daewoo. For more information, call us free on 0800 666 222. A free courtesy car? That'll be the Daewoo.

Fig 9.5 A 1995 advertisement for Daewoo consisting mainly of text.

3 a campaign theme
4 a variety of selling phrases.

Present your ideas in an oral presentation to the rest of your group.
    Remember: advertisements need to be eye-catching *and have* impact. *The* words *need to be* linked to images.

VISUALS

Visuals can help to get the message across by creating atmosphere. Visuals also demonstrate the product and break up the text. Illustrations take many different forms but the most commonly used are drawings and photographs. It is possible to obtain illustrations from a picture library. If illustrations are to be used in advertisements, the following should be considered:

1 Would the visual create:

 – the right image
 – atmosphere?

2 And if so, should the organisation use a drawing or a photograph, or a mixture of both?

By using certain images and a variety of techniques, it is possible to influence an audience.

1 *Soft focus* photography creates an atmosphere of romance.
2 If words which are *suggestive* – e.g. 'wholesome' – are used, it is implied that the product is 'good for you'.
3 The way the advertisement is *laid out* – its use of white space to break up the information and highlight aspects of the advertisement – has an effect.
4 The use of *'flashes'* with money-off vouchers/offers attracts attention and makes a statement about the company, i.e. 'cheap and cheerful' perhaps.

Advertisements usually set out to convey a specific message about the product, i.e. what this product can do for you as a consumer – what are the *benefits*.

In the early part of the 20th century, the AIDA model was developed when the psychology of selling was being analysed. This identifies the stages a prospective customer goes through when considering the purchase of a product/service.

1 *Attention* – gets the attention of the audience.
2 *Interest* – develops interest in the product/service being offered.
3 *Desire* – arouses a desire for the product/service stronger than the desire for competitors' products/services.
4 *Action* – the customer buys the product.

STUDENT ACTIVITY

CREATING THE HEADLINES AND VISUALS

You are to work in teams of three or four. Choose a product, then choose one main idea for an advertisement which you are to produce for that product. Brainstorm and produce a list of potential:

1 headlines
2 selling phrases
3 slogans
4 campaign themes.

Think about the different ways your ideas can be expressed.
    Try to identify the visuals you will use – try producing rough sketches.

Visual ideas

The most popular and most often used visual ideas/strategies include the following:

1 Show the product being used. If the product is, for example, a butter substitute, such as in the campaign for St Ivel's 'Utterly butterly' product, it is sensible to show the product being spread onto bread, or in this case cream cracker biscuits – in other words, the product is to be *demonstrated*.

173

Another example would be the 'Slap it on your...' campaign by the manufacturers of Golden Syrup:

'Slap it on your fruit'
'Slap it on your bread'

The advertisement demonstrates the product by showing the syrup being trickled onto a variety of products – banana etc. – which would not necessarily be associated with Golden Syrup. The music and rhyming of the verses helps to push the message home in the case of the Golden Syrup advertisement.

2 Show the product wrapped or unwrapped. In this case it is useful to highlight the benefit and use a metaphor to associate the product with something else. These advertisements usually speak about the product in terms usually associated with other things.

If the product is to be presented unwrapped, the words used in the advertisement are extremely important.

Fig 9.6 An advertisement for Ryvita which shows the product unwrapped but with dressing!

3 Sometimes a 'close-up' of part of the product is shown which is useful to highlight a unique selling proposition. In a toothpaste advertisement this might be done to emphasise the 'stripes', for instance.

4 Use may be made of one specific aspect of the product's story, such as the place where the product is 'harvested' or how the product has developed over time. For example, see the advertising for Evian mineral water on this and the next page.

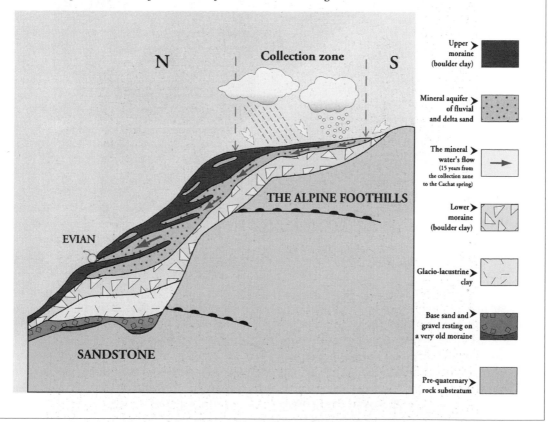

The flow of Evian water

Evian is a product of the French Alps. During the quaternary era, the Rhône glacier advanced and retreated on the northern side of the Alps leaving clay moraines between which glacial sands are found.

Evian's mineral aquifer is made up of a fluvio-lacustrine alluvium through which the water slowly

filters, protected on each side by a wide moraine of boulder clay several tens-of-metres thick.

Evian's spring is fed by rain water and melted snow which seep into the Vinzier plateau (Gavot region) at the foothills of the Chablais Alps (average altitude of 850m) far from any urban or industrial activity.

Evian water takes over 15 years to travel through this mineral filter, leading to an extremely stable composition and complete absence of chemical or microbiological contamination.

N   **Collection zone**   S

THE ALPINE FOOTHILLS

EVIAN

SANDSTONE

Upper moraine (boulder clay)

Mineral aquifer of fluvial and delta sand

The mineral water's flow (15 years from the collection zone to the Cachat spring)

Lower moraine (boulder clay)

Glacio-lacustrine clay

Base sand and gravel resting on a very old moraine

Pre-quaternary rock substratum

Fig 9.7 A leaflet produced by Evian which explains the origin of the water.

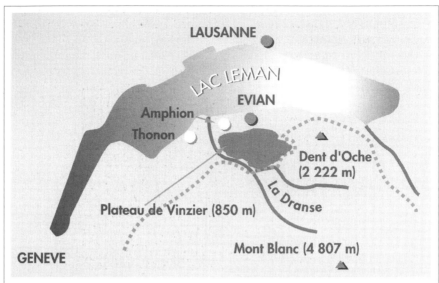

The speed that the water flows through the mineral aquifer has been calculated at about 300m per year, using hydrodynamic laws. Evian water takes more than 15 years to filter from the collection zone (feed basin) to Griffon (the spring rises at a constant temperature, 11.6°C -degree celsius- all year round).

Evian water is easily identifiable through its three unique characteristics:

• consistency of mineral content
• magnesium:calcium ratio
• content of dissolved silica

The Mg^{++} to Ca^{++} ratio of Evian water is 0.5 (calculated using milliequivalent concentrations). Evian water has a low mineral content (of bicarbonated, calcic and magnesian type). It is low in sodium, nitrates and sulphates, and has a neutral pH.

CHARACTERISTIC MINERAL CONTENT			
(milligrams per litre/*milliequivalents per litre*)			
Calcium	78 *3,9*	Bicarbonates	357 *5,83*
Magnesium	24 *2*	Sulphates	10 *0,21*
Potassium	1 *0,025*	Chlorides	4,5 *0,127*
Sodium	5 *0,217*	Nitrates (NO₃)*	3,8 *0,061*

Silica as SiO_2 = 13.5 mg/l,
dry residue at 180°C = 309 mg/l, pH=7.2

* Or Nitrates (as N):1.

5 Emphasis may be placed on the presentation, e.g. a celebrity may endorse the product or a famous figure from history may be used.

6 Emphasis may be placed on one aspect only of the product. In this case it is usual to highlight a special feature.

7 The advertiser may highlight what the benefit will be to the consumer if he or she used the product, e.g:

'You can lose 10lbs in a week by using this diet aid.'

8 By associating the product with an identified and specific lifestyle, the advertisement will show the attitude or state of mind which the product gives rise to.

9 A comparison can be made with a competitor's product by means of split-screen advertising. This technique is also used to project strong visual images on one half of the page and product information on the other half.

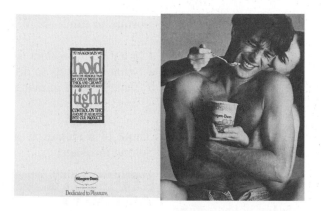

Fig 9.8 Illustrations of 'split' advertisements from Häagen-Dazs.

9.2 COPY AND COPYWRITING

The copy which is developed for a specific advertisement should communicate the advertiser's message effectively. The craft of copywriting is a skill which develops after much practice.

COPY

Good copy should include:

– facts about the product/service
– prices where relevant

but should not oversell the product or service by using superlatives. Just as when we tell a story, the copy should have a *beginning*, a *middle* and an *end*.

The beginning

The first line of copy which appears immediately after the headline is very important. This line of copy must make people want to find out more.

The middle

The copy here should include facts about the product or service being offered. The headline has grabbed the attention and now the audience wants to know more.

177

The end

Certain information should always be included, such as the telephone number to contact for further information. The advertisement should tell people how they can find out more.

SOME NOTES ON STYLE

Copywriters have their own distinctive styles, and therefore their messages should not sound the same. However, there are some fundamentals which all good copywriters observe in their writing:

1 Sentences should be written straightforwardly with correct use of grammar.
2 Make use of nouns and verbs but not adjectives and adverbs.
3 Give the reader the facts about the product.
4 Use only as many words as are necessary to convey the message.

The most important thing to remember is *keep it simple:* use short sentences where possible and keep the language as simple as possible. Make sure the advertisement says what you want it to say. There is no need to use clever words to do this! The copy should be informal – using 'you' as much as possible – and should not oversell the product/service.

The copy should encompass three main objectives:

1 *Sell.* The copy is there to sell the product/service. A description can be used to put forward a case which will result in someone wanting to purchase the product/service. However, the objective is not to 'tell a story'.
2 *Make a statement about the benefits.* Don't forget that the copy is there to sell the product/service. Copy should not be *about* product specifications or special features. Copy should be identifying the *benefits* of the specifications/special features.
3 *Promote the brand image.* Copy related to brand image, attitude and lifestyle does not sell the hardware, it sells feelings. Copy is there to sell the idea of the advertisement. This may be achieved by telling a story or using character sketches etc.

CREATING SLOGANS

One way to make a start here is to study the slogans used for a variety of different products/services. When attempting to create a slogan, it is important to think about:

1 what your product is
2 what is it likely to do for people
3 what kind of phrase can be used to sum up the product.

Think of a slogan as another way of creating a selling message.

STUDENT ACTIVITY

You are to work in pairs and produce slogans for the following:

1 tomatoes
2 jeans
3 walking boots
4 adventure holidays.

STUDENT ACTIVITY

You are to create a slogan for a basic product, e.g. bread. Use some of the techniques included in this chapter to help you to develop an appropriate slogan. Discuss your slogan with the rest of your group and explain how you went about developing it, i.e. the processes involved.

9.3 TYPOGRAPHY

The choice of the right style of type is crucial in helping to sell the product/service being advertised.

TYPEFACES

There are many different kinds of typeface. From the small selection shown in Figure 9.9, you can see some of the options.

SOME GENERAL RULES

1 Type can appear in a variety of weights, and in italics, small capitals or large capitals – and many more variations on a theme!

ABCDEFGHIJKLMNOPQRSTUVWXYZ
abcdefghijklmnopqrstuvwxyz
Times Roman Italic

ABCDEFGHIJKLMNOPQRSTUVWXYZ
abcdefghijklmnopqrstuvwxyz
Times Roman

ABCDEFGHIJKLMNOPQRSTUVWXYZ
abcdefghijklmnopqrstuvwxyz
Futura

ABCDEFGHIJKLMNOPQRSTUVWXYZ
abcdefghijklmnopqrstuvwxyz
Frutiger

ABCDEFGHIJKLMNOPQRSTUVWXYZ
abcdefghijklmnopqrstuvwxyz
Courier Regular

ABCDEFGHIJKLMNOPQRSTUVWXYZ
abcdefghijklmnopqrstuvwxyz
Abadi Regular

ABCDEFGHIJKLMNOPQRSTUVWXYZ
abcdefghijklmnopqrstuvwxyz
Helvetica Condensed

ABCDEFGHIJKLMNOPQRSTUVWXYZ
abcdefghijklmnopqrstuvwxyz
Sabon Roman

Fig 9.9 Examples of some different styles of typeface – there are many others.

179

2 A variety of typestyles might be used in one
   advertisement, but it is best to use a minimalist
   approach and stick with variations within one
   typeface or just two different faces.

3 Using capital letters for long headlines makes
   them hard to read – better, in this case, to use
   upper and lower case letters. All-capitals can
   be used effectively for short headlines.

4 Reversed-type headlines, i.e. white type which
   appears on a black surface, can give a dramatic
   effect but prove difficult to read.

5 If the headline is to be longer than one line,
   break up the headline at the end of a phrase.

STUDENT ACTIVITY

Study the following article by Dan Foulkes
from Ads International, *issue 23, Winter
1994/5, entitled 'Type':*

*H**arlem** is a Neville Brody typeface. What
images does that conjure up in your mind?
The jazz age? Jumping horn solos sent out
by the amphetamine fuelled lips of men in
sharp suits, over blue smoke filled
speakeasies? All evoked by the title of a
typeface, for Brody understands that letter-
forms possess visual personalities that
enormously influence our interpretation of
words written in that face. It's an oddity
then, that type – particularly in the context
of commercials – generally goes unnoticed,
and for an industry supposedly founded on
creativity the methods in which it is employed are exceptionally unimaginative. Is
it simply that type is incinerated by the
wattage of the big idea, and suddenly remembered at the last moment only because
the product name has to be flashed across
the screen? Or is it just that the ad industry
doesn't fully understand its potential? With
the ever increasing cross fertilisation of
ideas from one medium to another perhaps
the industry has something to learn from
the design community where typographic*

*solutions have long been integral to the sup-
port of brands, and an understanding and
appreciation of the creativity type presents
is a prerequisite for any designer worth
their Anglepoise.*

*TSLN (Tutssel St John Lambie-Nairn) is
an interesting hybrid, marrying the
renowned broadcast graphics' ability of
multi-award winning Lambie-Nairn with
the talent of design consultancy Tutssel's,
headed up by Glenn Tutssel, ex-creative director of Michael Peters', which was in the
eighties the Saatchi's of design. Each
company handles separate clients but will
merge their skills if required. Consequently
Tutssel's may soon be applying design sen-
sibilities to advertising convention, and
with their broadcast brethren they may
provide a genuine alternative to dreary on-
screen typographic solutions. Tutssel
states: 'I think in general on-screen typography in advertising is very, very weak.
Some of the creative work being done in
commercials is staggering, with a lot of extremely powerful imagery being created,
but typography invariably seems to be an
afterthought, whereas properly used it can
greatly enhance the communication of the
message. There is so much more scope for it
that has yet to be explored in commercials.'*

*Whilst Tutssel may not be telling us any-
thing we don't already know, his vision for
a new working model to create stronger on-
screen type is an interesting one.*

*'If designers who are experts in the typo-
graphic area worked more in conjunction
with agencies they would be able to more
strongly endorse the communication of an
advertising idea with a strong, relevant
typographic solution,' continues Tutssel. 'I
think we've all been far too rigid in the past,
viewing disciplines as the set domain of one
kind of person or company. It's illogical because by working together with complemen-
tary skills you can produce a better end
result, as I think we've found with our operation. Here we can offer our brand building
design skills coupled with Lambie-Nairn's
reputation for producing outstanding
screen graphics.'*

In the last eighteen months Lambie-Nairn has produced three excellent examples of creative thinking applied to on-screen type. Philip Dupée, creative partner and associate director, made all three spots, but acknowledges that commissions which actually include typographic considerations, let alone use type as the primary mode of communication, are few and far between. The spots – for Nike, the Economist and Johnnie Walker Black Label – demonstrate that a commercial which adopts a typographic route can be highly effective creatively, as Dupée notes: 'I think that what we did with Nike and The Economist is actually quite unusual because in both cases the respective logos were actually the stars of the commercials. But both are very strong ideas and maybe they're made even more memorable simply because commercials using type in an interesting way are such a rarity.'

The Wieden & Kennedy Amsterdam work for Nike used two simple ten second spots, with the Nike logo dribbling all over the place in the shape of a basketball in the first ad, and then in the second, smashed across the screen as a tennis ball. Dupée reveals his approach to the two spots: 'I started by designing the Nike logo into graphic shapes equivalent to a basketball and tennis ball. We animated them by taking them onto computer in a 3D environment because it looks so much better even though you only ever see them as a flat graphic shape. I think it worked so well because the idea is simple but captures what Nike's all about – a hard playing, hip, sporting brand.'

AMV BBDO's Economist work also revolved around the client's logo, using the dot of the 'i' in the magazine's title as a gun target to illustrate how accurate the editorial content is. Tutssel views this spot in particular as an example of the potential synergy between design and advertising, explaining: 'I believe where we as designers can help an agency is in creating for them unique, appropriate typefaces, and if they need it, on-screen identities. It isn't simply a question of going to a Mac and selecting something that looks nice and isn't going to look too out of place. If you have a beer product or a confectionery product obviously the character of the letterform is going to have to be very different. But that's not the end of the story because if you have a product like a photocopier you may not want a typeface that reflects the actual nature of that product but rather the tone of the ad, or something to underline and reflect the product benefits that have been presented.

'I accept that perhaps there is not the time in an agency to consider these things,' continues Tutssel, 'but what I don't understand is why they neglect a very important element from the creative mix, when I believe as a company with our dual aspect we could work on the tone of the type to support the brand in the most positive way possible. As a company our partnership works well, because where we understand the demands of static type, someone like Phil can bring a typographic idea to life, and can envisage how it will work in an animated context.'

Tutssel is quite clearly fired up by the idea of dismantling the barriers that currently separate the disciplines, as his hands start to dissect the air in ever more emphatic underlining movements. 'The Nike ad as a solution wouldn't actually look out of place in a design context, because opting for a creative typographic route is always a considered option by a designer if deemed appropriate. Having said that, translating a logo onto screen obviously carries with it its own set of problems because a lot of them were never designed to work in that format – you might get colour flare, or the type might bleed off-screen and so on, but again that's where the joint skills we possess as a company enable us to design things that will work both on- and off-screen.'

There is an air about Tutssel when he talks about type in commercials which suggests that, whilst he understands the reasons behind its sad neglect, he feels creatives should stop making excuses and *start looking at alternatives. A good designer will consider every element of a piece of design, from the material it's to be printed on and how the colours will reproduce, to the way the type complements the image. Judging by the results on television and in the cinema, most creatives generally don't regard type as an essential element in the creation of commercials. But why does a commercial full of beautiful images like Dunlop's 'Unexpected' – which Hoovered up so many awards – feature a bolted on type abomination at the end? Perhaps companies such as TSLN, and currently they are the only one offering this mix of design and broadcast graphics' skills, present a different way of working which will allow every element of a commercial to be truly creative.*

Discuss the issues.

9.4 LAYOUT

The ability to lay out a printed advertisement, i.e. the visuals and copy, requires visual skill. Some basic principles should be observed. An advertisement is made up of:

– headlines
– copy
– visuals
– slogans
– borders
– coupons etc.

These are all aspects of an advertisement's design.

The main components of an advertisement are:

1 the headline, subheadings and any other 'display' type
2 the main visual plus any other illustrations
3 the main copy
4 the logo style and symbol plus strapline
5 other aspects, i.e. coupons for instance.

The next stage is to decide which of these aspects are the most important and which are less important, visually, so that a hierarchy can be developed.

DESIGNING THE LAYOUT

The layout must follow a logical sequence. It is useful to produce a thumbnail sketch of the advertisement in different formats in order to identify the layout which offers the most balanced display. The visual is an important feature of the advertisement because it attracts people's attention. A visual can provide mood because it appeals to people's feelings, so the picture must be eye-catching. Pictures may be illustrations or photographs.

Some practical steps to follow when designing the layout of an advertisement:

1 Create a page which represents the size of the advertisement.
2 Move the various elements, i.e. headlines, copy, visuals etc., around on the page to see which combination works best.
3 Make use of white space to improve impact.

Advertisers must identify the main 'benefit' of their products and produce a headline from this. It is best (as already mentioned) to 'keep it simple' to ensure that it attracts the readers' attention. Eye-catching devices which might be used are:

1 bullet points – which make up a list of details the advertiser wishes to highlight about the product/service being offered
2 flashes – which can be seen in a variety of formats, and which draw attention to special offers or money-off vouchers.

Most companies have a corporate image which is partly represented by colour and partly by the logo. Using the company logo in an advertisement creates impact.

Company slogans should create a statement which tells the consumer something about that company.

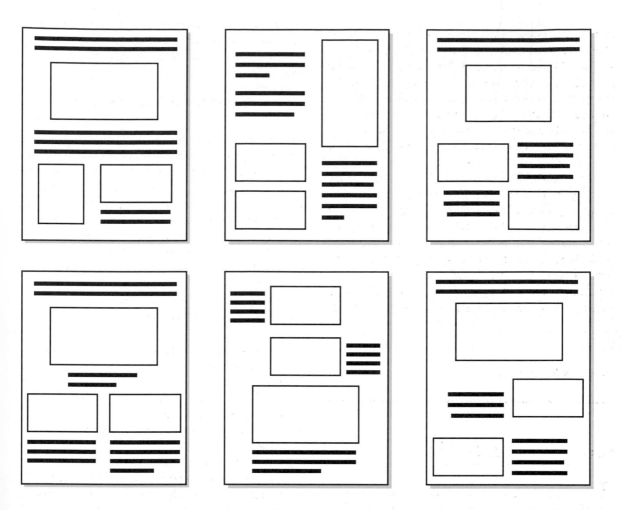

Fig 9.10 Thumbnail sketches of the stages of development of layouts for a printed advertisement.

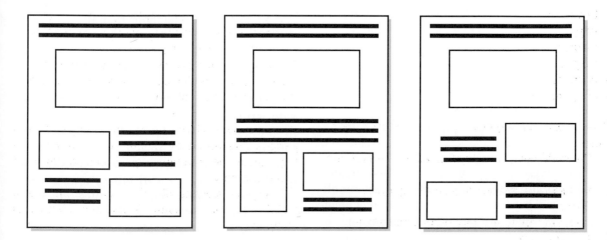

Fig 9.11 More detailed sketches of the most promising layouts.

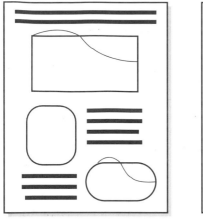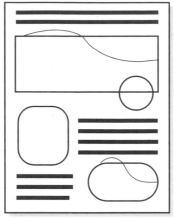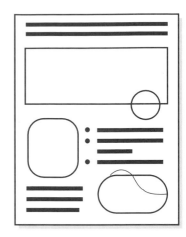

Fig 9.12 Stages in completing the final layout.

Create an appropriate slogan for each of the following:

1 a cut-price local fashion store
2 a newly opened pet shop with animal-grooming facilities
3 a retailer of second-hand computer game software which offers a part-exchange service.

9.5 FILM/CINEMA ADVERTISING

It is *music* that is crucial in film. Music creates mood and atmosphere and develops memorable associations between itself and the product being advertised. Music can be purchased from a music library.

It is important that advertisements in cinemas *entertain* the audience.

9.6 TELEVISION ADVERTISING

Advertisements which appear on television are mini versions of the extended films which appear on our cinema screens.

THE STORYBOARD

It is important to remember that advertisements which will appear on film, i.e. on television or in the cinema, are usually presented to the customer in the form of a *storyboard*, i.e. a minimum of eight or more pictures (not usually an accurate reproduction of the final film) drawn on a board with written commentary beneath. What do you need to remember when producing a storyboard for a television commercial?

In order to create an interesting television commercial it is necessary to create drama. Think about the strategy which is to be used. Is the advertisement selling a benefit or is the product/service going to *solve a problem?*

DIFFERENT FORMS OF TELEVISION COMMERCIALS

There are many forms a television commercial can take. Some of them are as follows:

1 *Demonstrations.* Television allows the advertiser to demonstrate a product and at the same time highlight the benefits to be derived from purchasing the product. What can the product do? The advertisement for the floor cleaner Flash demonstrates how quickly a floor can be mopped by using the product.
   The setting should be credible.
2 *The before-and-after strategy.* This technique is often used when advertising 'slimming' aids/products or hair-colour products where it is possible to show the individual both 'before' and 'after' his or her use of the product, in order to demonstrate its effects.
3 *The narrative.* The advertisement will deliver a story. The story may be serious, funny, sad etc. Nescafé Gold Blend uses this type of advertisement. Many household products are advertised using a comic storyline with a hard sell. The product itself might be demonstrated within the story line.

THE VISUALS

These need to be kept as simple as possible. Produce a storyboard with eight frames. Each frame should be underpinned with both a brief explanation of what is occurring in each shot and an indication of the narrative, music, sound effects etc. to be used. Try to make it clever – the idea needs to leap out of the screen at you. Ensure the idea appears within the first few seconds so that you 'hook' the audience. The product too should appear early on, possibly in close-up, and then regularly throughout, with a possible close-up at the end of the ad. Finally, there should be constant action, again to ensure the audience stays watching.

SOUND

It is important to ensure that the soundtrack is synchronised with the visuals. On television, there is usually less talking and more sound, whether it be music, special sound effects etc.
   Most advertisements which appear on television use music to create mood and atmosphere.

9.7 RADIO

Radio advertisements usually fall into one of the following categories:

1 *A dramatised commercial.* A situation is dramatised in a brief scene in which the product is introduced as a solution to a problem. The scene is usually followed by a commercial for the product, spoken by the announcer.
2 *A dialogue commercial.* The commercial is put across by the announcer, sometimes with assistance from others. The announcer may also converse with users of products/experts, or with a representative from the product's manufacturer.
3 *A straight commercial.* An advertisement is delivered by an announcer who praises the merits of the product in a straight advertising message.
4 *A gimmick commercial.* Listeners are attracted straightaway by an unusual noise, i.e. sound effect, music, a dramatic opening etc. It could be singing or a jingle for the product, or it could be a verse about the product.

Radio commercials usually use short words and short sentences.

STUDENT ACTIVITY

Listen to commercial radio for a period of one week and make notes about the content of four advertisements which you hear during this period. Analyse each in terms of:

– strategy
– target audience
– style and tone of the message.

Was the advertisement interesting? Did it grab your attention? If not, why not? If it did, what was it that made it memorable?
Discuss your findings with your group.

Soundtracks used on television are transferable to radio and are recognised by the audience. This can improve the impact of a television campaign. A radio campaign, on the other hand, should be written *specifically* for radio. The message on radio should not only be repeated over and over again – because there are no visuals to underpin the message being given – but should also be short and to the point.

9.8 CREATING THE UNIQUE MESSAGE

Creating an effective advertising message is not an easy task. It is easy to acquire techniques of layout and copywriting, and to study how companies can create unique selling propositions – in my opinion, something which can be learned – but you are either an ideas person or you are not. What's more, before an advertisement idea can be created, the individual has to have *full knowledge* of the product involved. Studying advertisements and looking at the relationship between words, music and images, will, however, help individuals to learn by example, i.e. by observation, experience and practice.

Each advertisement is unique and should be designed specifically for the advertising medium in which it is to appear.

STUDENT ACTIVITY

You have decided to produce an advertisement the size of an A4 page for a well-known branded product of your choice. The advertisement will include:

– *one photograph 6cm by 7cm*
– *two line drawings each 3cm by 3cm*
– *one headline of three words*
– *two three-line sentences for each of the two drawings*
– *a final one-line slogan.*

Produce a rough of the layout.

9.9 CASE STUDY: 'INFOMERCIALS'

Infomercials became legal in the USA in 1984, and it is estimated that they create sales of approximately $1 billion per year. However, a larger proportion of advertising spend is still on below-the-line media. Infomercials have not yet taken off in the UK.

The term 'infomercial' is interpreted in many ways, i.e. short advertisements which are crammed with information; short programmes which 'sell' the product etc. An infomercial consists of a short story about a product which might be funny, dramatic etc. The story has to be strong enough to keep the audience's attention for possibly 30 minutes and have a beginning, a middle and an end. Story lines are based around a well-known fictitious or other character to advertise a product or service.

Most major agencies in the USA are investigating this type of commercial. Saatchi and DMB&B have apparently set up departments working in the field of infomercials. Infomercials may last for 5, 10, 15 or 20 minutes or more instead of 30 or 60 seconds, so they will need to be cost effective.

Between 1988 and 1994, the number of infomercials made in the USA grew from 100 to 400. The approximate cost of an infomercial in the USA is $250,000. The product type with the largest sales in 1992 was that of exercise equipment: sales totalled approximately $245 million. Celebrities who are willing to take part in infomercials earn large sums 'upfront' and usually enjoy a percentage of the sales revenue.

In the UK there have been very few companies producing infomercials. One recent campaign was the Land Rover 'worldwide' spots. The story line will need to be strong, there will need to be a structure and costs will need to be kept down if this type of commercial is to grow in the UK. It is likely that the larger advertisers will push this new medium.

(Adapted from an article by Greg Sheridan which appeared in *Ads International*, issue 23, Winter 1994/5)

Infomercial Facts:

Infomercials started on TV as often unintentionally humorous sales pitches for products such as body shapers.

Singer Cher is called the 'Queen of Infomercials' for her endorsements of hair and beauty products that have reportedly earned her a million dollars in fees plus a percentage of the profits.

The number of infomercials made a year increased from 100 in 1988 to about 400 in 1994.

New-style infomercials aiming to convince viewers they are learning as they are laughing cost an average of $250,000 to produce.

Presidential candidate Ross Perot paid $500,000 for each live thirty minute infomercial he did on network time to sell himself and his ideas to American people.

The average cost of airing an infomercial in a late night regional market is $20,000 for thirty minutes.

In June 1993 the Federal Trade Commission settled a lawsuit with a California TV producer. He was charged with false advertising in the content of programme-length infomercials made between 1987-89 and instructed to refund $3.5 million to customers.

Building product familiarity often requires airing infomercials 10-20 times per week and gradually increasing that to 40-50, with sometimes as many as 200-300.

In 1992 infomercials sold about $245 million in exercise equipment – the largest product type.

The average product needs to recoup $1.50 for every $1 spent on air time Celebrities can receive anything from $10,000 upwards upfront plus 2.5% of sales. Even the 'live studio audience' is packed with extras who get $40+ each to look amazed. Senior citizens from nearby retirement homes have been bussed in to see the stars and get a free lunch.

Fig 9.13 Some facts and TV-screen stills from an Ads International article on 'infomercials'.

STUDENT ACTIVITY

Work in teams of three or four. Produce an idea for an infomercial for a product/service of your choice. Then, either:

1 role-play the scenario or
2 produce a television storyboard for your 'infomercial'.

Role-play or present your ideas to the rest of your group. Your role-play or presentation should last 20 minutes.

1 What different forms might headlines take?
2 Identify as many visual ideas as possible which might be used in advertising.
3 What are the rules when producing good copy?
4 Why is the typography used in advertisements important?
6 How would you approach the task of producing a strong storyboard for a television advertisement?
7 What are the important issues when producing a radio advertisement?

10

The role of the advertising agency

AIMS

- to define the role of the agency
- to look at how the role of the agency has developed over time

UNIT 20 ADVERTISING
Working towards:

- **Element 20.4**

  - Performance Criteria:
    1 Describe the advertising services offered by types of agencies
    2 Explain the criteria used to select advertising agencies
    3 Describe the roles of advertising agency personnel

10.1 THE AGENCY

The agency has a large role to play in creating and developing advertisements for a variety of large organisations. These organisations pay sizeable fees for the expertise which is to be found in-house at an advertising agency. Competition is fierce between agencies, who have to provide a unique service to each client and continue to develop new ideas which will promote products/services in line with their clients' ethos.

In December 1994 a number of clients were reviewing their agency requirements. Table 10.1 shows a list of these clients which appeared in *Campaign* magazine in December 1994.

THE AGENCY IN THE PAST

As mentioned briefly in Chapter 1, the agency's job was initially to sell, to prospective advertisers, space in newspapers/magazines for which they were paid commission – and at first they worked more on behalf of the publications themselves. However, by starting to offer more help to prospective advertisers about how they should produce their advertisements, agencies effectively increased both their scope of operation and their commission earnings potential.

THE AGENCY NOW

Advertising agencies now work on behalf of a variety of clients to whom they offer a unique and confidential service. Agencies produce appropriate advertisements for their clients' products/services and seek to identify the most cost-effective and relevant media in each case.

An advertising agency employs a variety of people who have specialist skills to offer. These may include:

1 The **account director** – usually responsible for a specific client group. He or she will also negotiate new client accounts.

2 The **account executive** – responsible for a small number of accounts, possibly just one or two. The account executive, who usually reports to the account director, will work closely with the client to develop an understanding of both the client's business and the client's specific needs. He or she must get as much information as possible about the product/service being offered by the client company. It is likely that there will be several meetings, and the account executive will need to identify:

– the size of the budget spend
– detailed information about the product/service
– the market – the client may have identified a specific segment, or may need help in doing this
– the distribution channels for the product/service
– the name of the product, its price and its packaging design
– who the competitors are.

The account executive will liaise with the account director and possibly other directors within the agency to clarify whether the client's product or service fits into the agency's 'business profile'. The account executive will also liaise with personnel in the agency about the specific requirements of his or her client(s).

The account executive will confirm in writing discussions/agreements reached after each meeting with the client. These reports form a record for reference purposes, as well as the basis of a report which is submitted to the client usually once a year.

3 The **marketing manager** – offers a marketing service to clients who do not have a marketing executive in-house. The marketeer will offer advice on market research, branding, segmentation etc.

4 The **media planner/buyer**. In a small agency the roles of media planner and media buyer will be combined. In larger agencies the two roles are likely to be carried out by different individuals. These individuals will have a comprehensive knowledge of all media available, and will offer advice regarding the most appropriate primary/secondary media (see Chapters 4 and 5) for a specific client in a particular circumstance.

The planner will use statistics regarding

Table 10.1 Agency accounts under review as at December 1994.

Clients	Budget £m	Past 12 months Register-MEAL	Incumbent	Shortlist
Alitalia (global)	N/A	N/A	various	O&M, Lintas, DMB&B, Publicis FCB, JWT, Armando Testa, Lowes, McCannis
Allied Carpets	4.5	4.5	Mighty Mouse Communications	N/A
Allinson	N/A	1.2	BST	N/A
Avis	0.5	0.16	Howell Henry	N/A
BBC (corporate)	N/A	N/A	N/A	N/A
Beauty International	5.0	2.9	BMP	Publicis, Rainey Kelly, Burkitt Weinreich, Bates Dorland
Blockbuster	N/A	6.0	Y&R	Y&R, GGT, BMP, Leo Burnett, O&M, DMB&B
British Horseracing Board	1.0	N/A	N/A	N/A
CIC Video UK	1.0	1.0	Brompton	N/A
Duckhams Motor Oil	0.3	0.3	Duckworth Finn	N/A
EC against Aids	N/A	N/A	N/A	McCanns Scotland and others
European Passenger Services	3.5	N/A	N/A	Y&R and others
Femidom	N/A	0.6	Laing Henry	N/A
HEA	8.0	5.0	BMP, AMV, Laing Henry, BDDH	BMP, AMV BBDO, Laing Henry and others
Health Education Board for Scotland	2.0	0.8	Leith	N/A
Healthy Options	N/A	2.2	O&M	N/A
Hoverspeed	N/A	1.4	AMV, McBain Noel-Johnson	Arc, Leagas Delaney, Simons Palmer, the McWilliams Consultancy
Intersport	1.0	N/A	Target Advertising	N/A
JFM	1.5	0.3	Leagas Delaney	Leagas Delaney, WMGO, DMB&B, JWT M'chester, Davies Little Cowley
Keds (pan-Euro)	10.0	N/A	N/A	BDDP, DDB Needham
LEB	3.0	N/A	N/A	Chiat Day, GGK, DMB&B
Mates	1.0	0.5	N/A	N/A
Matthew Clark	1.5	0.7	N/A	N/A
Miller Pilsner	6.0	2.0	BMP	N/A
N&P Building Society	N/A	8.0	GGK	N/A
National Football League	1.0	N/A	N/A	N/A
NatWest (media)	23.5	23.5	CIA Medianetwork, BBH	CIA Medianetwork, BBH
Neutrogena	2.5	1.8	N/A	N/A
PPP	4.0	N/A	N/A	N/A
Phillips (global)	N/A	N/A	N/A	N/A
Portman Building Society	1.0	N/A	N/A	N/A
Radio 1	2.0	N/A	Arc Advertising	Rainey Kelly, Saatchi, Chiat Day
Radio Rentals	N/A	9.5	WCRS	WCRS, DMB&B, Publicis
Rockport	N/A	2.7	BBH	N/A
Royal Armouries	1.0	N/A	N/A	Faulds, BDH, McCanns M'chester, Advertising Principles, Poulters, Brahm
Ryvita	2.0	0.8	Lansdown Conquest	Simons Palmer, O&M, CDP, Lansdown Conquest
Sega (pan-Euro)	25.0	25.0	N/A	AMV, DMB&B, Lowe Howard-Spink, McCann-Erickson
Southern Comfort	N/A	2.3	Lowe Howard-Spink	Y&R, Burkitt Weinreich
Thomson Directories	5.0	0.5	DMB&B	N/A
Turkish Tourist Board	1.0	N/A	Dovetail and R&D	Banks Hoggins O'Shea, Dovetail and R&D
TV Licensing	2.5	2.5	Hall Harrison	Hall Harrison and others
UIP (pan-Euro)	16.0	N/A	Y&R	Lintas, Y&R
Union Bank of Switzerland	2.0	0.7	DMB&B Financial	DMB&B Financial, TBWA, Y&R
United Friendly Assurance	3.0	N/A	N/A	Banks Hoggins O'Shea, Burkitt Weinreich, Roose and Partners
Wedgwood (global)	N/A	N/A	DFSD Bozell	BBH, WCRS
Wispa	N/A	3.5	GGT	N/A
World of Leather	3.5	3.7	First City BBDO	N/A

Source: *Campaign, 23 December 1994.*

circulation figures for newspapers/magazines and viewing/listening figures for television and radio. The planner will also be able to look carefully at costs and compare these across different media types. He or she will draw up a media schedule which will identify the dates and sizes and costs of principle advertising. This plan will be included in the presentation to the client of the whole campaign. When the schedule has been agreed, the media planner/buyer or media buyer (depending on the size of the agency) will negotiate the best rates possible with each of the media identified.

The media buyer will also be able to identify the most effective advertising slots for, say, television or radio, and these may need to be booked far in advance to ensure the right slots are secured.

5 The **copywriter** – responsible for producing all wording for all advertising.

6 The **art director** – responsible for the art studio in a large agency. He or she will have a number of specialists reporting to him or her:

- the **visualiser** will be responsible for interpreting the message in a visual way
- the **layout artist** will produce a detailed plan of the advertisement
- the **typographer** will choose the style of type to be used, working with the layout, visuals and copy produced by his or her colleagues

7 The **production manager** – responsible for ensuring that advertising is produced on time for all clients of the agency, and that the advertisements are delivered on time to all media. He or she will act as a progress chaser, and is responsible for supplying the finished artwork, copy and layout to be used for a particular advertisement.

In addition:

1 Marketing/research/planning – mainly responsible for analysing the market-research information collected to ensure that it is used to generate an appropriate creative strategy for the client's product.

2 Other departments will include an accounts section responsible for billing the client for services, as well as others such as personnel, contracts, art/picture buying, public relations, sales promotions and a whole host of other activities which can be found in most organisations, i.e. general administration etc.

Agencies often employ freelance specialists to help them should they receive a brief which falls outside their in-house team of expertise; and most small agencies use a variety of specialists on a subcontract basis, i.e. exhibition designers etc.

POST-CAMPAIGN

The advertisement(s) will be studied closely to see if the message has not suffered in reproduction and whether it appeared in the right place, i.e. on the right page etc. The printing quality, style of type used etc. will also be checked for accuracy.

Recall research will usually be carried out, and an adjustment made to the campaign should this prove necessary. In addition, at the end of the campaign the team and the client will wish to know:

- whether the campaign has met the objectives
- whether the message was correct
- whether the message reached the target audience
- whether the media selected was appropriate in each case

The answers to these and other questions will be analysed to ensure that future campaigns benefit from the findings.

STUDENT ACTIVITY

Work in pairs and scan a variety of the magazines which are aimed at marketeers, i.e. Campaign magazine etc. Choose four advertisements which have been produced by different agencies.

1 Can you identify, from examples of the work of these agencies, what kind of approach has been used in each of the advertisements you have chosen?

2 Is there a particular marketplace which each agency appears to favour?

Compare your findings with those of other members of your group/class.

The main job of the agency is to create a *unique* and *effective* advertising campaign for each of its clients.

10.2 DO I NEED AN AGENCY?

Companies either:

- use an advertising agency for all their advertising needs, or
- never use an agency, or
- use a combination of agency and in-house expertise.

STUDENT ACTIVITY

Saatchi & Saatchi were responsible for changing the image of Mrs Thatcher during her period as prime minister beginning in 1979. Working in small teams, research this change in her image. Try to identify how significant a change was achieved.

Compare your findings with the rest of your group.

ISSUES TO CONSIDER WHEN DECIDING TO USE AN AGENCY

Whether an agency is used or not will depend on a number of key queries, i.e.:

- Has the company in-house specialists who have all-round ability?

- Will these specialists be able to handle every aspect of any advertising brief on behalf of the company?
- Would an agency be able to bring something new to this specialist team?
- Would an agency be interested in handling the account (size will sometimes have an impact on this decision).
- Can the company afford the specialist services of an agency?

10.3 INDUSTRIAL AGENCIES

Industrial agencies specialise in advertisements which appear in *trade/technical* journals as well as at trade exhibitions. These agencies consist of experts in industrial and technical products. Payment to such agencies is usually by fee because of the specialist nature of their field of operation. In addition, clients tend to stay with these agencies for a longer term than perhaps is the case in the more commercial agency field.

10.4 MEDIA INDEPENDENTS

Media independents tend to purchase advertising space at the keenest price possible and sell to a variety of clients. It is likely that these independent operators are paid commission by the media only. However, they *may* also attract commission from the client.

10.5 CASE STUDY: SAATCHI & SAATCHI

One of the most successful agencies in the UK is Saatchi & Saatchi. Below is a potted history of Maurice Saatchi who left the company in December 1994.

Maurice Saatchi was born in 1946 in Baghdad. In 1947 his family moved to the UK and settled in London. Having gained a Major in Sociology at the London School of Economics, graduating with first-class honours in 1964, he joined

Haymarket Publishing as a junior assistant to Michael Heseltine and Lindsey Masters on a salary of £2,000 per annum. He helped to plan the launch of *Campaign* magazine and *Accountancy Age*.

In 1970, Maurice joined his brother at the Cramer Saatchi agency, and the agency was re-launched using an advertisement in the *Sunday Times*. The new name was Saatchi & Saatchi, Cramer having departed. It began with £1 million in billings and just five accounts.

In 1974 Saatchi took over Norley's and effectively doubled in size. Martin Sorrell was recruited as Finance Director by Maurice in 1976, and in 1978 the agency won the Conservative Party account. Billings in 1979 reached £67.8 million, making Saatchi the largest agency in the UK. In 1981 Saatchi purchased Dorland Advertising, paying £7 million.

In 1982 Saatchi acquired Compton Advertising of New York, and in 1985 Maurice replaced Ken Gill as Chairman of Saatchi.

In 1986 Saatchi acquired the $876 million billing of Dancer Fitzgerald Sample (DFS) for $75 million and opened up negotiations to acquire the Ted Bates Group. The money was raised through a rights issue totalling £406 million.

In 1987 a bid for the Midland Bank was aborted. DFS merged with Saatchi Compton to become Saatchi & Saatchi Worldwide. Billings totalled £2.3 billion. Maurice gained a 68 per cent salary increase to £500,000 per annum.

In 1989 profits were £50 million lower than expected. Maurice and Charles announced they were to step down as Joint Chief Executives and make way for Robert Louis-Dreyfus. At this point Charles Scott became Group Finance Director.

In 1990 Maurice announced cuts in the broth-ers' £625,000 per annum salaries in order to placate shareholders. A rescue package totalling £400 million saved the Group in 1991, and in 1993 Scott replaced Louis-Dreyfus.

In 1994 it was reported that there was 'antagonism' between Scott and Maurice. The Group announced pre-tax profits of £19 million for 1993. Shareholders who had become disaffected by Maurice and who were led by David Hero of fund managers Harris Associates called for Maurice's resignation. In a boardroom coup, Maurice was forced to quit and was offered the post of Honorary President of the holding company. He was given until January 3 to decide.

(Adapted from information supplied by Saatchi & Saatchi)

DISCUSSION POINT

Carry out some further research of the press reporting of the incidents which led up to Maurice leaving Saatchi & Saatchi.

In your opinion, why was Maurice effectively removed from Saatchi & Saatchi and what were the consequences of this move subsequently?

REVIEW YOUR PROGRESS

1 What was the main role of agencies earlier in the 20th century?

2 How has the role changed during recent years?

3 List the kind of specialists an agency is likely to employ.

4 What are the main considerations to be taken into account before a company employs the services of an agency?

The advertising budget

AIMS

- to identify and understand the different methods used to produce a budget
- to prepare, present and justify an advertising budget spend

UNIT 20 ADVERTISING

- **Element 20.1**

  - Performance Criteria:
    3 Describe how a given budget may be allocated for the campaign

- **Element 20.2**

  - Performance Criteria:
    4 Produce a media plan within a budget

11.1 THE BUDGET

The size of the budget which is allocated to a company's advertising, usually for a period of 12 months, will determine the criteria against which the success of the campaign can be judged. If a company is using an advertising agency, the agency will certainly need to know at the start of a project what the budget is for that specific project.

There are several methods which can be used to determine the size of budget. The budget relating to advertising expenditure is usually termed the 'proportion'. Methods for setting budgets include those relating to:

1 sales
2 competitors' activities
3 market theories.

Whenever companies spend money, they attach a 'value for money' evaluation which is undertaken to establish whether the expenditure has been justified. Allocating valuable financial resources to support an advertising campaign may be considered an investment of a kind which can be measured against certain specific results.

HOW IMPORTANT IS ADVERTISING FOR THE PRODUCT?

Some products will need only a small advertising budget, i.e. staple foods such as bread, whereas a 'luxury' item may need to be advertised extensively because sales will depend on this, i.e. beauty products, perfumes etc. It might therefore be argued that:

- commodities attract a low advertising spend
- image-building products attract a high spend.

STUDENT ACTIVITY

The following includes extracts from an article by Jeremy Prescot (Managing Director of Kilmartin Baker) which appeared in Admap *magazine dated March 1995 entitled 'Measuring the impact of a small budget – a national diabetes campaign, and the invaluable role of research.'*

This case history of British Diabetic Association advertising shows how a small research programme gave the Association the confidence to spend the vast majority of its advertising budget on a nationwide symptoms awareness campaign. The research helped in modifying the advertising, and provided additional information about public perceptions of diabetes and the proportion of the population suffering from the symptoms. The advertisements were positioned as educational and informational and did not use the shock tactics common in public health campaigns. Market research was used alongside clinical research to give an overall picture of the effectiveness of the campaign.

...the idea for the advertising and research was conceived in a doctor's surgery ... doctors were concerned about the low public awareness of the symptoms of diabetes given that one in ten of the population are ultimately affected by it ... The doctors had recently conducted two research studies to try and determine people's levels of awareness of the symptoms of diabetes. In the first study they analysed 100 consecutive newly-diagnosed patients who had non-insulin dependent diabetes and found that only 39 per cent of these patients had reported major symptoms to the referring doctor ... When these same patients were asked to complete a symptom enquiry form, 80 per cent recognised further symptoms and the more severe cases recognised that they had been showing the symptoms of diabetes for many years.

The second study consisted of street interviews in Hammersmith and Fulham. Of 480 respondents, only 52 per cent were able to name a symptom of diabetes ...

In view of the findings of the research undertaken, Kilmartin Baker devised a campaign which was aimed at raising awareness of symptoms associated with 'non-insulin dependent diabetes' as well as increasing the number of 'self-referrals' to GPs. Kilmartin Baker felt that the campaign would be 'very relevant' to the British Diabetic Association for the following reasons:

- it would be a very public demonstration of what the BDA stand for
- it would be relevant to existing and potential diabetics (all previous advertising appeared to be aimed at non-diabetics)
- it would be a useful vehicle to raise awareness of the BDA to the public at large in an informative way
- and a way of encouraging existing diabetics to retain their membership for a longer period of time.

The campaign strategy was to raise awareness of the symptoms of diabetes to the target audience, chiefly the whole adult population, (symptoms include: thirst, tiredness, blurred vision, sudden weight loss, an increase in urination and irritation), but also to reassure the audience that diabetes can be controlled. The ad should also be 'optimistic'.

The test of the media took place in Wolverhampton and Basingstoke. The two areas had differing socio-economic profiles and the doctors wished to identify the number of new patients who sought their GP's advice with symptoms of diabetes.

...four sheet posters and local press were selected, because they provided the best possible discrete coverage of all adults living in Basingstoke and Wolverhampton at a cost-level that could be replicated on a national basis. The budget for media and production was set at £25,500.

Research was carried out by a research company using questionnaires which used short questions. The research produced some surprising results but in terms of the original objectives of the campaign, the following can be identified:

...the awareness figure increased to 100 per cent immediately after the advertising and remained at this figure even at the post-post research stage. Awareness of diabetes advertising quadrupled over the campaign period from 10 per cent to 41 per cent ... The research indicated that in addition to recalling the test campaign, respondents were actually remembering details of the advertising and that their awareness symptoms had actually increased ... Over 70 per cent of those recalling symptoms claimed to have seen the advertisement as a poster, while a further 17 per cent said they had seen it in their local paper. Surprisingly, a high percentage of respondents claimed to have seen the advertising in a national paper (22 per cent) ... Prior to the campaign, 75 per cent of respondents had heard of the BDA ... The BDA was so impressed with the results of the research that it decided to repeat the campaign nationally...

We decided to base the national advertising campaign on the 'If you suffer from the following symptoms...' advertisement, rather than the man looking tired advertisement as there was a greater recall of this in the research. We adapted this advertisement to produce a series of three advertisements, and made these even more effective than the test advertisement by:

- reducing the number of symptoms advertised to concentrate on the four main symptoms
- putting increased urination first in the list of symptoms, as the research indicated that recall of increased urination was relatively low compared with the other main symptoms
- including an advertisement design specifically to draw attention towards increased urination as a symptom
- the addition of a freephone number.

We backed up the national campaign by mailing packs to GPs in advance so that they were aware of the campaign...

Initial reaction to the national campaign has been very positive ... around 3,500 *people have contacted the BDA's freephone number requesting additional information ... membership for the BDA has increased by seven per cent over the campaign period ... There have also been a number of unsolicited letters from the public supporting the national campaign.*

DISCUSSION POINT

How many of your fellow students were aware of the main symptoms of diabetes? Do you think this knowledge is useful to the adult general public? What impact did a small budget have on the campaign achieving its objectives?

WHAT SIZE OF BUDGET?

The various methods which can be used to identify the size of budget spend include the following:

The Rule of Thumb method

The Rule of Thumb method relates advertising expenditure consistently to some other company activity which is also measured. It may also relate it to an external objective which the company wishes to achieve. There are several Rule of Thumb methods:

1 *Percentage-of-sales method*. This method is based on either:

   – a percentage of last year's sales revenue, or
   – a percentage of next year's forecast sales revenue.

The latter is the one most often used. This method relates advertising spend to sales and ultimately to income. If the projected sales are achieved as a direct result of the advertising spend, advertising is planned from income, and profit is achieved.

Advertising is the prime cost of selling in this instance.

Estimates will identify basic costs, and the advertising spend will be set against every form of expenditure within the organisation. Very often, a percentage will be identified for each.

This method takes no account of the dynamics of the marketplace or of competitive activity.

2 *Expenditure-per-unit method*. This involves allocating a specific amount to the advertising budget based on the number of products the organisation expects to sell. This method results in a percentage advertising budget based on sales forecasts.

3 *Task method*. The company identifies its objectives and then allocates to an advertising budget sufficient money to achieve these objectives. The most usual tasks identified relate to media, i.e. which consumer groups are being targeted and how frequently the advertising should appear over a given period of time. The cost of accomplishing the plan determines the size of the budget allocation. The task method also incorporates some analysis and planning.

It is difficult to identify how much an advertising budget should be, and a picture derived from information produced on the basis of objectives may be just as misleading as any other. However, the task method *is* appropriate for the introduction of a *new* product, and it also suits a situation where a major shift is occurring in the way an established product will be advertised and marketed in the future. In this situation, an analysis of existing relationships between advertising and sales is of no use.

4 *Share-of-sales method*. This method relates the advertising budget to the size of market share the organisation expects to achieve.

Other Rule of Thumb methods exist but the above represent the ones mostly commonly used.

The competitor-based method

It is sometimes wise to spend in proportion to what either competitors or the market spend. For example:

A company's major competitor may spend £2 million, and it may therefore be necessary for the company to spend a similar amount.

The market as a whole spends, £x million on advertising. A company may enjoy a 20 per cent share of that market, and therefore the advertising spend will need to be 20 per cent of £x.

The advertising spend will match the competition spend in a competitive market environment. And there is a relationship between share of market and share of market expenditure.

The percentage-of-overheads-and-profit method

There are certain costs which a company incurs which are *fixed*. Money left after paying these fixed costs may be diverted to other needs within the company, including advertising. Thus, advertising itself is not a fixed cost.

This method bears no relationship to the market or to sales.

The size of the company's advertising budget will ultimately depend on the company's total financial situation. The budget must be affordable, and expenditure on advertising, however determined, should be monitored and assessed in order to ensure that the most effective results are achieved with the minimum spend possible.

11.2 CASE STUDY: NESTLÉ

Nestlé identifies advertising as a 'positive way' of reminding people of its brands which it feels will help both to maintain and increase the sales required to make the product economic and profitable, and to underline the *benefits* of the product. The company's campaigns span television, posters and the press, and at retail level include price cuts and special promotions.

Nestlé's advertising budget is worked out as follows. The company sets costs against income earned from sales for each brand. After fixed and variable costs, as well as overheads, have been deducted, an advertising allowance is identified for each brand. The budget spend is relative to the amount of profit the brand earns: if the profit is small the advertising budget is also small.

The size of the budget is determined by the marketing function within the organisation, although guidance is also sought from financial experts within the company. (Nestlé will not disclose the exact size of its budget spend.) The brand's history and current progress in terms of the brand's position in its marketplace are also considered together with pressures from competitive products and the brand's projected future position.

The budgets are discussed during the Summer months and finally agreed in the Autumn in good time for the following year. Discussion also takes place with the company's agents, who advise how best the budget can be spent.

(Adapted from information supplied by Nestlé)

DISCUSSION POINT

Nestlé produces a wide range of products. Do you think their approach to advertising budgeting is the most appropriate, or can you identify an alternative method which you feel would be more relevant for the different product ranges they offer?

REVIEW YOUR PROGRESS

1 Identify and explain each method, for determining the size of the budget spend, found under the broad heading 'Rule of Thumb'.

2 Which method is most often used and why?

3 Explain what you understand by each of the following approaches to setting an advertising budget:

(a) competitor based
(b) based on a percentage of overheads and profit.

4 Is there one method which is preferable to the others?

12

Stages in planning an advertising campaign

AIMS

- to identify the various stages of an advertising campaign
- to explain what is involved in each stage
- to produce an advertising campaign from a given brief

UNIT 20 ADVERTISING

- **Element 20.1**

    - Performance Criteria:
        1 Identify objectives from a given campaign brief for a target audience
        2 Recommend focus of appeal to be used for target audience
        4 Select appropriate media for reaching audience

- **Element 20.2**

    - Performance Criteria:
        3 Select a suitable media mix to reach target audience
        4 Produce a media plan within a budget

- **Element 20.3**

    - Performance Criteria:
        1 Identify, from an advertising brief, product features and benefits to be communicated
        2 Prepare a suitable style of advertisment for a chosen media
        3 Conform with legal and voluntary advertising constraints
        4 Describe appropriate methods to pre-test the advertisement

This chapter is designed to consolidate all aspects of the **advertising campaign plan.** In addition, there is an opportunity for the reader to produce an advertising campaign plan from a given brief. If it is necessary for the reader to produce Evidence for Advertising Unit No. 22 of the BTEC Advanced GNVQ in Business, included at the end of the chapter is an Assessment Exercise which when completed will achieve this aim.

12.1 STAGES OF AN ADVERTISING CAMPAIGN

1 **Define the objectives**. The objectives of a campaign can be numerous and might include:

- the launch of a new product or re-launch of an existing one
- to maintain market share
- to improve market share
- to remind, i.e. to maintain awareness of the product
- to explain the uses to which a product can be put
- to test a product. This may be done on a regional basis before a full national campaign is launched
- to sell a product directly to the public
- to recruit personnel for the company's workforce
- to promote the company's image – i.e. large companies which offer a range of products may find it easier to promote the company itself rather than the range of products

2 **Clarify the brief**. The client's brief must be clear. Full information about the product/service to be advertised must be obtained from the client company. The kind of information which must be sought would include the following:

- how large is the budget for the campaign
- the specific product/service to be advertised

- the name of the product
- who the customers are
- where the product/service is to be distributed
- who the competition are

3 **Set the budget**. The advertising 'appropriation' is usually part of the overall marketing budget. The size of the appropriation will depend upon the method the company uses to allocate monies for this activity. See Chapter 11 for more information.

4 **Research**. Researching both the target market and the competition is of prime importance if the campaign is to be successful. Both primary and secondary research will usually be carried out.

5 **Evaluate the media**:

- **above-the-line**, i.e. television, radio, the press, magazines etc.
- **below-the-line**, i.e. direct response, direct mail, sales promotions, exhibitions etc.

6 **Choose the media** most suitable for the target audience identified.

7 **Create the advertisement**:

- create a unique selling proposition
- compose the copy/script
- design the visuals
- choose the music (if being used)
- decide on layout, use of headlines, typescript etc.

8 **Produce a media schedule** which meets the customer's needs and is cost effective and within budget.

9 **Present the campaign proposition** to the client. Before the campaign can go ahead the client company will need to be presented with full information about the campaign. Adjustments may need to be made in the light of the client's response prior to the campaign being implemented.

10 **Carry out pre-campaign testing**. Impact/recall studies should be carried out after the first showing of the advertisement so that the campaign can be adjusted if necessary.

11 If necessary, **adjust the campaign** in the light of feedback gained during pre-campaign testing.

12 **Execute the campaign**.

13 **Evaluate the results**. Use impact/recall studies, tracking studies etc. to test whether objectives have been met.

12.2 CASE STUDY: HOW TERRY'S SUCHARD CREATE AN ADVERTISING CAMPAIGN

1 *The Copy Strategy.* The copy strategy is all about deciding what we want the advertising to achieve. Before creating an advertisement, we must decide who our audience is, what we want to say to them about our product, and how we want them to react. This is what we then use to brief our advertising agency, and later to evaluate advertising scripts brought to us by them, checking whether the new ad meets our business and marketing objectives or not.

In preparing the copy strategy we will take into consideration any research we have on our marketplace and consumers, both qualitative (small groups having an in-depth discussion) and quantitative (numerical data about people's buying habits).

2 *The Creative Brief.* The copy strategy is primarily a business document talking about business objectives. From this our advertising agency develops a creative brief, which translates our requirements into a form that can be used to stimulate their creative teams and spark off exciting ideas.

3 *Advertising Script and Storyboard.* After considering our brief for a period of time (usually approx. six weeks), our advertising agency will come back to us with a suggested advertising script. To help us visualise how the finished ad will look, they show us a storyboard, which is basically a cartoon strip of the ad. They may also use music, pictures and other effects to 'set the mood', so that we can have as good an idea as possible how the finished ad will be.

4 *Media Choice.* The advertisement need not necessarily be for television. We also consider press, poster and cinema advertising. Different types of media are good at attracting the attention of particular target segments of the population, e.g. women's magazines are good for advertising to women! Since chocolate is eaten by virtually everybody, however, television, being a mass media (it reaches a lot of people very quickly), is ideal for most of the Terry's Suchard brands.

5 *The Shoot.* If Terry's Suchard approves the advertising agency's recommended script, the next stage is the shoot. Before filming takes place, a meeting is held at which both Terry's Suchard and its advertising agency agree the final details of the film, such as the set, the cast, and the actors' clothes. The person who will be directing and producing the film on behalf of the advertising agency is also present at this meeting. (Advertising agencies do not film ads. This is done by specialised production companies as different types of film require different skills. The advertising agency will commission the production company best suited to film each individual ad on behalf of Terry's Suchard.)

6 *Pre-testing.* A TV commercial costs up to £2 million to produce and put on air for six weeks. We do not want to spend this amount of money on an ineffective campaign. Pre-testing may therefore be used on a new advertisement. There are various types of pre-testing techniques, which involve showing selected consumers the new ad either in cartoon ('animatic') form, or as a finished film, and testing their responses via a questionnaire or in-depth discussion.

7 *On-Air.* We can buy television air-time according to what types of people will be watching at that time. So our target market is women, social categories ABC1, aged 25–45. We can buy air-time only during programmes that are considered to be liked by those people.

Television air-time is bought in units called 'television ratings', or TVRs. A TVR equates to 1 per cent of the target audience watching once. A typical six week advertising campaign might comprise 500–800 TVRs.

Tracking. We want to see whether or not our advertising is a success. Again, we use consumer research in the shape of a 'tracking study', which tracks consumers' attitudes to our brands over time. We will then be able to see whether there was any shift in consumers' opinion during and after the advertising campaign. The key things we will be looking out for might be as follows:

- Branding – i.e. more people than before remember the brand name
- Persuasion Shift – i.e more people than before claim that they are likely to buy the product
- Key Communication – i.e. more people than before see the product as being fun, or delicious (this must match the things we said we wanted to communicate in our copy strategy documents, and is different for every brand)

Brands and marketplace are changing all the time, so now we start the process all over again!

(Adapted from information supplied by Terry's Suchard)

REVIEW YOUR PROGRESS

1 Identify the stages in planning an advertising campaign.
2 What is the purpose of clarifying the client brief?
3 Identify as many different kinds of media as you can in each of the following categories:

   – above-the-line media
   – below-the-line media.

4 How many different ways of identifying budget spend can you name? Give a brief explanation of each.
5 What methods are available to assist in pre-testing advertisements?
6 What kind of studies can be undertaken post-campaign to test the effectiveness of the campaign?

BTEC ADVANCED GNVQ IN BUSINESS

Additional Option Unit No. 20 – Advertising

ASSIGNMENT: 'THE ICE CREAM WARS'

- Hand Out: to be advised by your tutor
- Hand In:

  - Task 1 Orals: see your tutor
  - Task 2 Orals: see your tutor
  - Task 3 Orals: see your tutor
  - Task 4 and Portfolio: see your tutor

You are employed by the 'Imaginative Advertising Agency' which has been approached by a number of luxury ice cream manufacturers. You will need to choose one of these manufacturers and gather information about:

- the company
- its products
- its pricing policy
- its distribution channels
- its promotional ethos.

The brief

You are to produce an **advertising campaign plan** for the ice cream manufacturer you have chosen. The aim is to raise awareness and increase sales, initially in the UK and later in Europe. **You are to concentrate on the UK market *only*.**

Assume that the sales revenue for last year was £15 million. The company wishes to increase its sales revenue by 25 per cent per annum over the next three years.

Task 1

Deliver an oral presentation to a representative of the ice cream manufacturer (your tutor) which details the following:

You are to create and produce an **advertising plan**. You will need to:

1. find out as much information as you can about the company's ice cream products and range
2. carry out research to identify the target audience
3. carry out research to find out more about competitors in the same market
4. produce an idea for an advertising campaign
5. create a **unique selling proposition**
6. produce a 'mock-up' of the press advertisement, television storyboard, radio script, poster advertisement etc. as appropriate, taking into account legal and ethical constraints on advertising.

You will present your ideas orally (to last 10 minutes), backing them up with appropriate text, visuals etc., and allow time within that allocated period for questions.

(Performance Criteria: 20.1.1, 20.1.2.)
(Performance Criteria: 20.1.2, 20.3.1, 20.3.2.)

Task 2

Deliver an oral presentation to a representative of the ice cream manufacturer (your tutor) which lasts 10 minutes and which details the following:

Your original ideas for the promotion have been accepted by the board of the ice cream manufacturer, and you are now to make further recommendations with regard to the timing of the campaign, suggested budget spend etc.

You must now prepare a **comprehensive portfolio** which includes **budget information** and a detailed **media plan**.

1. Based on your original group ideas and taking into account any comments made by the representative of the company regarding the **advertising proposal** you recently presented, you must research the different types of media and decide upon and recommend:

   (a) the **primary** media, and
   (b) the **secondary** media

   that you propose should be used.
2. Produce appropriate **visuals/copy/storyboard/script.**

3 Suggest the timing of the advertising campaign, a time span and the frequency of appearance of the adverts in each of your chosen media.
4 Explain how you propose to pre-test the advertisement for effectiveness, i.e. **impact and recall.**
5 You must produce a detailed costing of the **campaign plan** – i.e. you must not only detail the costs for media but also identify the resources which will be required in order to produce the copy and visuals (layout costs, etc.) on the basis of **primary research** which you have carried out.
6 You will need to identify lead times for certain media timings as appropriate.

(Performance Criteria: 20.1.3.)
(Performance Criteria: 20.1.4, 20.2.1, 20.2.2.)
(Performance Criteria: 20.3.4 Range: Methods.)

Task 3

Deliver an oral presentation to a representative of the ice cream manufacturer (your tutor) which lasts 20 minutes and which details the following:

You must identify and explain the following methods for deciding the size of the advertising budget:

(a) **Rule of Thumb**
(b) **proportion of previous sales**
(c) **proportion of forecast sales**
(d) **the task approach**.

You must recommend those of the above methods which, in your opinion, would be most appropriate for the ice cream manufacturer you have chosen, and work out the size of the resulting advertising budget on the basis of information contained earlier in this Assignment. You must then use the resulting budget spend, as determined by the method you have chosen, to constrain your proposed **advertising campaign**.

(Performance Criteria: 20.1.3, 20.2.4.)

Task 4

Produce a brief report to explain how you would test both the impact and the effectiveness of the campaign, after having first detailed the alternative methods available to you.

(Performance Criteria: 20.3.4.)

Please note: the complete portfolio which you are to produce should include (in fully documented form) the following:

1 a customer profile
2 details of competitors
3 the unique selling proposition
4 visuals and copy/storyboard/script, as appropriate
5 an explanation of how you will pre-test the impact of the advertising communication you have produced
6 those media identified and selected as appropriate for the audience targeted
7 a media plan
8 a budget which details full costings for the media plan you propose and identifies how you calculated the size of the budget spend available
9 some notes about the legal and voluntary constraints imposed on advertisers by various bodies.

(Performance Criteria: 20.2.3, 20.3.3 and all other Performance Criteria and all aspects of all Ranges.)

The complete portfolio is to be submitted by: a date to be agreed by your tutor.

Below is a brief resumé of some aspects of advertising which might act as reminders while you are developing your advertising campaign:

What is the purpose of advertising?

1 for the advertiser to gain acceptance of a product/service
2 to raise the profile of a product/service
3 to introduce a new product/service or to communicate a change to an existing product/service
4 to stimulate demand for a product/service
5 to support the efforts of the sales staff
6 to announce promotion/competitions etc.

Which media?

1 the press (local/national)
2 television (regional/national)
3 radio (local/national)
4 posters (on hoardings, transport etc.)
5 direct mail/direct response etc.

Media can be classified in a number of ways

1 news, general interest, specialist etc.
2 circulation size, area, type (bought, free, subscription)
3 type of reader (socio-economic group, lifestyle etc.)
4 frequency of publication (daily, weekly, monthly, annually etc.)
5 production (colour, black and white, glossy etc.)
6 cost (per page, per word, for display etc.).

The message needs to:

1 attract the attention of the audience
2 hold the attention of the audience
3 persuade the audience by stimulating a desire which motivates the reader/viewer to take action and buy the product/service

Decide on a selling 'theme' or 'angle'

1 Start by making a list – see Chapters 8 and 9.
2 Highlight those features of the product which are new or unique to the product.
3 Identify features which are relevant to the needs of the audience (remember: don't use negatives).
4 What benefit can the customer expect if he or she buys the product/service?

5 Decide on the unique selling proposition/benefit that will most effectively persuade the customer to buy the product/service. Is it:

- price
- quality
- convenience

or some other benefit which it is possible to identify?

Some reminders about the advertising copy

1 Keep it simple

- use short sentences
- avoid the use of jargon

2 Make it interesting

- attract attention
- be enthusiastic
- arouse curiosity
- focus on the benefits to the customer

3 Be brief

- get to the point
- use small areas of text – this keeps the readers interested

4 Be positive

- don't use negatives

5 Give out facts

- try to keep to the real world when highlighting features

6 Be honest

- remember the voluntary Codes of Practice and the Advertising Standards Authority

7 Be original

- use designs/images which create impact

8 A word about themes

- keep to one or two only

9 Be instructive

- state as often as possible:

  – why
  – where
  – when, and
  – how

  the product can be ordered

10 Be self-contained

- don't compare your product/service with that of another manufacturer or service-sector organisation

BIBLIOGRAPHY

Adams, J R, *Media Planning* (2nd Edn), Business Books Ltd, 1977.

Adcock, D, Bradfield, R, Halborg, Al and Ross, Caroline, *Marketing Principles & Practice* (2nd Edn), Pitman, 1995.

Borrie, G and Diamond, A L, *The Consumer, Society and the Law*, Penguin, 1966.

Crompton, Alastair, *The Craft of Copywriting* (2nd Edn), Hutchinson, 1987.

Curran, James and Seaton, Jean, *Power Without Responsibility, The Press and Broadcasting in Britain*, Routledge, 1993.

Davis, M P, *The Effective Use of Advertising Media*, Business Books Ltd, 1981.

Davis, Martyn P, *The Effective Use of Advertising Media* (3rd Edn), Hutchinson, 1988.

Douglas, Torin, *The Complete Guide to Advertising*, Macmillan, 1984.

Enis, B M *et al*, (8th Edn) *Marketing Classics*, Prentice-Hall, 1991.

Fairlie, R, *Direct Mail: Principles and Practice*, Kogan Page, 1979.

Farbey, A D, *How to Produce Successful Advertising*, Kogan Page, 1994.

Felton, George, *Advertising. Advertising Concept and Copy*, Prentice-Hall, 1994.

——, *Marketing Without Frontiers* (2nd Edn), Royal Mail International, 1992/93.

Goldman, Robert, *Readings Ads Socially*, Routledge, 1992.

Hague, P and Jackson, P, *Marketing Research in Practice, A Practitioner's Guide to Effective Applications and Key Strategies*, Kogan Page, 1992.

Hutchings, Andy, *Marketing, A Resource Book*, Pitman, 1995.

Ingman, Dan, *Television Advertising*, Business Publications, 1965.

Kent, Raymond, *Marketing Research in Action*, Routledge, 1993.

Kotler, Philip, *Marketing Management – Analysis, Planning, Implementation and Control* (16th Edn), Prentice-Hall, 1988.

Morden, A R, *Elements of Marketing* (2nd Edn), DP Publications, 1991.

Morgan, Eric, *Choosing and Using Advertising Agencies*, Business Books Ltd, 1974.

Nevitt, Dr T R, *Advertising in Britain – A History*, Heinemann, 1982.

Ogilvy, David, *Confessions of an Advertising Man*, Longman, 1964.

Oliver, Gordon, *Marketing Today* (2nd Edn), Prentice-Hall, 1986.

Peattie, Ken, *Environmental Marketing Management – Meeting the Green Challenge*, Pitman, 1995.

Schudson, Michael, *Advertising the Uneasy Persuasion, Its Dubious Impact on American Society*, Routledge, 1993.

Smelt, Maurice, *What Advertising Is*, Pelham Press, 1972.

Starch, D, *Measuring Advertising Readership and Results*, McGraw-Hill, 1966.

Stokes, David, *Discovering Marketing, An Active Learning Approach*, DP Publications, 1994.

Walsh, LS, *International Marketing M&E Handbooks* (3rd Edn), Longman, 1993.

Wilson, Ian, *Marketing Interfaces, Exploring the Marketing and Business Relationship*, Pitman, 1994.

Woolley, Diana, *Advertising Law Handbook* (2nd Edn), Business Books Ltd, 1976.

Worcester, R, *Consumer Market Research Handbook*, McGraw-Hill, 1972.

Worsam, Mike and Wright, D Berkeley, *Marketing in Management, Basic Principles*, Pitman 1995.

Index